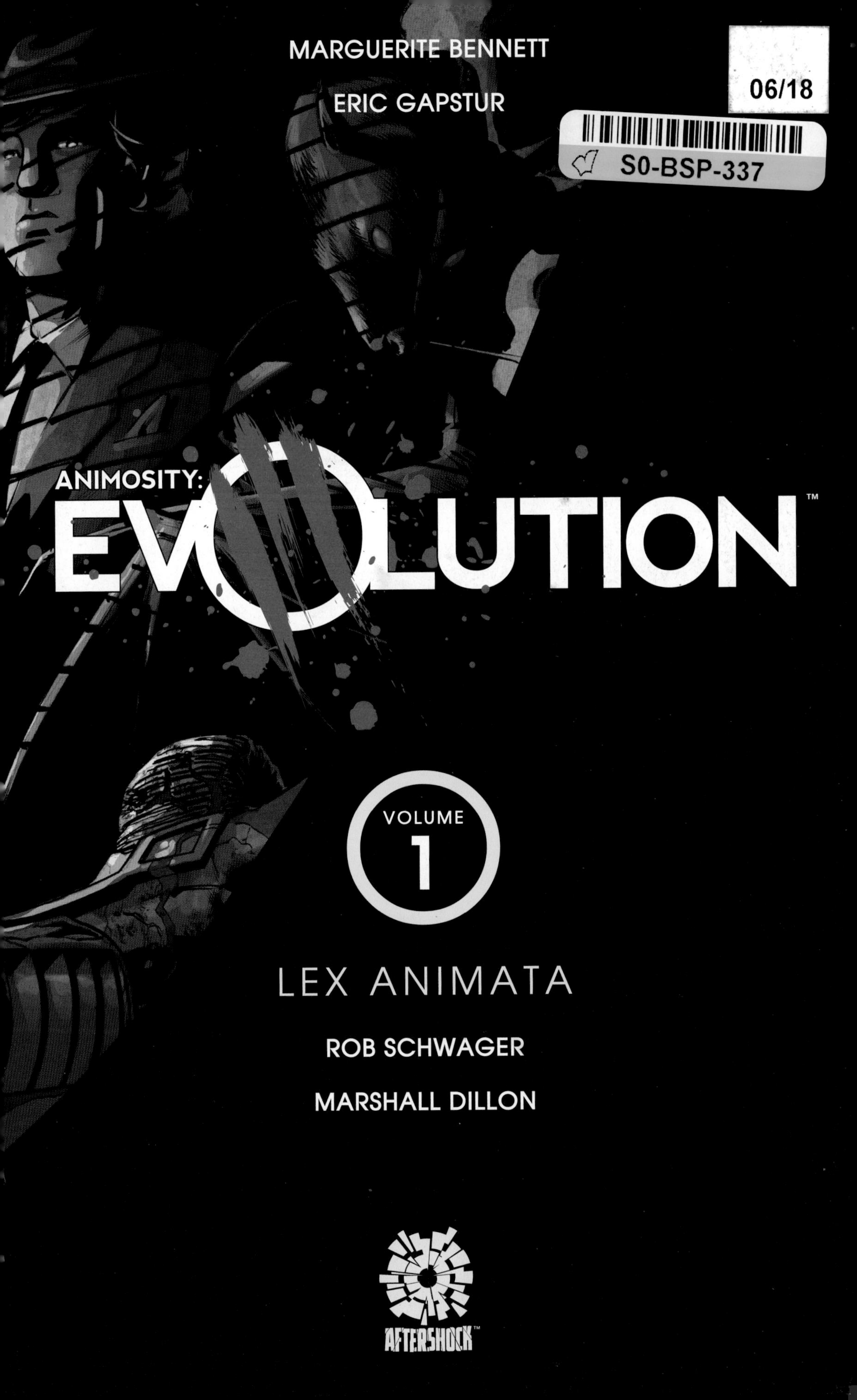

MARGUERITE BENNETT

ERIC GAPSTUR

ANIMOSITY: EVOLUTION™

VOLUME 1

LEX ANIMATA

ROB SCHWAGER

MARSHALL DILLON

AFTERSHOCK™

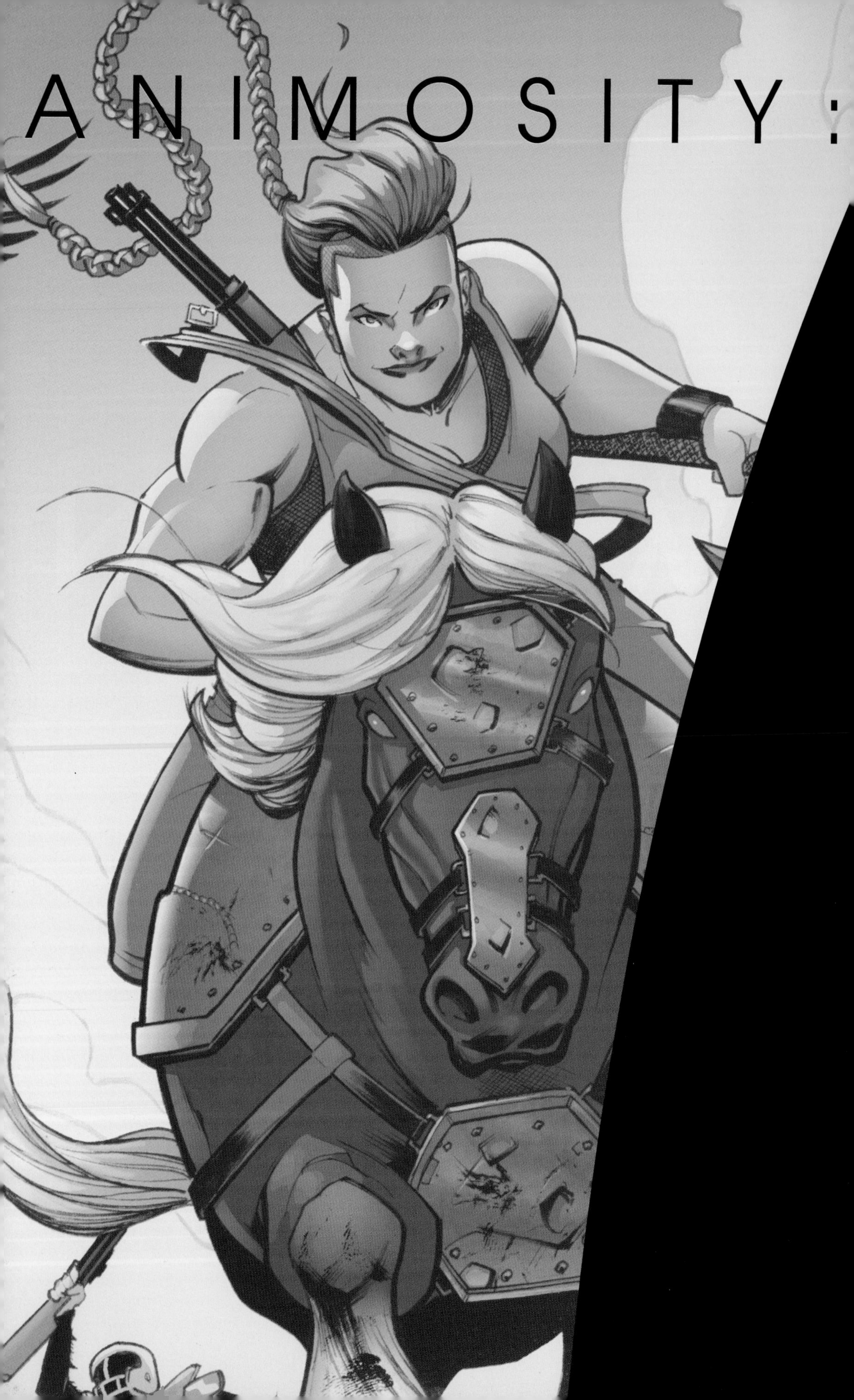
ANIMOSITY:

EVOLUTION

VOLUME 1
LEX ANIMATA

MARGUERITE BENNETT creator & writer

ERIC GAPSTUR artist

ROB SCHWAGER colorist

MARSHALL DILLON letterer

ERIC GAPSTUR w/ **ROB SCHWAGER** front cover

ERIC GAPSTUR w/ **ROB SCHWAGER** & **GUY MAJOR** original series covers

RAFAEL DE LATORRE w/ **MARCELO MAIOLO**, **ERIC GAPSTUR** w/ **ROB SCHWAGER**, **BLAKE OVARD** & **MIKE ROOTH** variant covers

COREY BREEN book designer

JOHN J. HILL logo designer

MIKE MARTS editor

AFTERSHOCK™

MIKE MARTS - Editor-in-Chief • JOE PRUETT - Publisher/ Chief Creative Officer • LEE KRAMER - President
JAWAD QURESHI - SVP, Investor Relations • JON KRAMER - Chief Executive Officer • MIKE ZAGARI - SVP, Brand
JAY BEHLING - Chief Financial Officer • STEPHAN NILSON - Publishing Operations Manager
LISA Y. WU - Retailer/Fan Relations Manager • ASHLEY WYATT - Publishing Assistant

AfterShock Trade Dress and Interior Design by JOHN J. HILL • AfterShock Logo Design by COMICRAFT
Original series production (issues 1-5) by CHARLES PRITCHETT • Proofreading by DOCTOR Z.
Publicity: contact AARON MARION (aaron@publichausagency.com) & RYAN CROY (ryan@publichausagency.com)
Special thanks to CHRIS LA TORRE, SVEN LARSEN, TEDDY LEO, LISA MOODY & KIM PAGNOTTA

First Printing: October 2016. 10 9 8 7 6 5 4 3 2 1

AFTERSHOCKCOMICS.COM Follow us on social media

INTRODUCTION

I took a chance in 2016—stepping away from a seventeen-year journey to syndicate my own comic strip to pursue work drawing comic books. I'd always known I wanted to make a living drawing comics, and if I'm honest with myself, I think my initial path had a lot to do with me at age twelve thinking a drawing of Snoopy looked manageable, while a Steve Rude drawing looked like a goddamn mystery. Turns out syndicating a comic strip was more of the latter, too.

So, I blew up everything I had worked for and started over. Trading facility and confidence in your work for clumsiness and doubt is never an easy thing, but working in a new style was exhilarating. I had learned a thing or two picking up some work inking other people in recent years, and comic books seemed a little less mysterious.

After about a year of samples sent to anyone who would give me the time of day, Mike Marts took a chance on me. "Comics" didn't even know I worked in comics, and he gave me not just any opportunity, but an opportunity to draw a spinoff of one of AfterShock's best sellers—Marguerite Bennett's ANIMOSITY: EVOLUTION. I was, and still am, honored.

So, I want to take a second to thank you for taking a chance on this book. New series and new creators can be a hard sell in this business, so know that it's really appreciated. I hope you enjoy this volume as much as I enjoyed drawing it.

ERIC GAPSTUR
March 2018

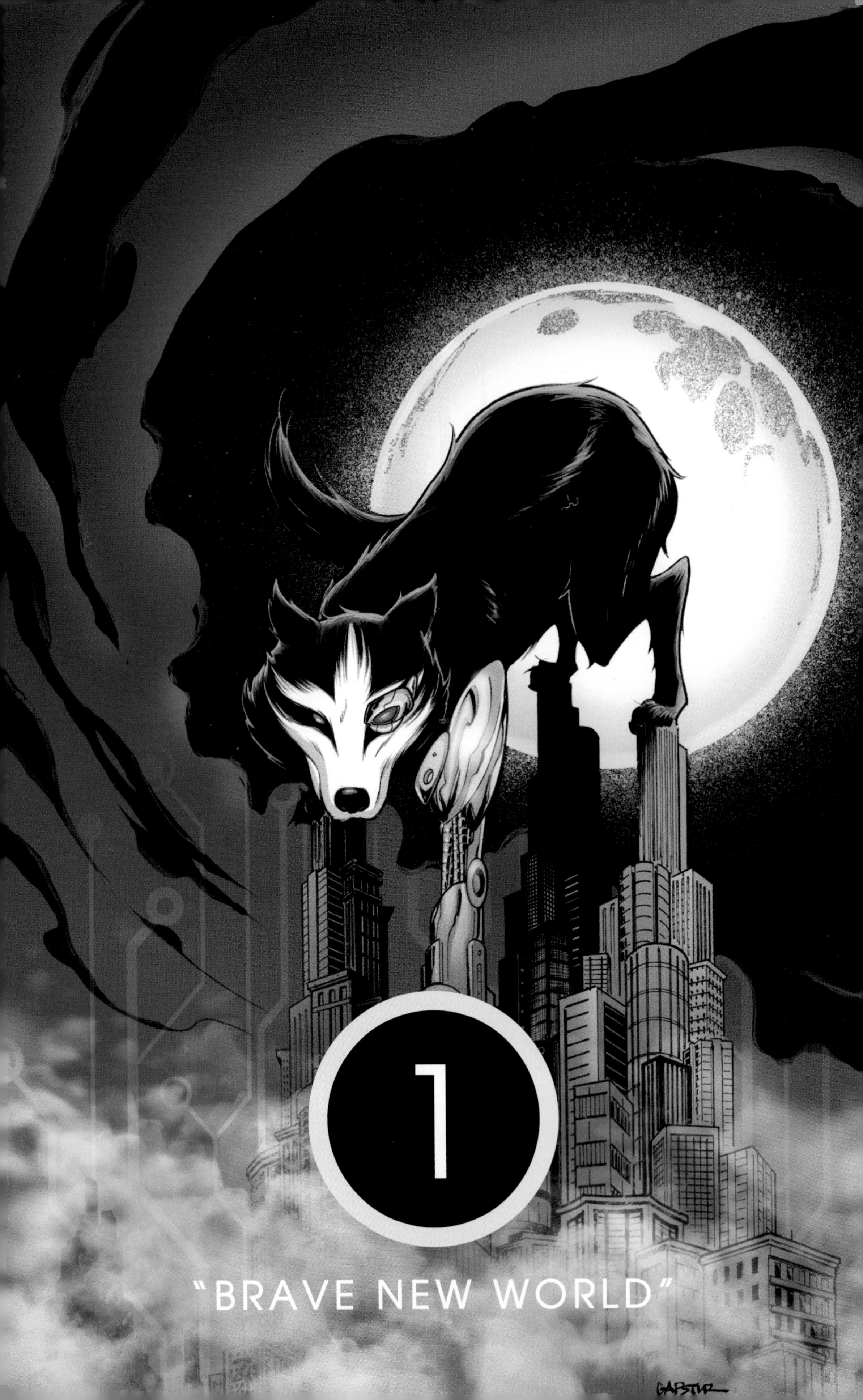
1
"BRAVE NEW WORLD"

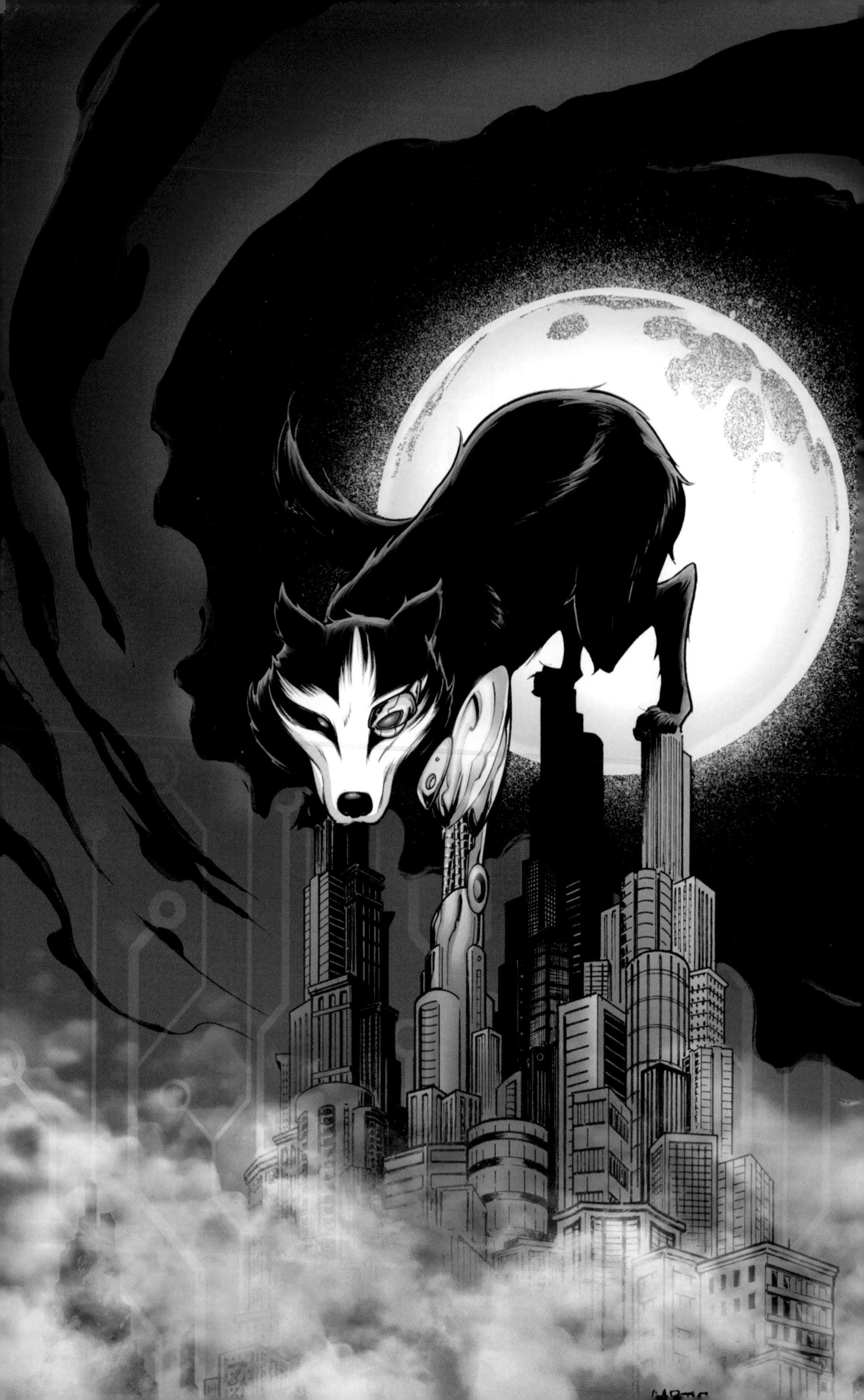

ANIMOSITY: EVOLUTION

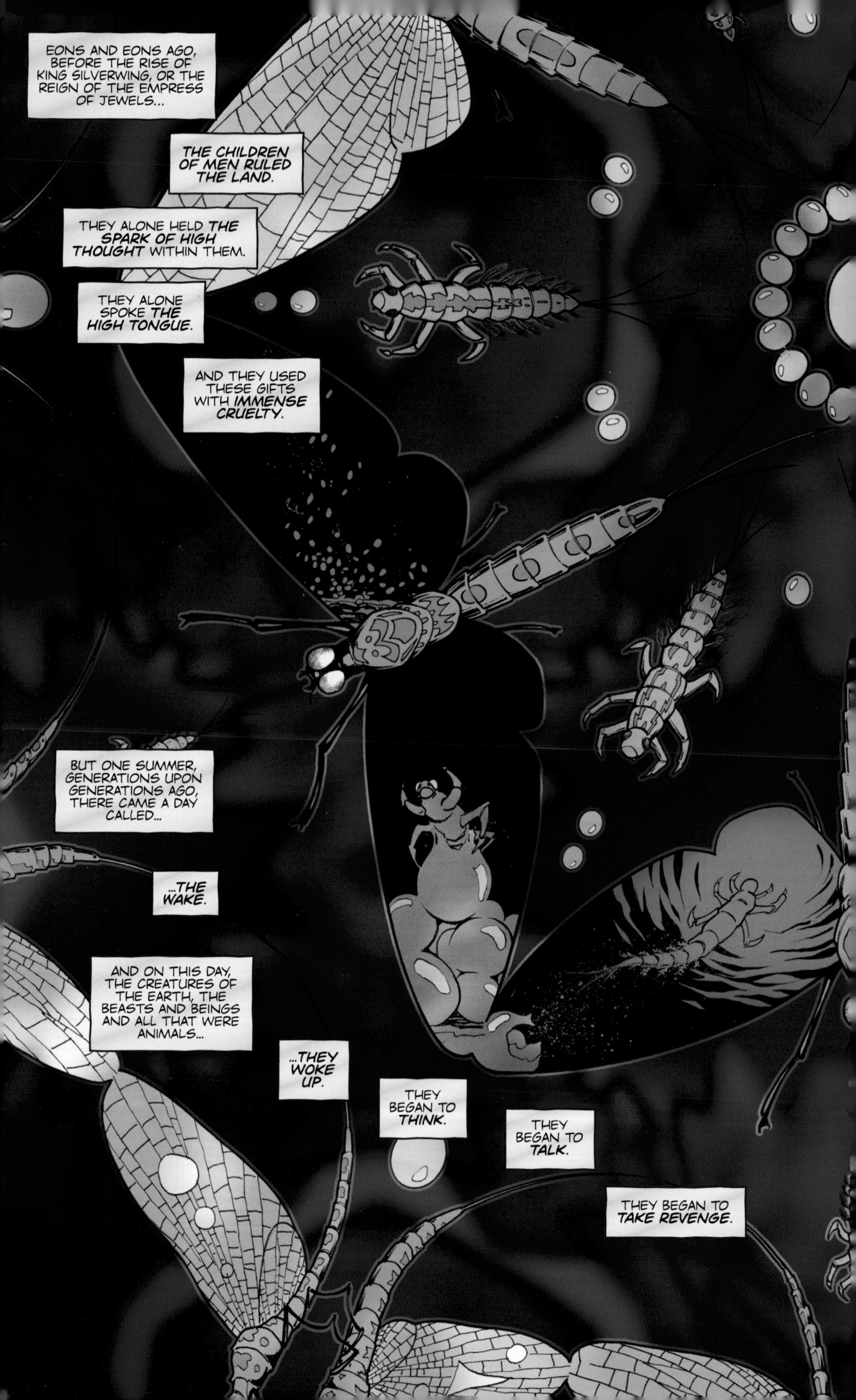
EONS AND EONS AGO, BEFORE THE RISE OF KING SILVERWING, OR THE REIGN OF THE EMPRESS OF JEWELS...
THE CHILDREN OF MEN RULED THE LAND.
THEY ALONE HELD THE SPARK OF HIGH THOUGHT WITHIN THEM.
THEY ALONE SPOKE THE HIGH TONGUE.
AND THEY USED THESE GIFTS WITH IMMENSE CRUELTY.
BUT ONE SUMMER, GENERATIONS UPON GENERATIONS AGO, THERE CAME A DAY CALLED...
...THE WAKE.
AND ON THIS DAY, THE CREATURES OF THE EARTH, THE BEASTS AND BEINGS AND ALL THAT WERE ANIMALS...
...THEY WOKE UP.
THEY BEGAN TO THINK.
THEY BEGAN TO TALK.
THEY BEGAN TO TAKE REVENGE.

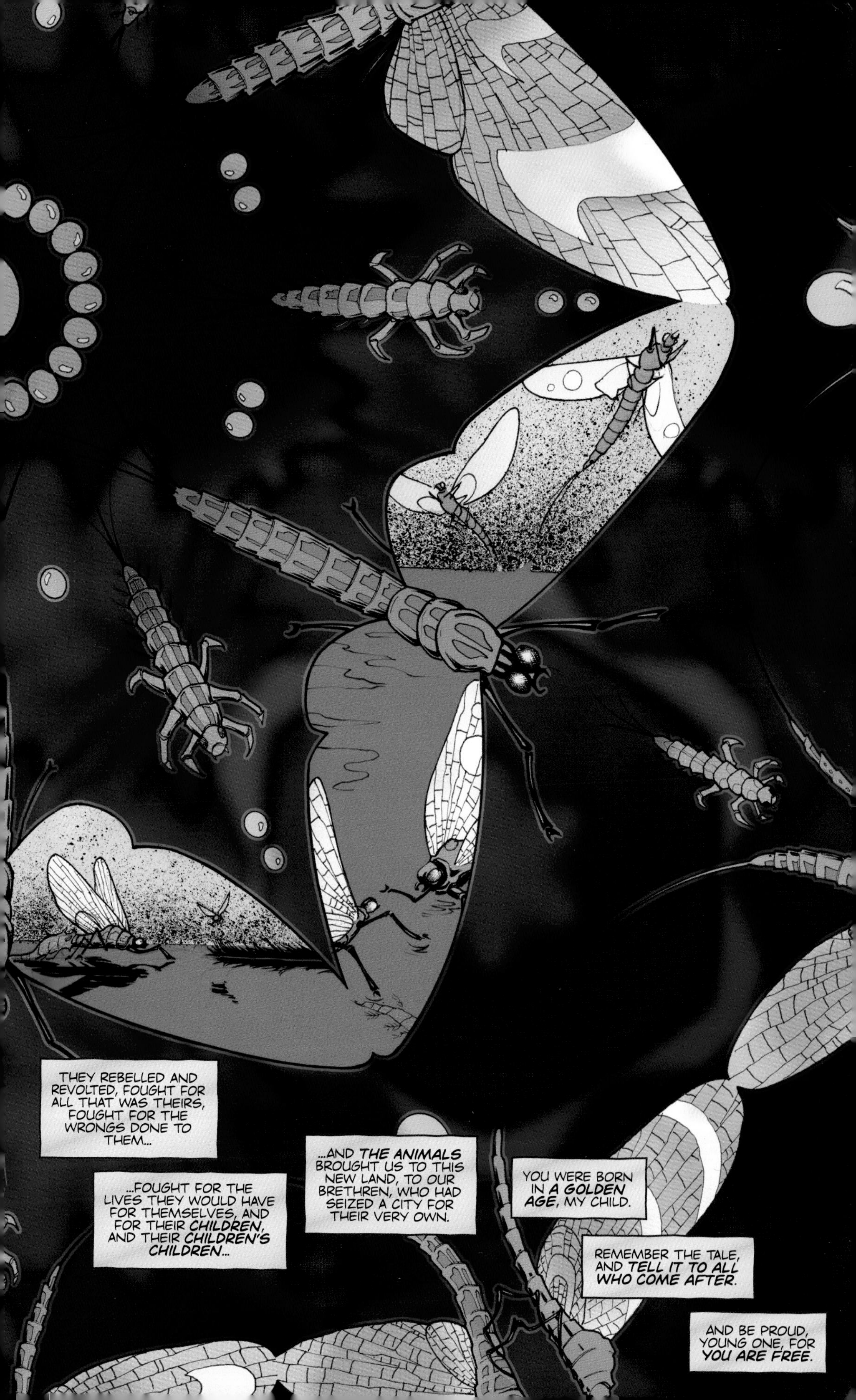
THEY REBELLED AND REVOLTED, FOUGHT FOR ALL THAT WAS THEIRS, FOUGHT FOR THE WRONGS DONE TO THEM...
...FOUGHT FOR THE LIVES THEY WOULD HAVE FOR THEMSELVES, AND FOR THEIR CHILDREN, AND THEIR CHILDREN'S CHILDREN...
...AND THE ANIMALS BROUGHT US TO THIS NEW LAND, TO OUR BRETHREN, WHO HAD SEIZED A CITY FOR THEIR VERY OWN.
YOU WERE BORN IN A GOLDEN AGE, MY CHILD.
REMEMBER THE TALE, AND TELL IT TO ALL WHO COME AFTER.
AND BE PROUD, YOUNG ONE, FOR YOU ARE FREE.

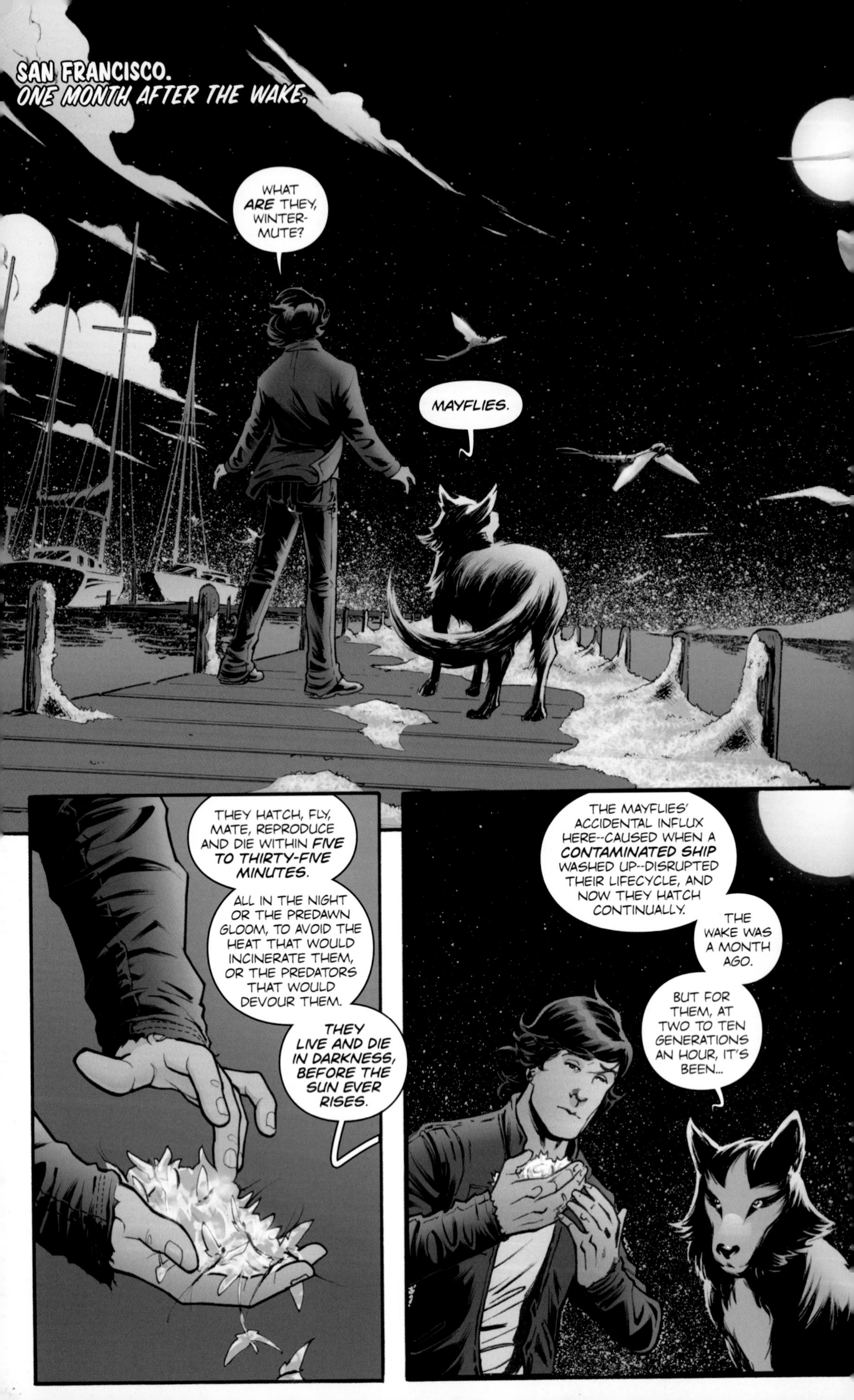
SAN FRANCISCO.
ONE MONTH AFTER THE WAKE.
WHAT ARE THEY, WINTER-MUTE?
MAYFLIES.
THEY HATCH, FLY, MATE, REPRODUCE AND DIE WITHIN FIVE TO THIRTY-FIVE MINUTES.
ALL IN THE NIGHT OR THE PREDAWN GLOOM, TO AVOID THE HEAT THAT WOULD INCINERATE THEM, OR THE PREDATORS THAT WOULD DEVOUR THEM.
THEY LIVE AND DIE IN DARKNESS, BEFORE THE SUN EVER RISES.
THE MAYFLIES' ACCIDENTAL INFLUX HERE--CAUSED WHEN A CONTAMINATED SHIP WASHED UP--DISRUPTED THEIR LIFECYCLE, AND NOW THEY HATCH CONTINUALLY.
THE WAKE WAS A MONTH AGO.
BUT FOR THEM, AT TWO TO TEN GENERATIONS AN HOUR, IT'S BEEN...

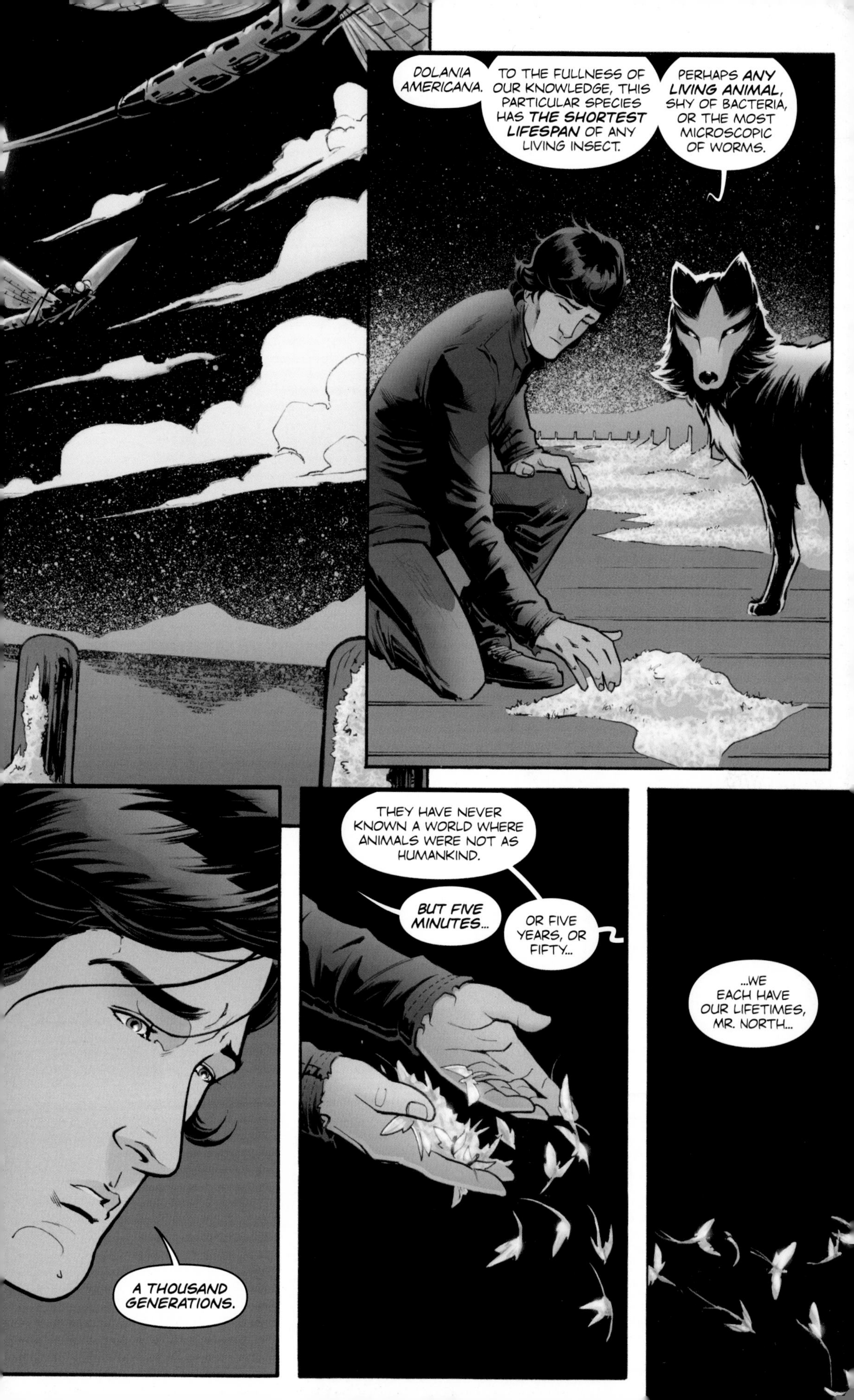
DOLANIA AMERICANA.
TO THE FULLNESS OF OUR KNOWLEDGE, THIS PARTICULAR SPECIES HAS **THE SHORTEST LIFESPAN** OF ANY LIVING INSECT.
PERHAPS **ANY LIVING ANIMAL**, SHY OF BACTERIA, OR THE MOST MICROSCOPIC OF WORMS.
A THOUSAND GENERATIONS.
THEY HAVE NEVER KNOWN A WORLD WHERE ANIMALS WERE NOT AS HUMANKIND.
BUT FIVE MINUTES...
OR FIVE YEARS, OR FIFTY...
...WE EACH HAVE OUR LIFETIMES, MR. NORTH...

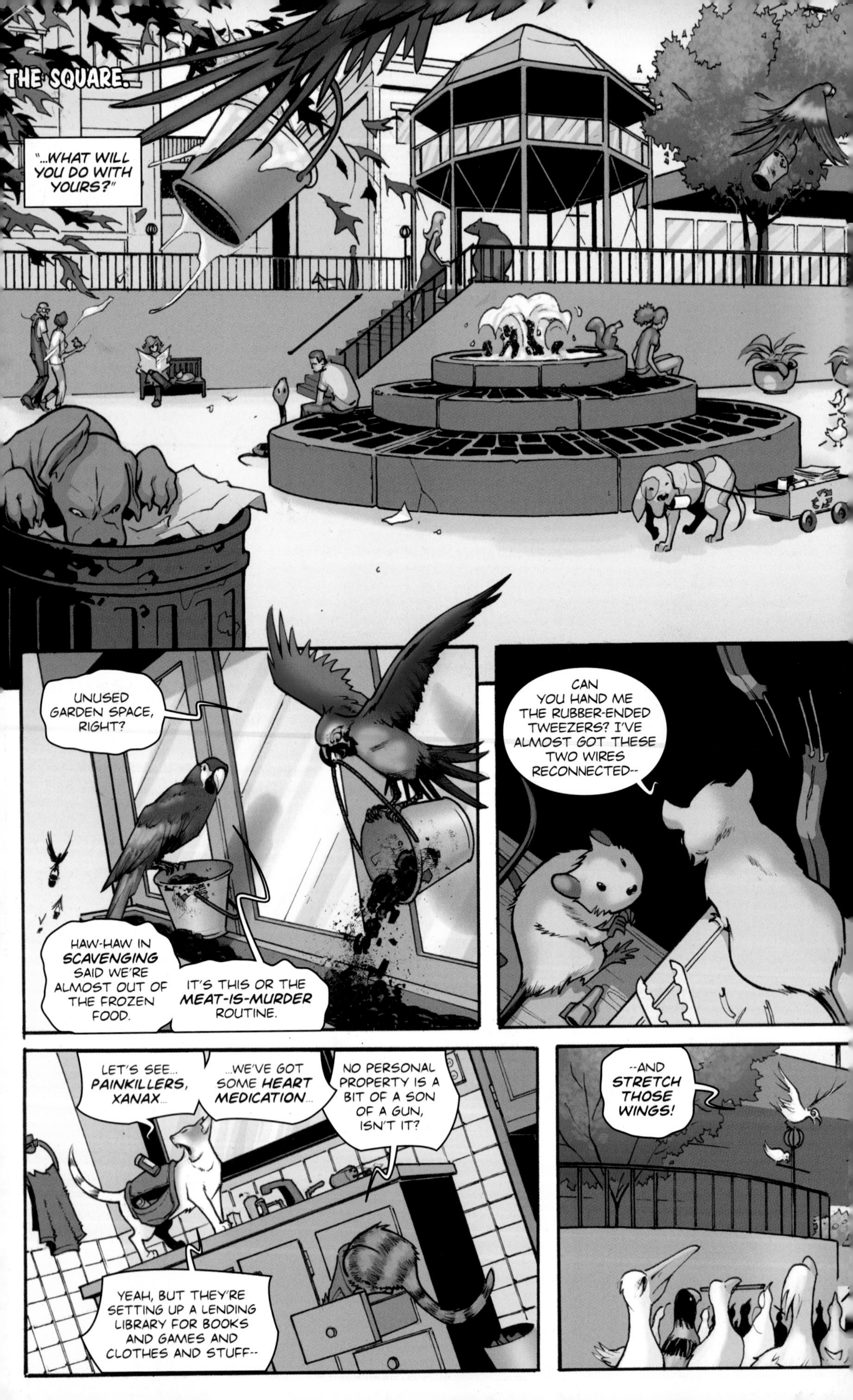
THE SQUARE.
"...WHAT WILL YOU DO WITH YOURS?"
UNUSED GARDEN SPACE, RIGHT?
HAW-HAW IN SCAVENGING SAID WE'RE ALMOST OUT OF THE FROZEN FOOD.
IT'S THIS OR THE MEAT-IS-MURDER ROUTINE.
CAN YOU HAND ME THE RUBBER-ENDED TWEEZERS? I'VE ALMOST GOT THESE TWO WIRES RECONNECTED--
LET'S SEE... PAINKILLERS, XANAX...
...WE'VE GOT SOME HEART MEDICATION...
NO PERSONAL PROPERTY IS A BIT OF A SON OF A GUN, ISN'T IT?
YEAH, BUT THEY'RE SETTING UP A LENDING LIBRARY FOR BOOKS AND GAMES AND CLOTHES AND STUFF--
--AND STRETCH THOSE WINGS!

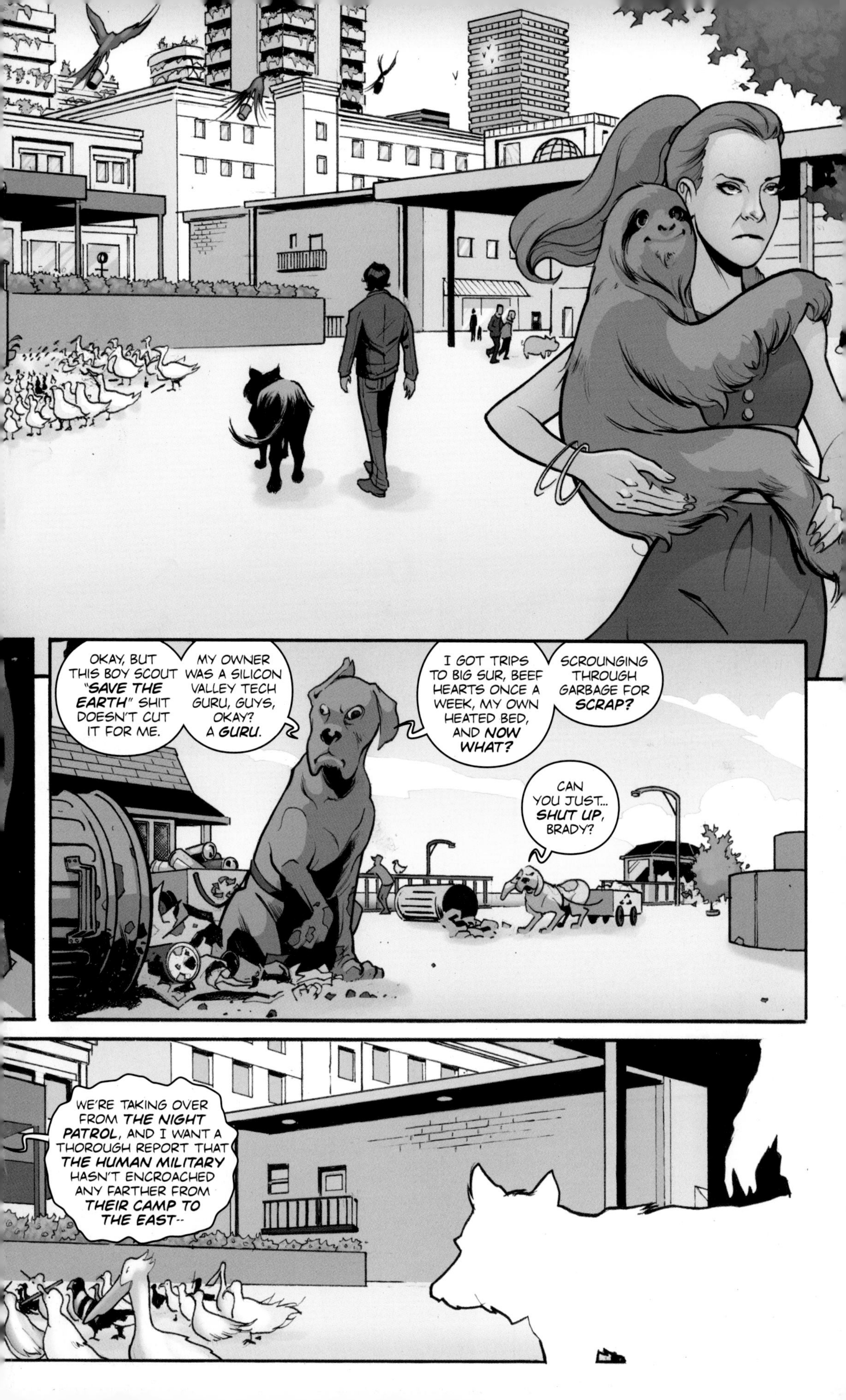
OKAY, BUT THIS BOY SCOUT "SAVE THE EARTH" SHIT DOESN'T CUT IT FOR ME.
MY OWNER WAS A SILICON VALLEY TECH GURU, GUYS, OKAY? A GURU.
I GOT TRIPS TO BIG SUR, BEEF HEARTS ONCE A WEEK, MY OWN HEATED BED, AND NOW WHAT?
SCROUNGING THROUGH GARBAGE FOR SCRAP?
CAN YOU JUST... SHUT UP, BRADY?
WE'RE TAKING OVER FROM THE NIGHT PATROL, AND I WANT A THOROUGH REPORT THAT THE HUMAN MILITARY HASN'T ENCROACHED ANY FARTHER FROM THEIR CAMP TO THE EAST--

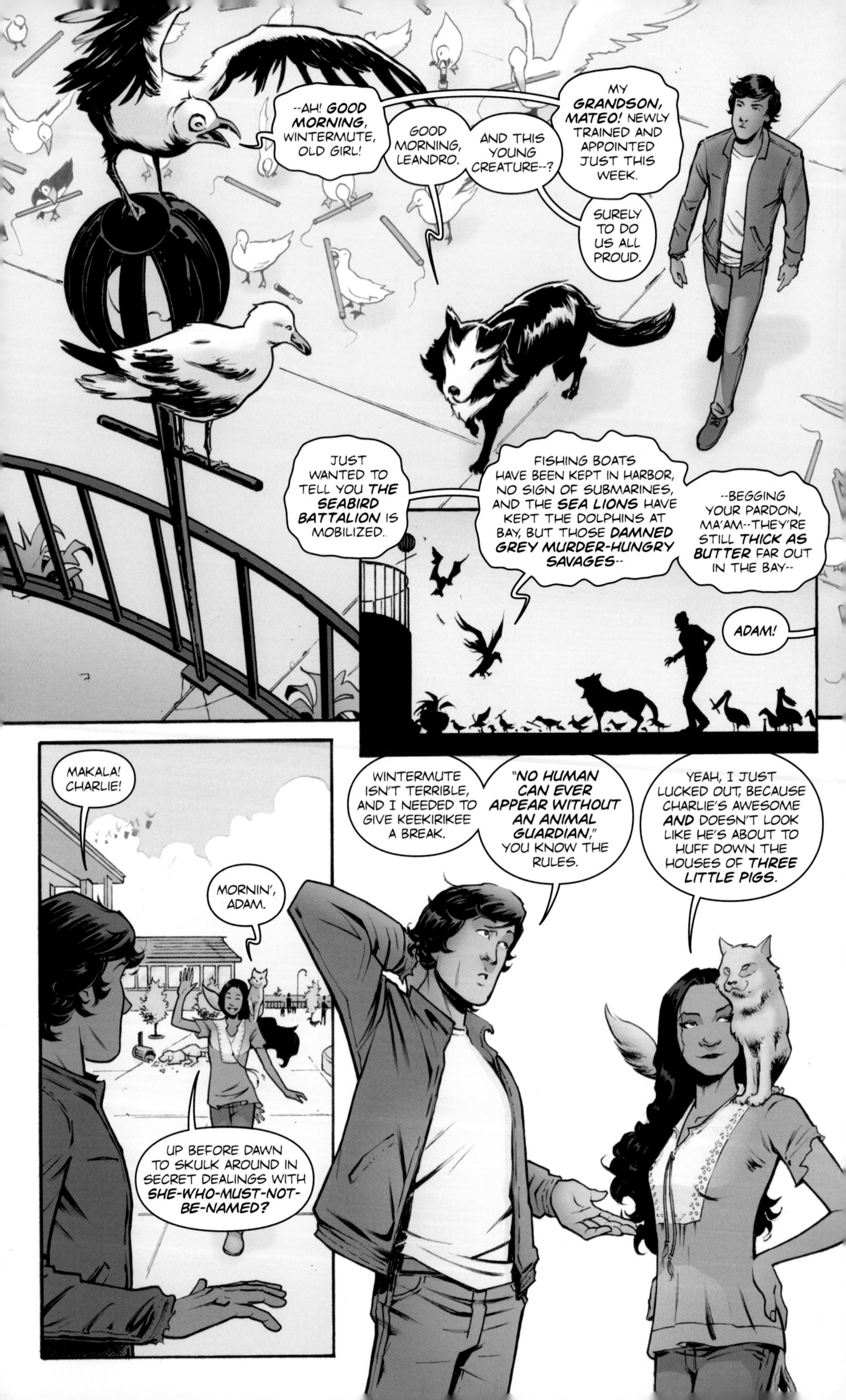
--AH! GOOD MORNING, WINTERMUTE, OLD GIRL!
GOOD MORNING, LEANDRO.
AND THIS YOUNG CREATURE--?
MY GRANDSON, MATEO! NEWLY TRAINED AND APPOINTED JUST THIS WEEK.
SURELY TO DO US ALL PROUD.
JUST WANTED TO TELL YOU THE SEABIRD BATTALION IS MOBILIZED..
FISHING BOATS HAVE BEEN KEPT IN HARBOR, NO SIGN OF SUBMARINES, AND THE SEA LIONS HAVE KEPT THE DOLPHINS AT BAY, BUT THOSE DAMNED GREY MURDER-HUNGRY SAVAGES--
--BEGGING YOUR PARDON, MA'AM--THEY'RE STILL THICK AS BUTTER FAR OUT IN THE BAY--
ADAM!
MAKALA! CHARLIE!
MORNIN', ADAM.
UP BEFORE DAWN TO SKULK AROUND IN SECRET DEALINGS WITH SHE-WHO-MUST-NOT-BE-NAMED?
WINTERMUTE ISN'T TERRIBLE, AND I NEEDED TO GIVE KEEKIRIKEE A BREAK.
"NO HUMAN CAN EVER APPEAR WITHOUT AN ANIMAL GUARDIAN," YOU KNOW THE RULES.
YEAH, I JUST LUCKED OUT, BECAUSE CHARLIE'S AWESOME AND DOESN'T LOOK LIKE HE'S ABOUT TO HUFF DOWN THE HOUSES OF THREE LITTLE PIGS.

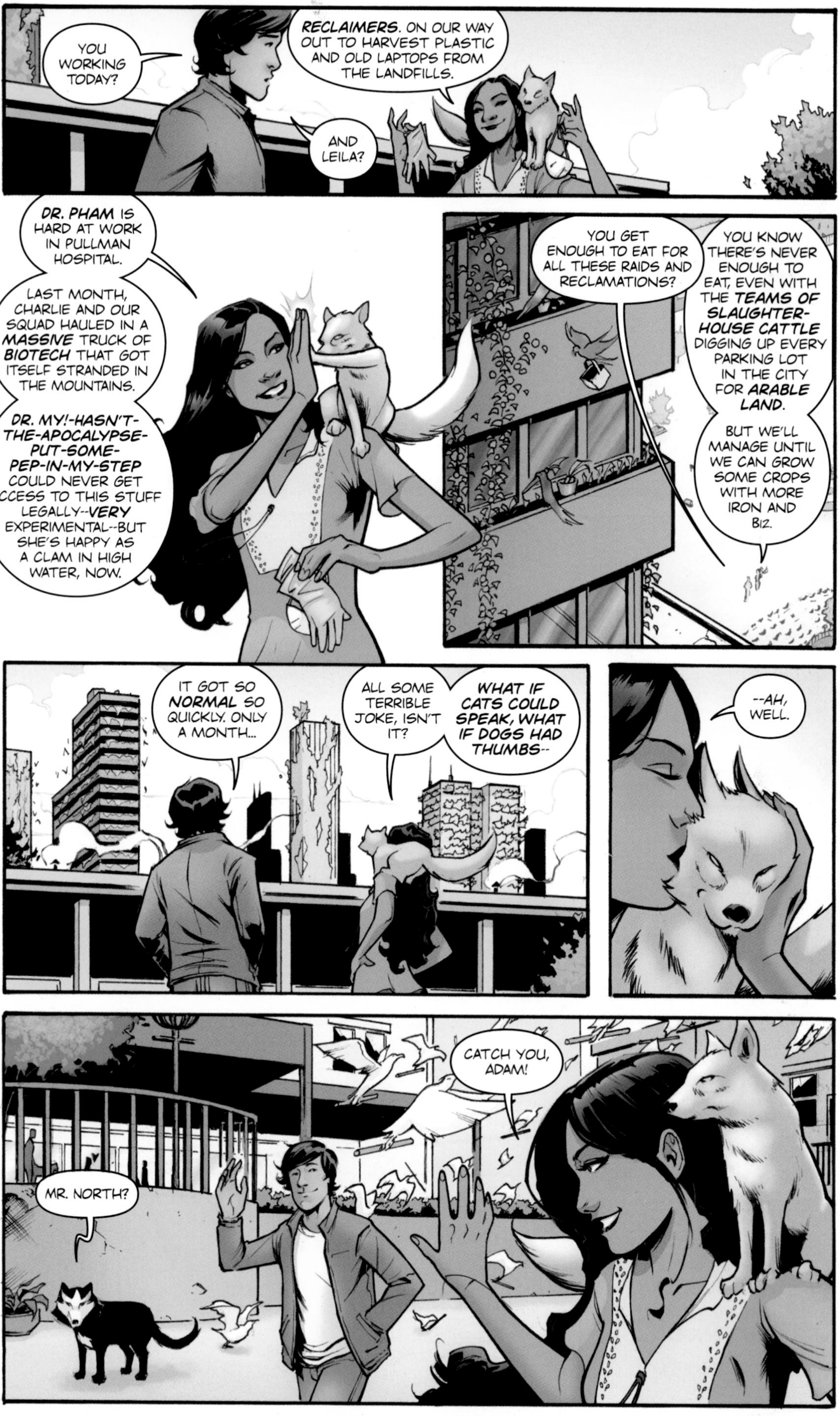
YOU WORKING TODAY?
RECLAIMERS. ON OUR WAY OUT TO HARVEST PLASTIC AND OLD LAPTOPS FROM THE LANDFILLS.
AND LEILA?
DR. PHAM IS HARD AT WORK IN PULLMAN HOSPITAL.
LAST MONTH, CHARLIE AND OUR SQUAD HAULED IN A MASSIVE TRUCK OF BIOTECH THAT GOT ITSELF STRANDED IN THE MOUNTAINS.
DR. MY!-HASN'T-THE-APOCALYPSE-PUT-SOME-PEP-IN-MY-STEP COULD NEVER GET ACCESS TO THIS STUFF LEGALLY--VERY EXPERIMENTAL--BUT SHE'S HAPPY AS A CLAM IN HIGH WATER, NOW.
YOU GET ENOUGH TO EAT FOR ALL THESE RAIDS AND RECLAMATIONS?
YOU KNOW THERE'S NEVER ENOUGH TO EAT, EVEN WITH THE TEAMS OF SLAUGHTER-HOUSE CATTLE DIGGING UP EVERY PARKING LOT IN THE CITY FOR ARABLE LAND.
BUT WE'LL MANAGE UNTIL WE CAN GROW SOME CROPS WITH MORE IRON AND B12.
IT GOT SO NORMAL SO QUICKLY. ONLY A MONTH...
ALL SOME TERRIBLE JOKE, ISN'T IT?
WHAT IF CATS COULD SPEAK, WHAT IF DOGS HAD THUMBS--
--AH, WELL.
CATCH YOU, ADAM!
MR. NORTH?

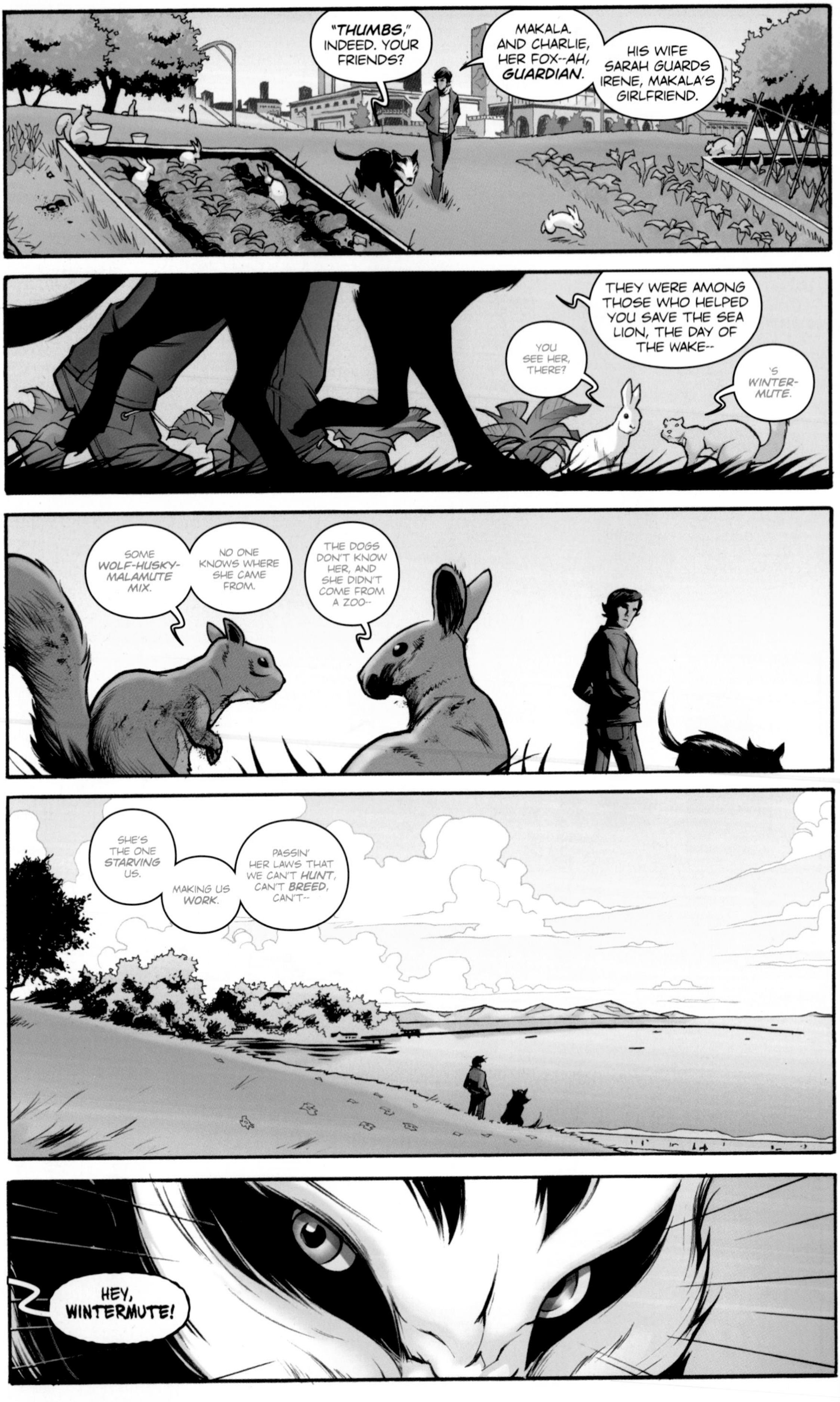
"THUMBS," INDEED. YOUR FRIENDS?
MAKALA. AND CHARLIE, HER FOX--AH, GUARDIAN.
HIS WIFE SARAH GUARDS IRENE, MAKALA'S GIRLFRIEND.
THEY WERE AMONG THOSE WHO HELPED YOU SAVE THE SEA LION, THE DAY OF THE WAKE--
YOU SEE HER, THERE?
'S WINTERMUTE.
SOME WOLF-HUSKY-MALAMUTE MIX.
NO ONE KNOWS WHERE SHE CAME FROM.
THE DOGS DON'T KNOW HER, AND SHE DIDN'T COME FROM A ZOO--
SHE'S THE ONE STARVING US.
MAKING US WORK.
PASSIN' HER LAWS THAT WE CAN'T HUNT, CAN'T BREED, CAN'T--
HEY, WINTERMUTE!

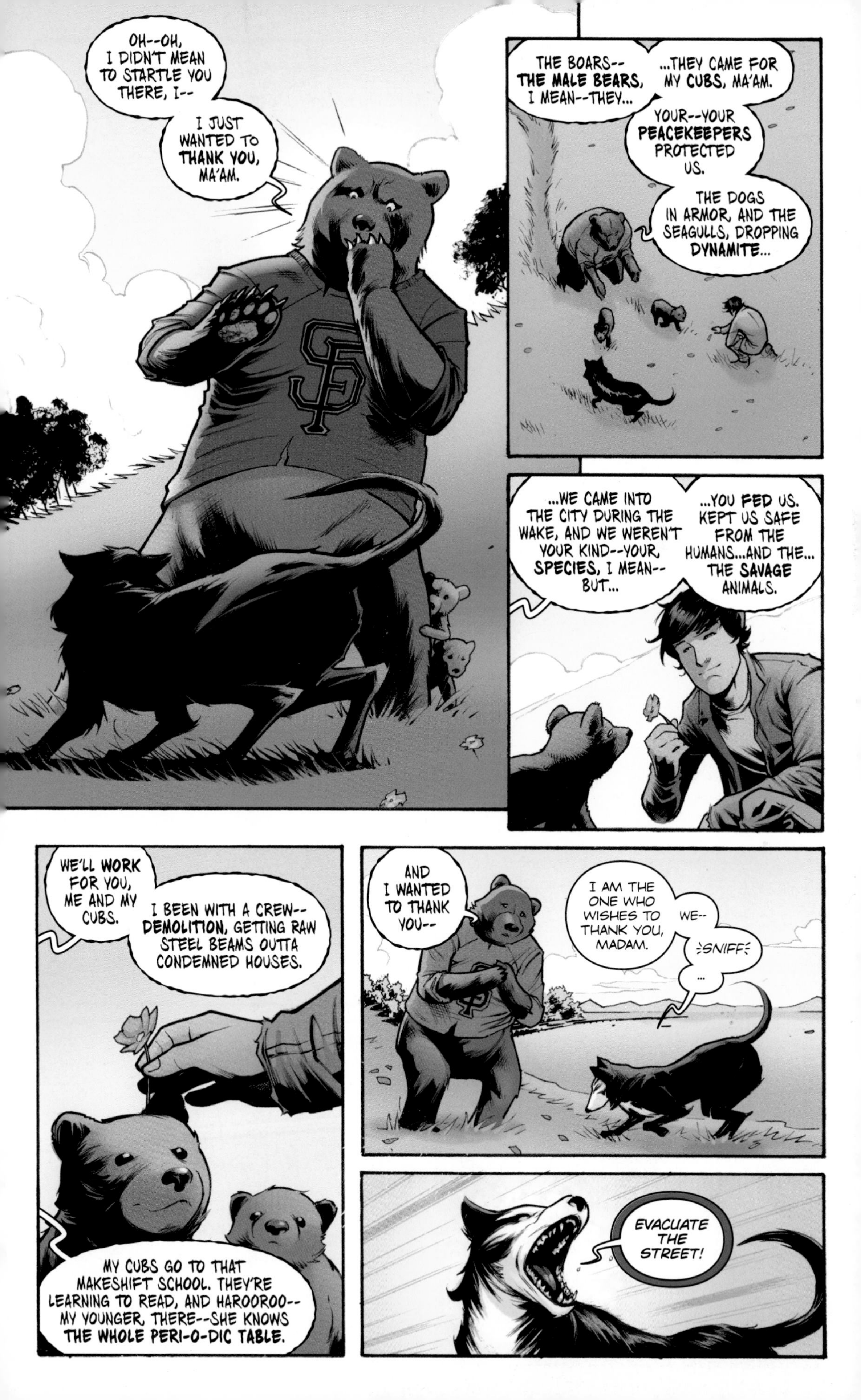
OH--OH, I DIDN'T MEAN TO STARTLE YOU THERE, I--
I JUST WANTED TO THANK YOU, MA'AM.
THE BOARS-- THE MALE BEARS, I MEAN--THEY...
...THEY CAME FOR MY CUBS, MA'AM.
YOUR--YOUR PEACEKEEPERS PROTECTED US.
THE DOGS IN ARMOR, AND THE SEAGULLS, DROPPING DYNAMITE...
...WE CAME INTO THE CITY DURING THE WAKE, AND WE WEREN'T YOUR KIND--YOUR, SPECIES, I MEAN-- BUT...
...YOU FED US. KEPT US SAFE FROM THE HUMANS...AND THE... THE SAVAGE ANIMALS.
WE'LL WORK FOR YOU, ME AND MY CUBS.
I BEEN WITH A CREW-- DEMOLITION, GETTING RAW STEEL BEAMS OUTTA CONDEMNED HOUSES.
MY CUBS GO TO THAT MAKESHIFT SCHOOL. THEY'RE LEARNING TO READ, AND HAROOROO-- MY YOUNGER, THERE--SHE KNOWS THE WHOLE PERI-O-DIC TABLE.
AND I WANTED TO THANK YOU--
I AM THE ONE WHO WISHES TO THANK YOU, MADAM.
WE--
SNIFF
...
EVACUATE THE STREET!

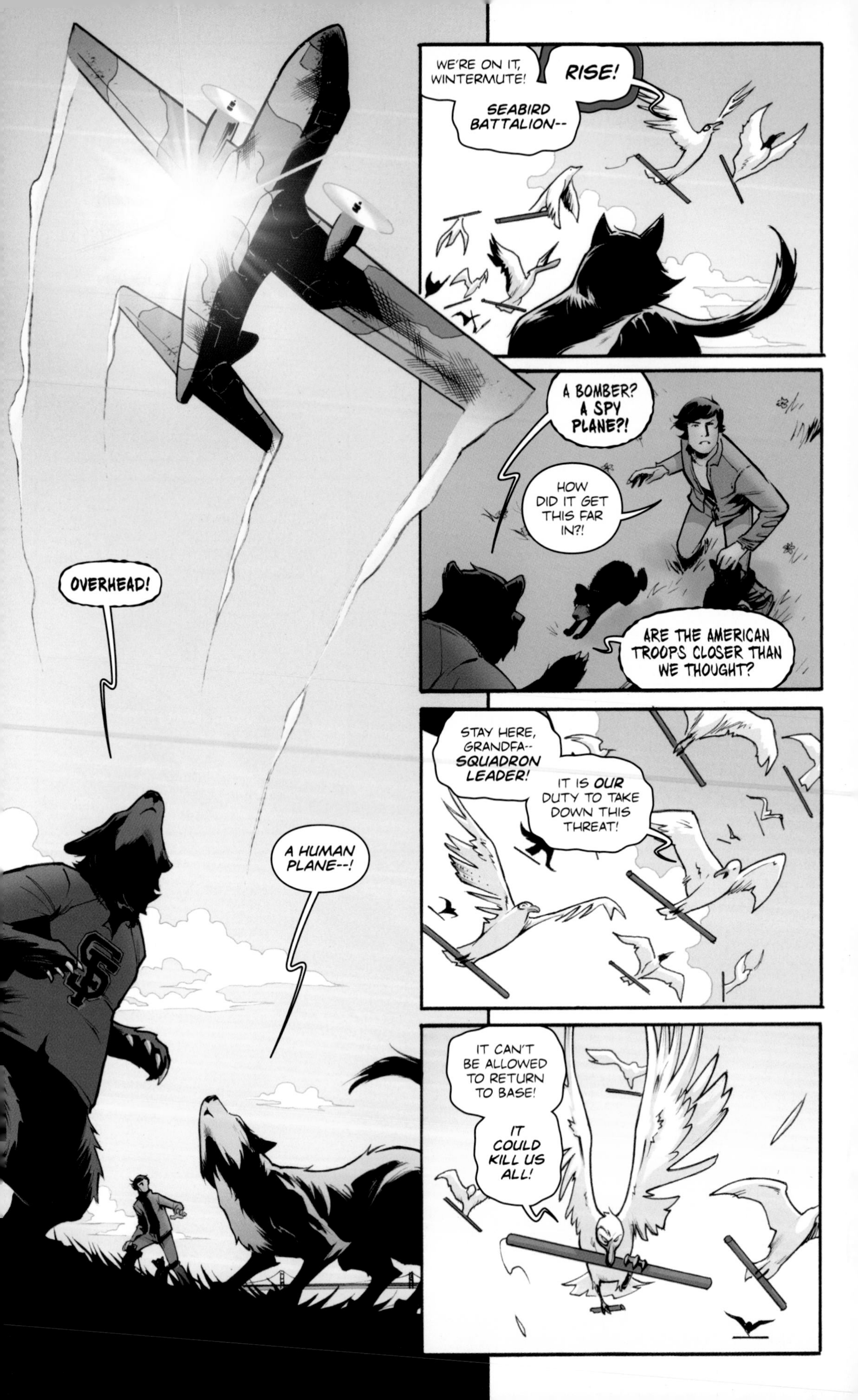
OVERHEAD!
A HUMAN PLANE--!
WE'RE ON IT, WINTERMUTE!
SEABIRD BATTALION--
RISE!
A BOMBER? A SPY PLANE?!
HOW DID IT GET THIS FAR IN?!
ARE THE AMERICAN TROOPS CLOSER THAN WE THOUGHT?
STAY HERE, GRANDFA-- SQUADRON LEADER!
IT IS OUR DUTY TO TAKE DOWN THIS THREAT!
IT CAN'T BE ALLOWED TO RETURN TO BASE!
IT COULD KILL US ALL!

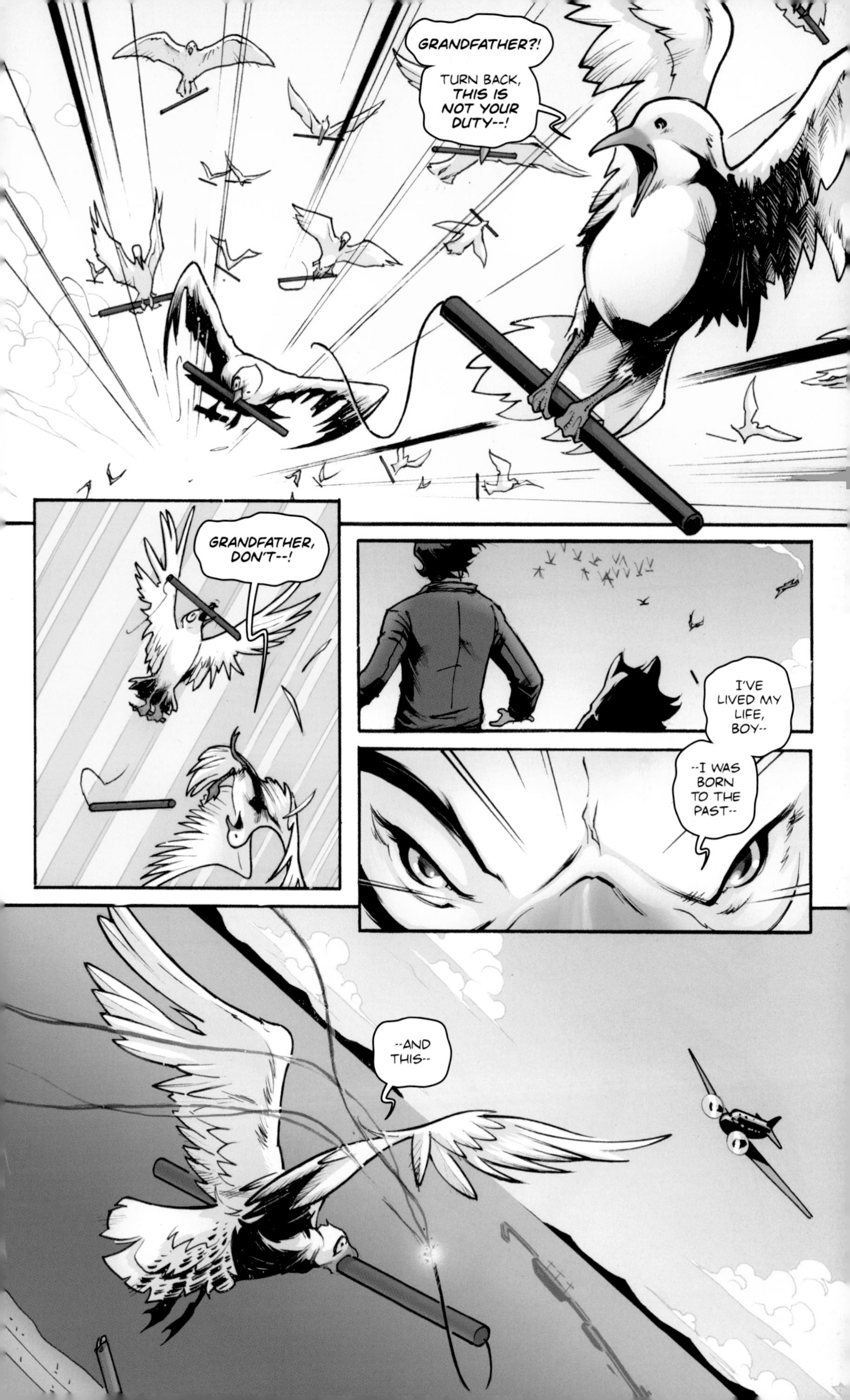
GRANDFATHER?!
TURN BACK, THIS IS NOT YOUR DUTY--!
GRANDFATHER, DON'T--!
I'VE LIVED MY LIFE, BOY--
--I WAS BORN TO THE PAST--
--AND THIS--

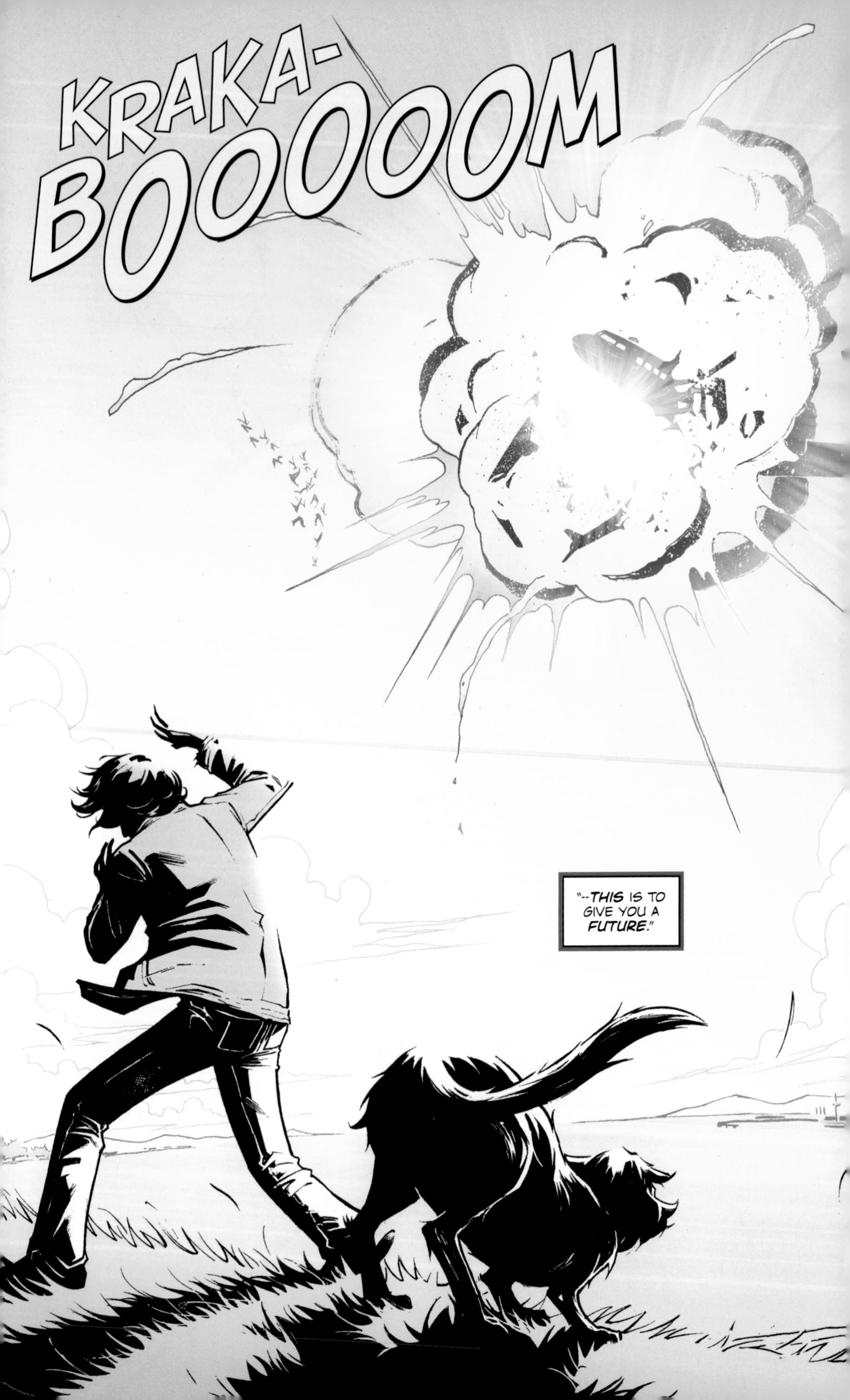
KRAKA-
BOOOOOOM
"--THIS IS TO GIVE YOU A FUTURE."

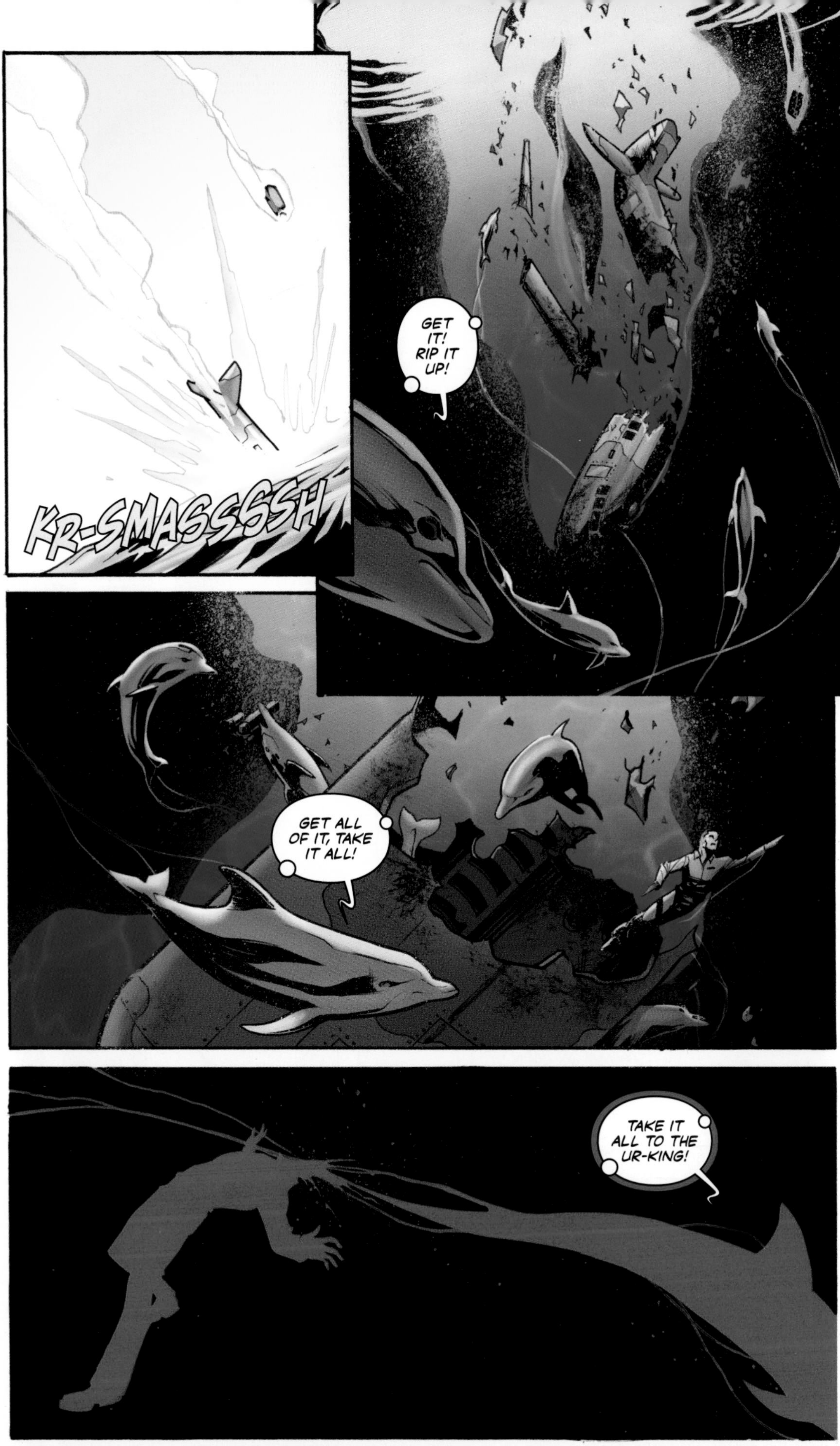
KR-SMASSSSSH
GET IT! RIP IT UP!
GET ALL OF IT, TAKE IT ALL!
TAKE IT ALL TO THE UR-KING!

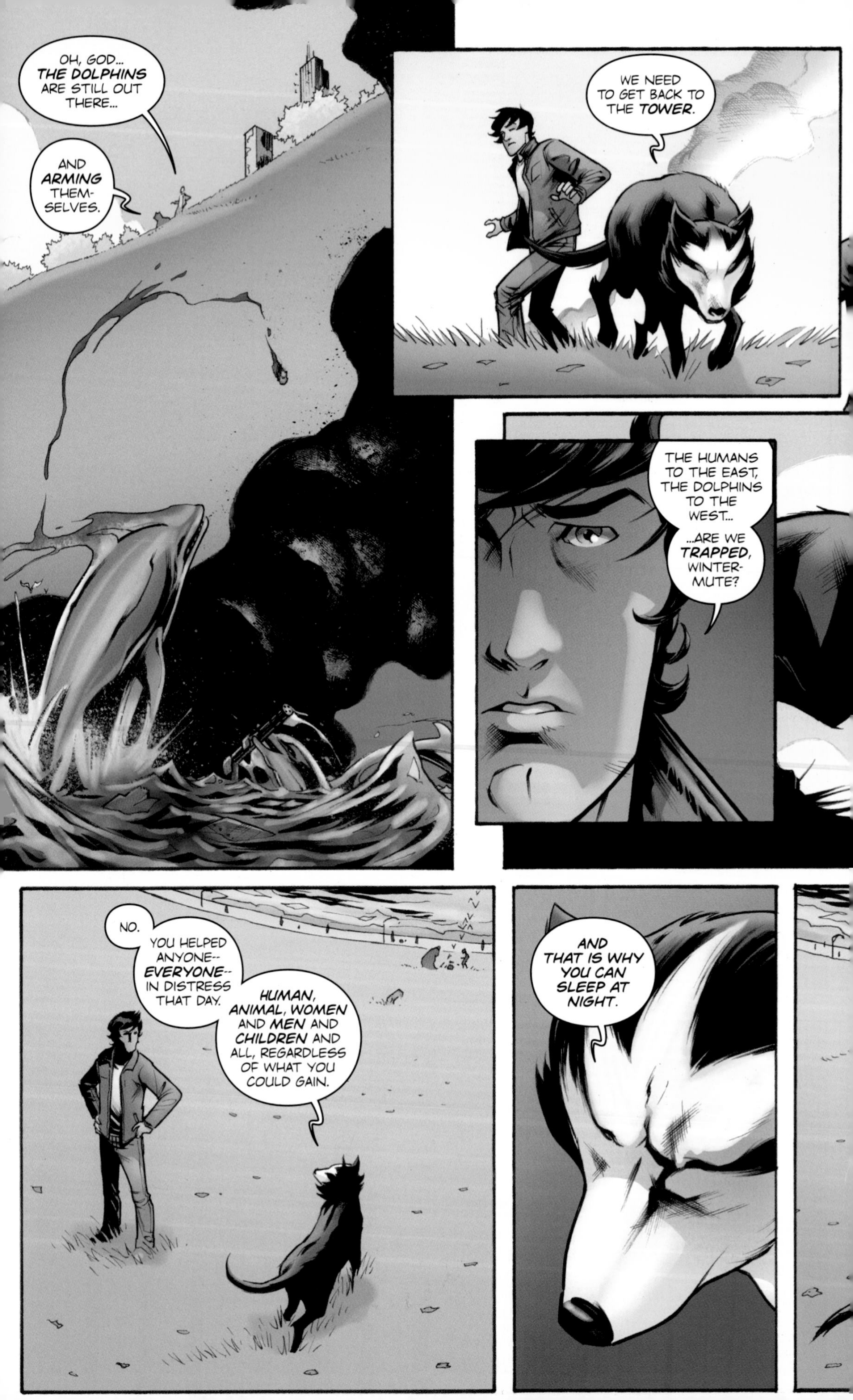
OH, GOD... THE DOLPHINS ARE STILL OUT THERE...
AND ARMING THEM-SELVES.
WE NEED TO GET BACK TO THE TOWER.
THE HUMANS TO THE EAST, THE DOLPHINS TO THE WEST...
...ARE WE TRAPPED, WINTER-MUTE?
NO.
YOU HELPED ANYONE-- EVERYONE-- IN DISTRESS THAT DAY.
HUMAN, ANIMAL, WOMEN AND MEN AND CHILDREN AND ALL, REGARDLESS OF WHAT YOU COULD GAIN.
AND THAT IS WHY YOU CAN SLEEP AT NIGHT.

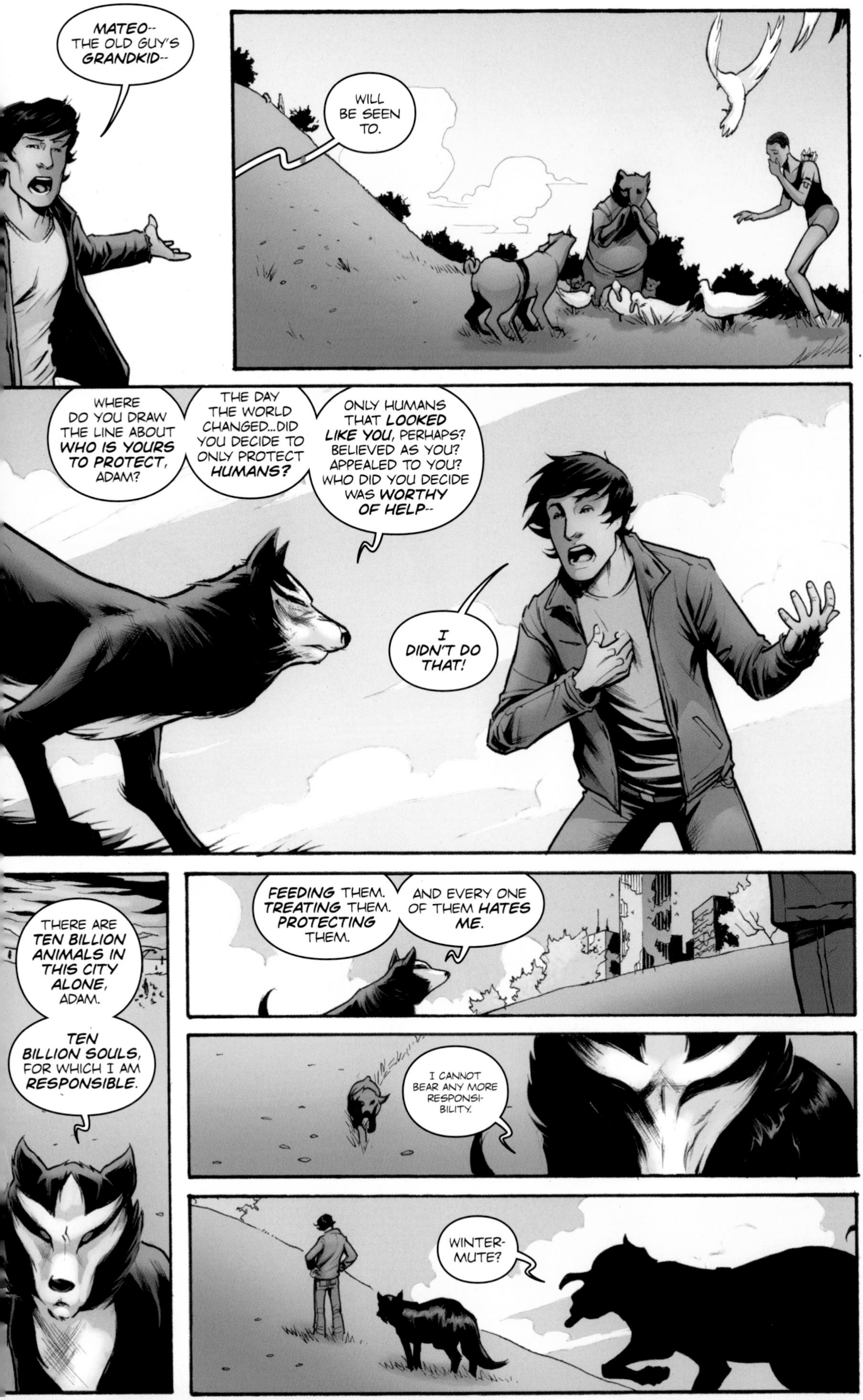
MATEO-- THE OLD GUY'S GRANDKID--
WILL BE SEEN TO.
WHERE DO YOU DRAW THE LINE ABOUT WHO IS YOURS TO PROTECT, ADAM?
THE DAY THE WORLD CHANGED...DID YOU DECIDE TO ONLY PROTECT HUMANS?
ONLY HUMANS THAT LOOKED LIKE YOU, PERHAPS? BELIEVED AS YOU? APPEALED TO YOU? WHO DID YOU DECIDE WAS WORTHY OF HELP--
I DIDN'T DO THAT!
THERE ARE TEN BILLION ANIMALS IN THIS CITY ALONE, ADAM.
TEN BILLION SOULS, FOR WHICH I AM RESPONSIBLE.
FEEDING THEM. TREATING THEM. PROTECTING THEM.
AND EVERY ONE OF THEM HATES ME.
I CANNOT BEAR ANY MORE RESPONSI- BILITY.
WINTER- MUTE?

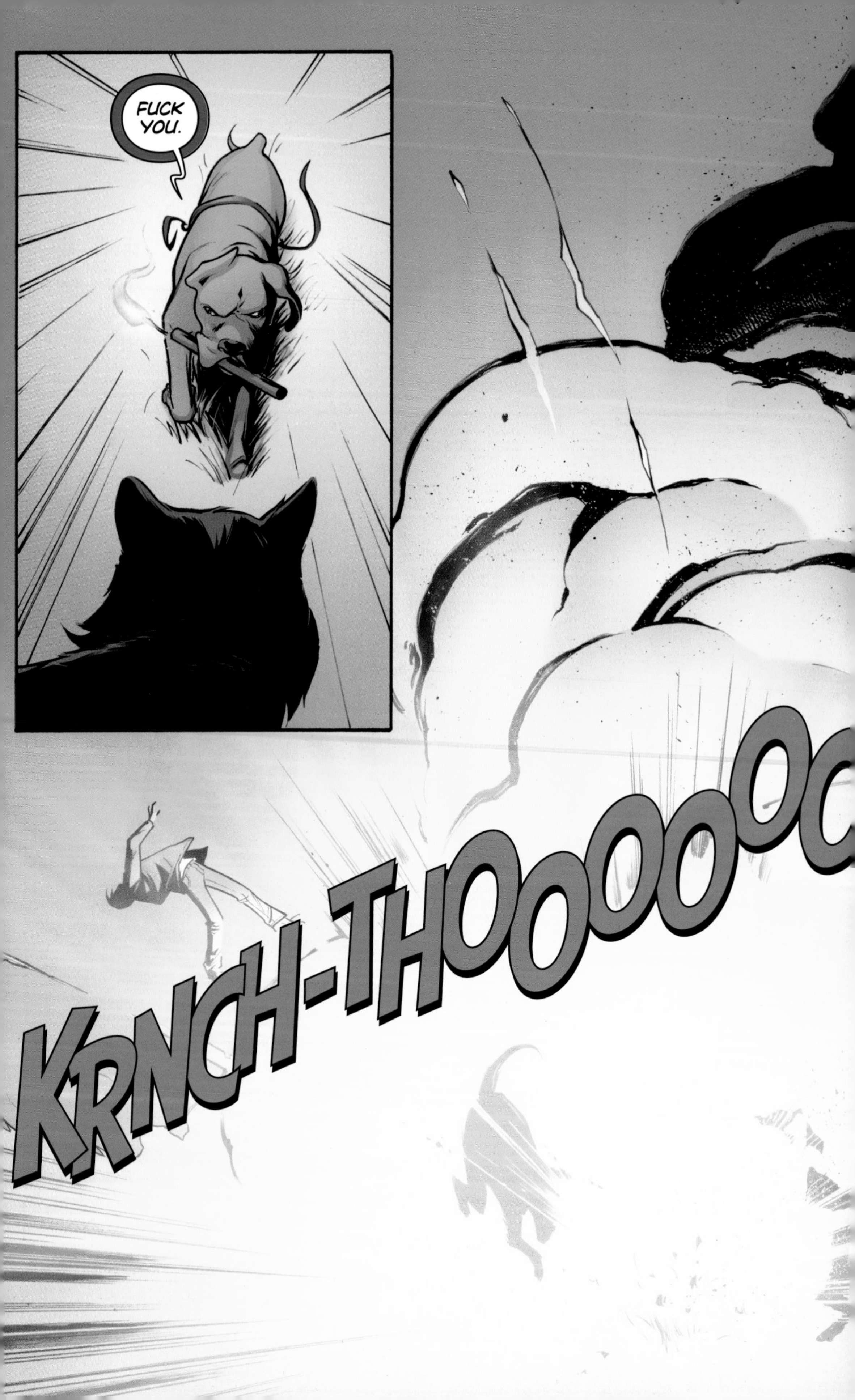
FUCK YOU.
KRNCH-THOOOOOO

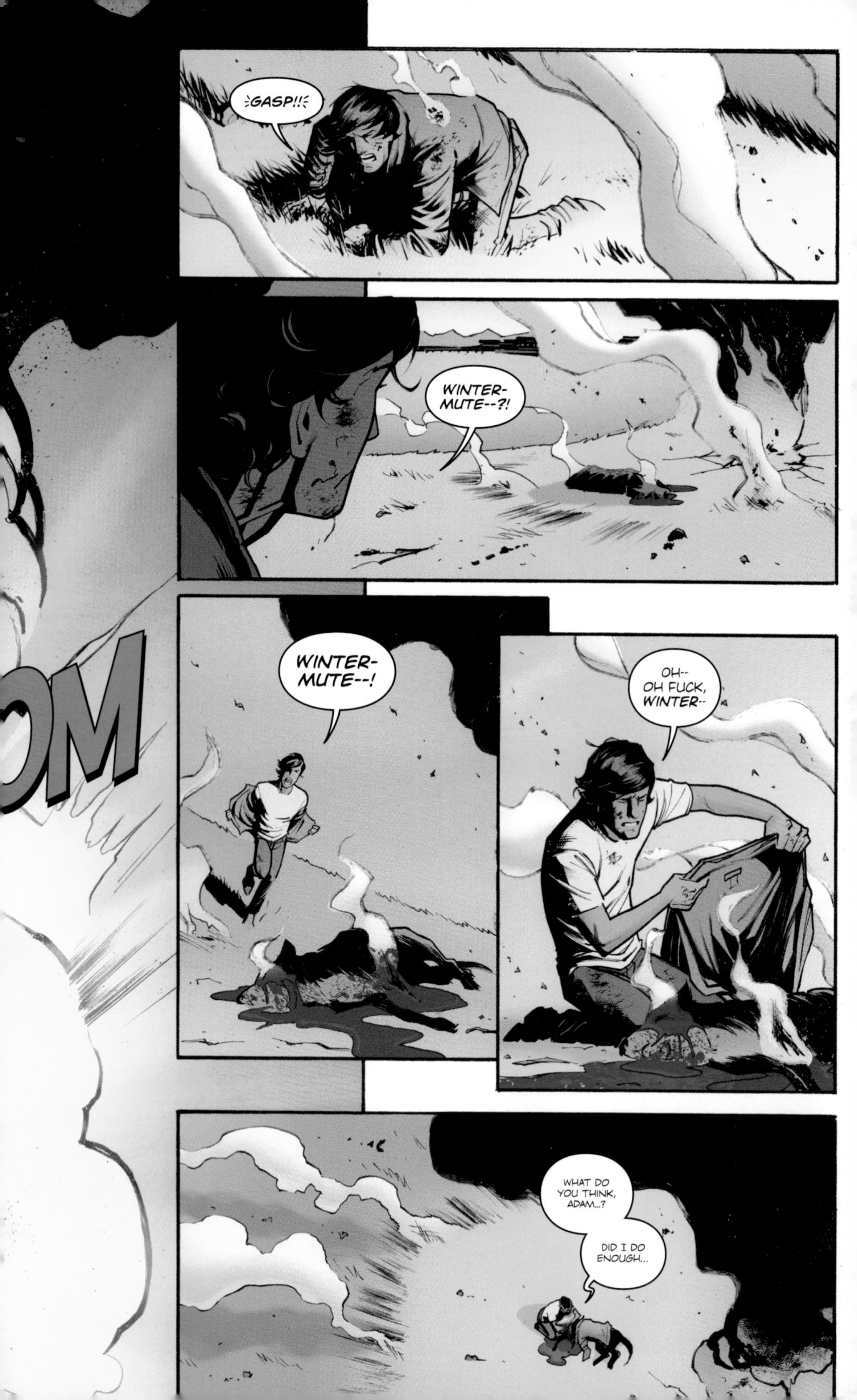
GASP!!
WINTER-MUTE--?!
WINTER-MUTE--!
OH-- OH FUCK, WINTER--
WHAT DO YOU THINK, ADAM...?
DID I DO ENOUGH...

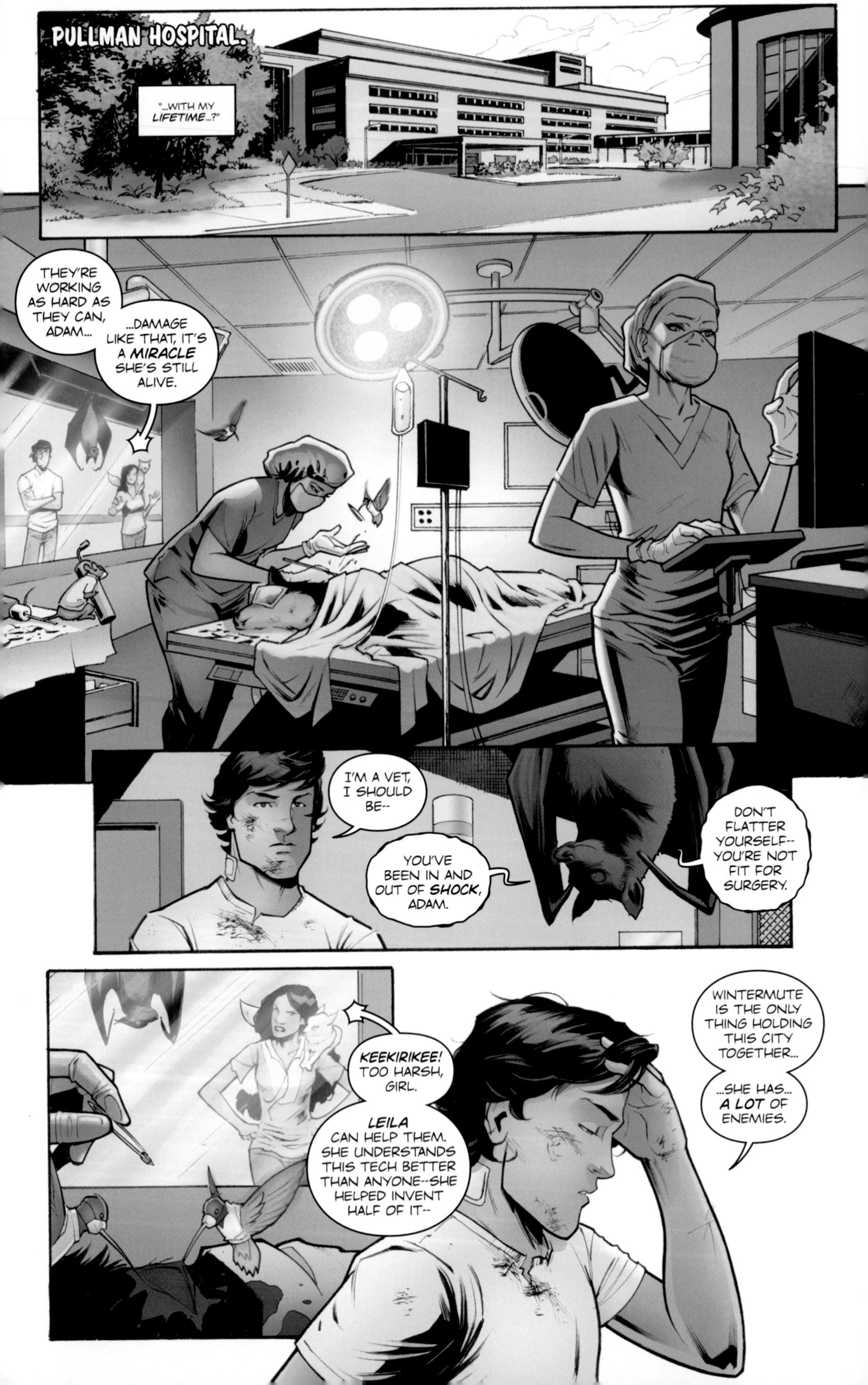
PULLMAN HOSPITAL.
"...WITH MY LIFETIME...?"
THEY'RE WORKING AS HARD AS THEY CAN, ADAM...
...DAMAGE LIKE THAT, IT'S A MIRACLE SHE'S STILL ALIVE.
I'M A VET, I SHOULD BE--
YOU'VE BEEN IN AND OUT OF SHOCK, ADAM.
DON'T FLATTER YOURSELF--YOU'RE NOT FIT FOR SURGERY.
KEEKIRIKEE! TOO HARSH, GIRL.
LEILA CAN HELP THEM. SHE UNDERSTANDS THIS TECH BETTER THAN ANYONE--SHE HELPED INVENT HALF OF IT--
WINTERMUTE IS THE ONLY THING HOLDING THIS CITY TOGETHER...
...SHE HAS... A LOT OF ENEMIES.

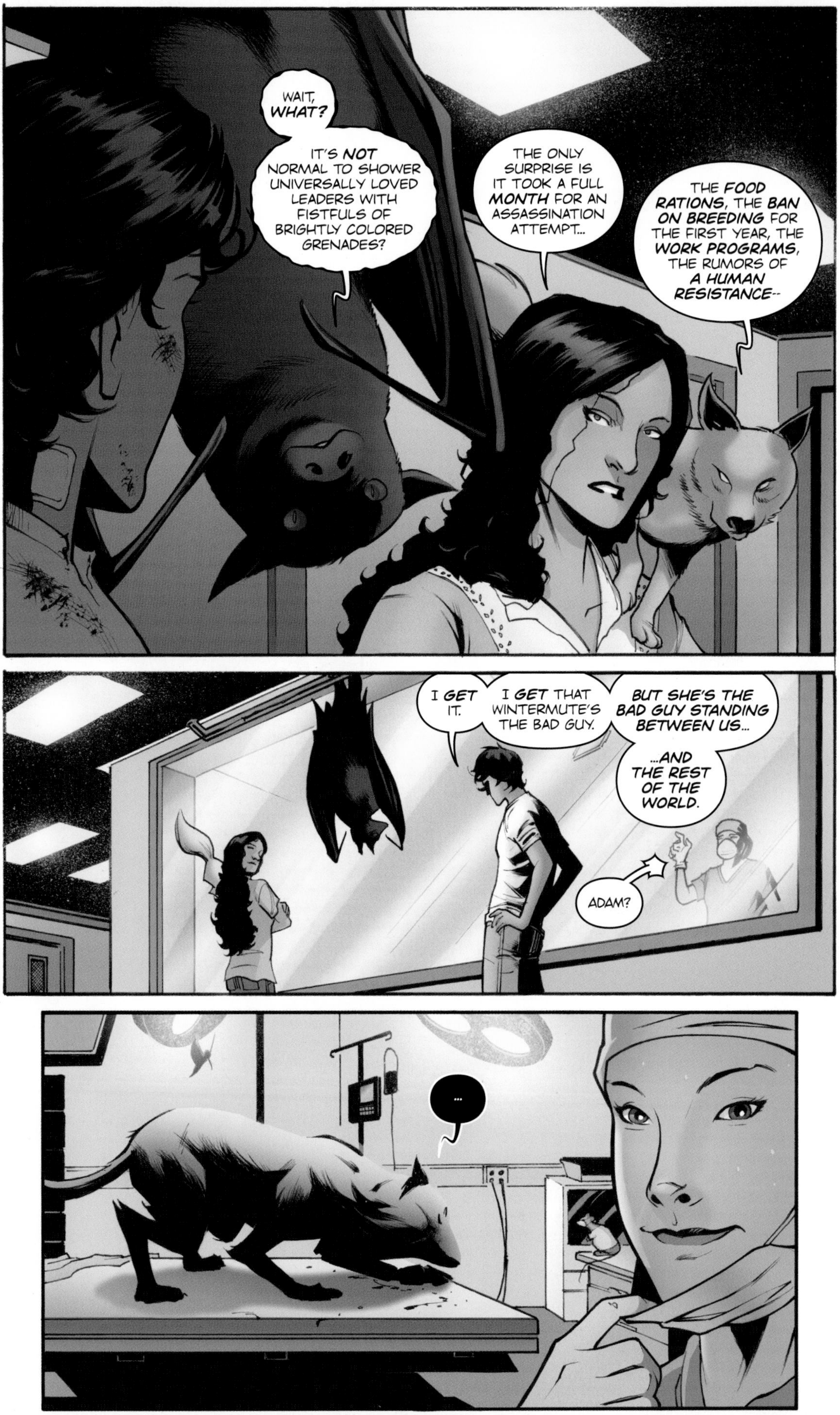
WAIT, WHAT?
IT'S NOT NORMAL TO SHOWER UNIVERSALLY LOVED LEADERS WITH FISTFULS OF BRIGHTLY COLORED GRENADES?
THE ONLY SURPRISE IS IT TOOK A FULL MONTH FOR AN ASSASSINATION ATTEMPT...
THE FOOD RATIONS, THE BAN ON BREEDING FOR THE FIRST YEAR, THE WORK PROGRAMS, THE RUMORS OF A HUMAN RESISTANCE--
I GET IT.
I GET THAT WINTERMUTE'S THE BAD GUY.
BUT SHE'S THE BAD GUY STANDING BETWEEN US...
...AND THE REST OF THE WORLD.
ADAM?
...

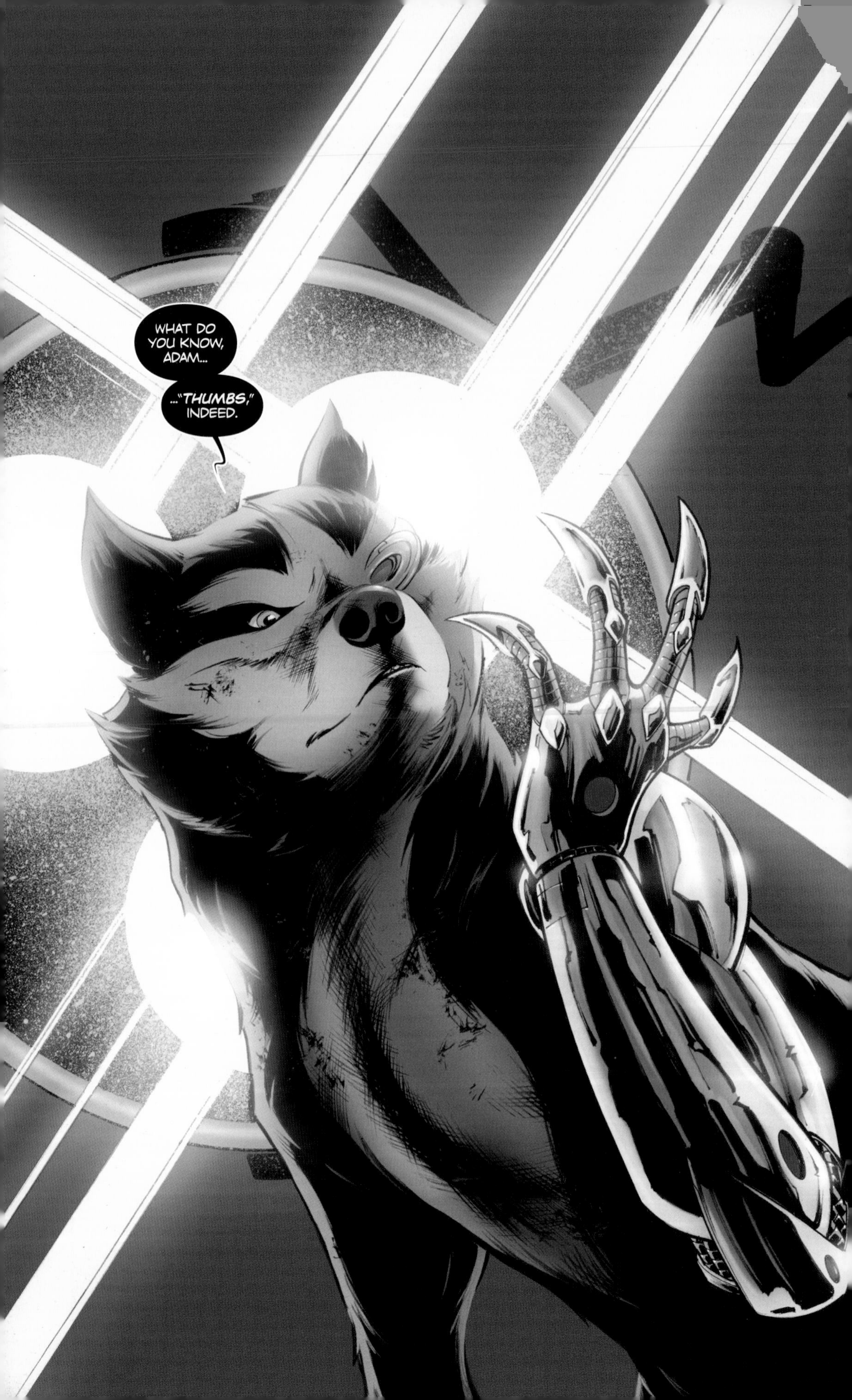
WHAT DO YOU KNOW, ADAM...
..."THUMBS," INDEED.

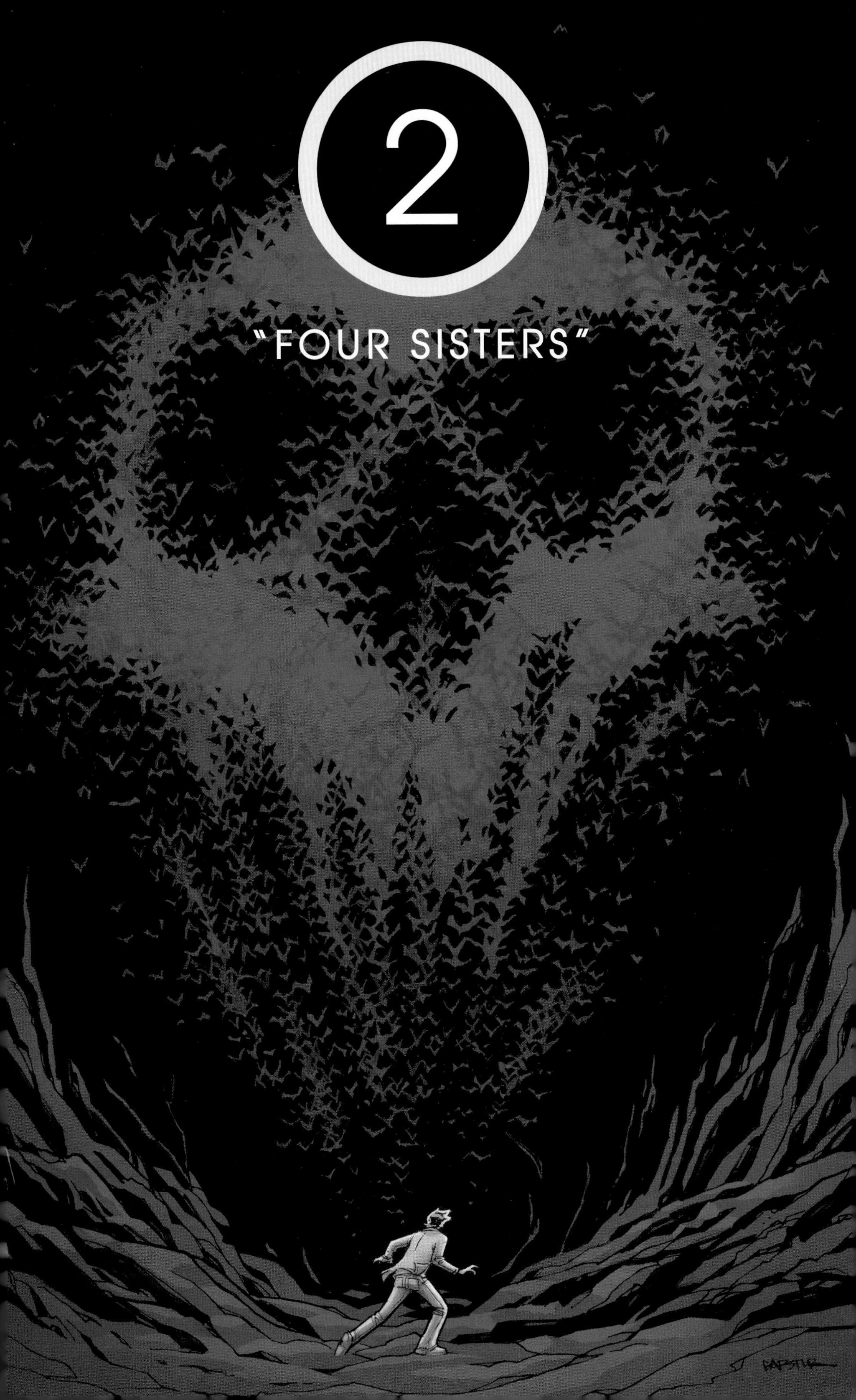
2
"FOUR SISTERS"

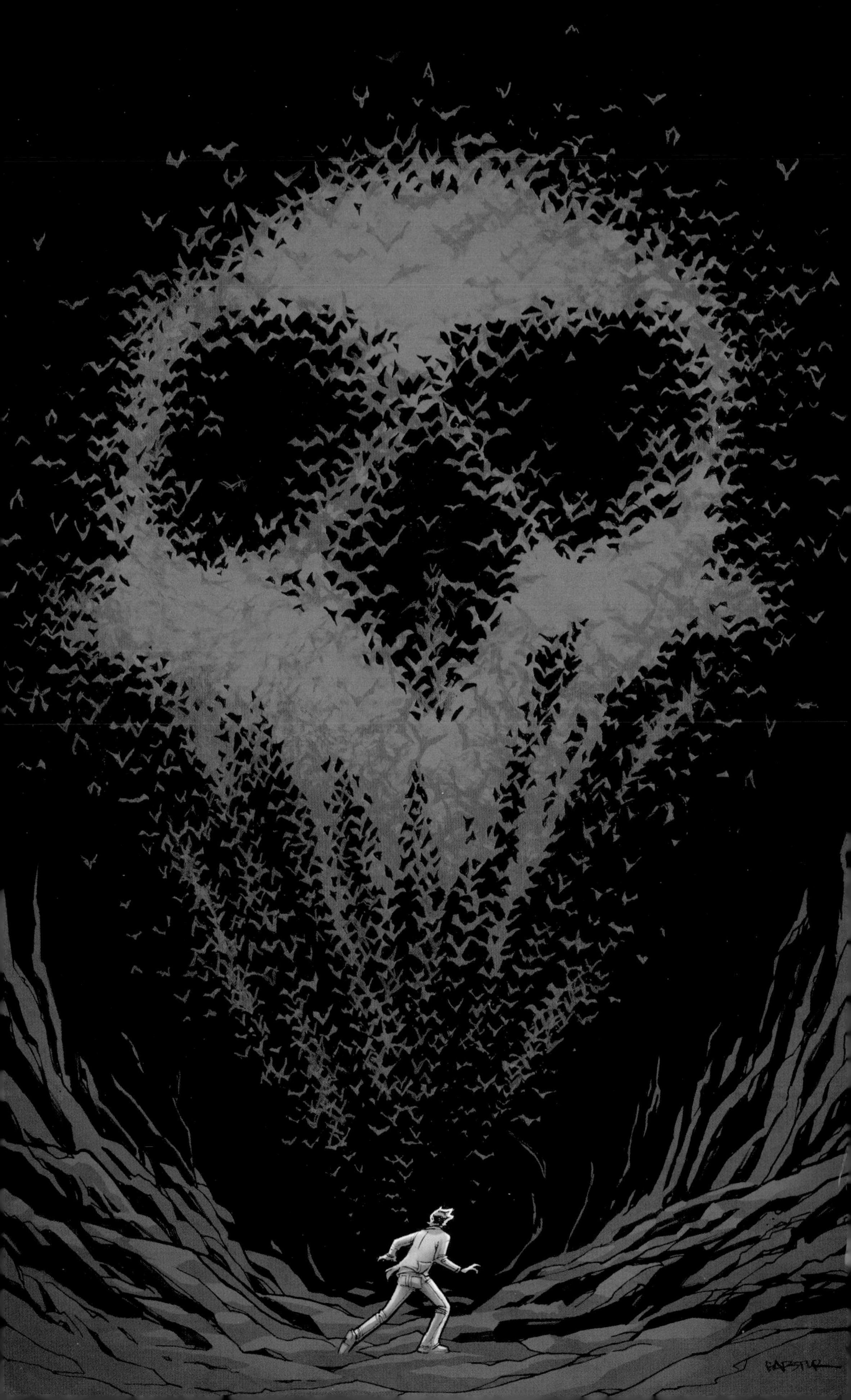

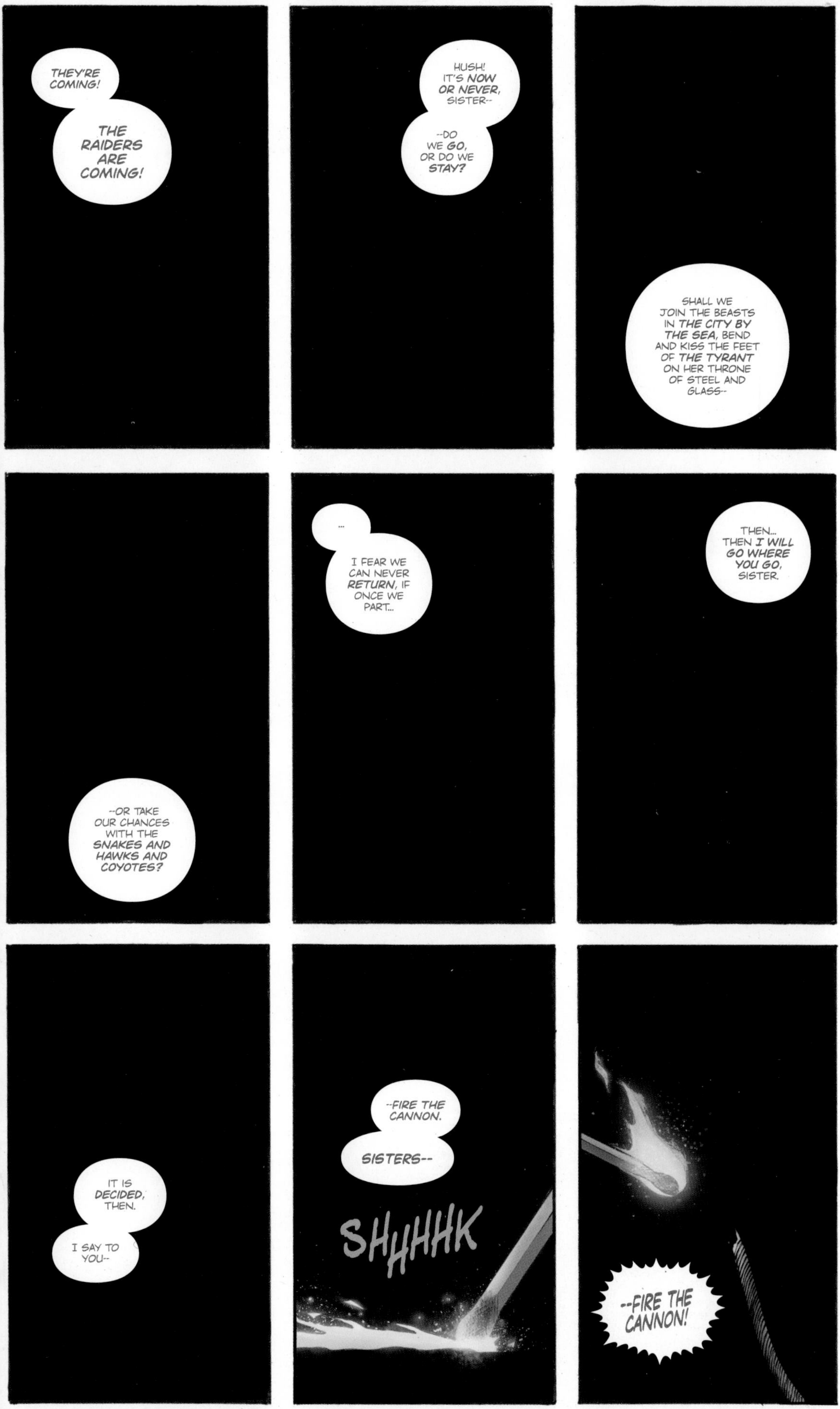
THEY'RE COMING!
THE RAIDERS ARE COMING!
HUSH! IT'S NOW OR NEVER, SISTER--
--DO WE GO, OR DO WE STAY?
SHALL WE JOIN THE BEASTS IN THE CITY BY THE SEA, BEND AND KISS THE FEET OF THE TYRANT ON HER THRONE OF STEEL AND GLASS--
--OR TAKE OUR CHANCES WITH THE SNAKES AND HAWKS AND COYOTES?
...
I FEAR WE CAN NEVER RETURN, IF ONCE WE PART...
THEN... THEN I WILL GO WHERE YOU GO, SISTER.
IT IS DECIDED, THEN.
I SAY TO YOU--
SISTERS--
--FIRE THE CANNON.
SHHHHK
--FIRE THE CANNON!

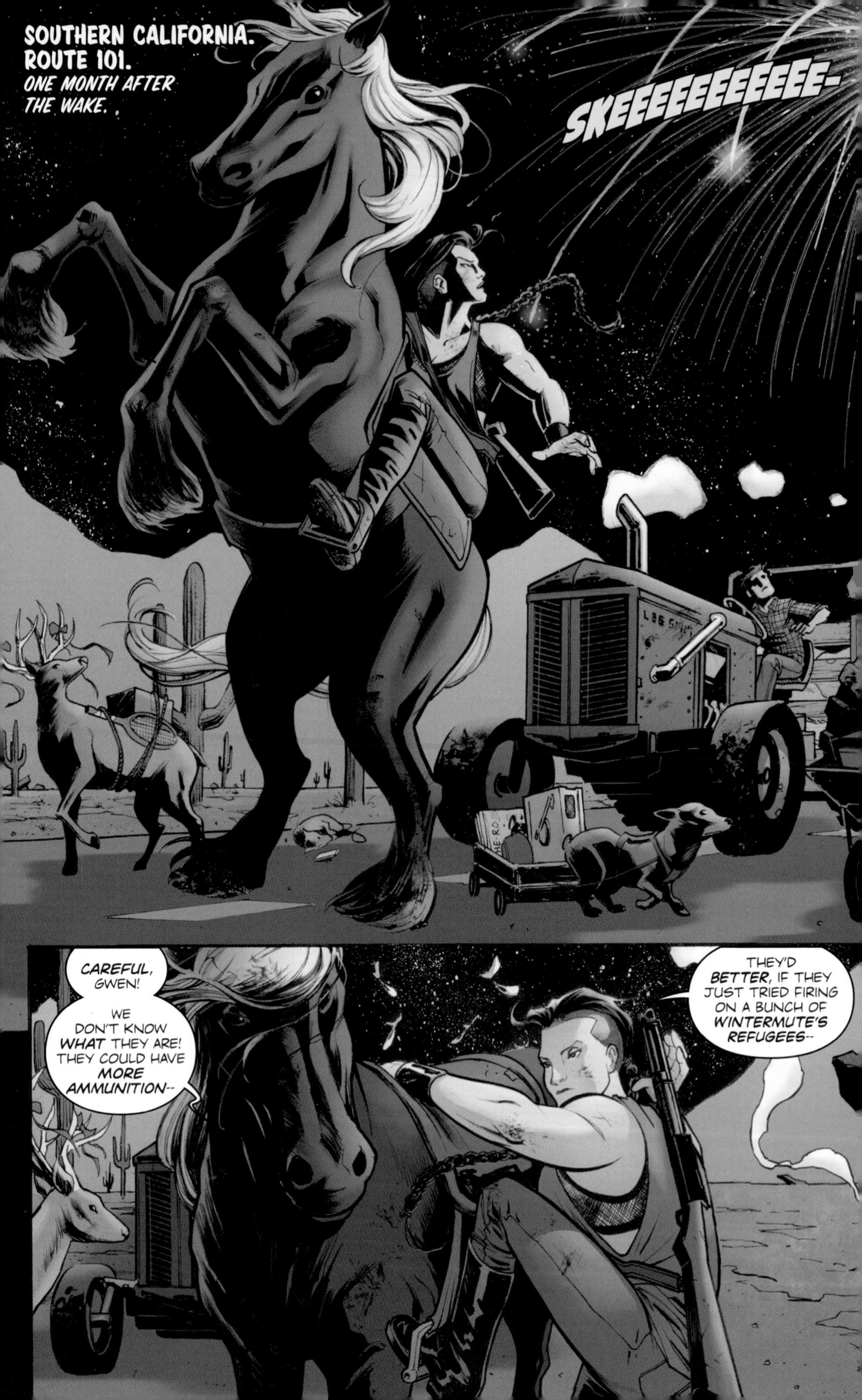
SOUTHERN CALIFORNIA.
ROUTE 101.
ONE MONTH AFTER THE WAKE.
SKEEEEEEEEEEE-
CAREFUL, GWEN!
WE DON'T KNOW WHAT THEY ARE! THEY COULD HAVE MORE AMMUNITION--
THEY'D BETTER, IF THEY JUST TRIED FIRING ON A BUNCH OF WINTERMUTE'S REFUGEES--

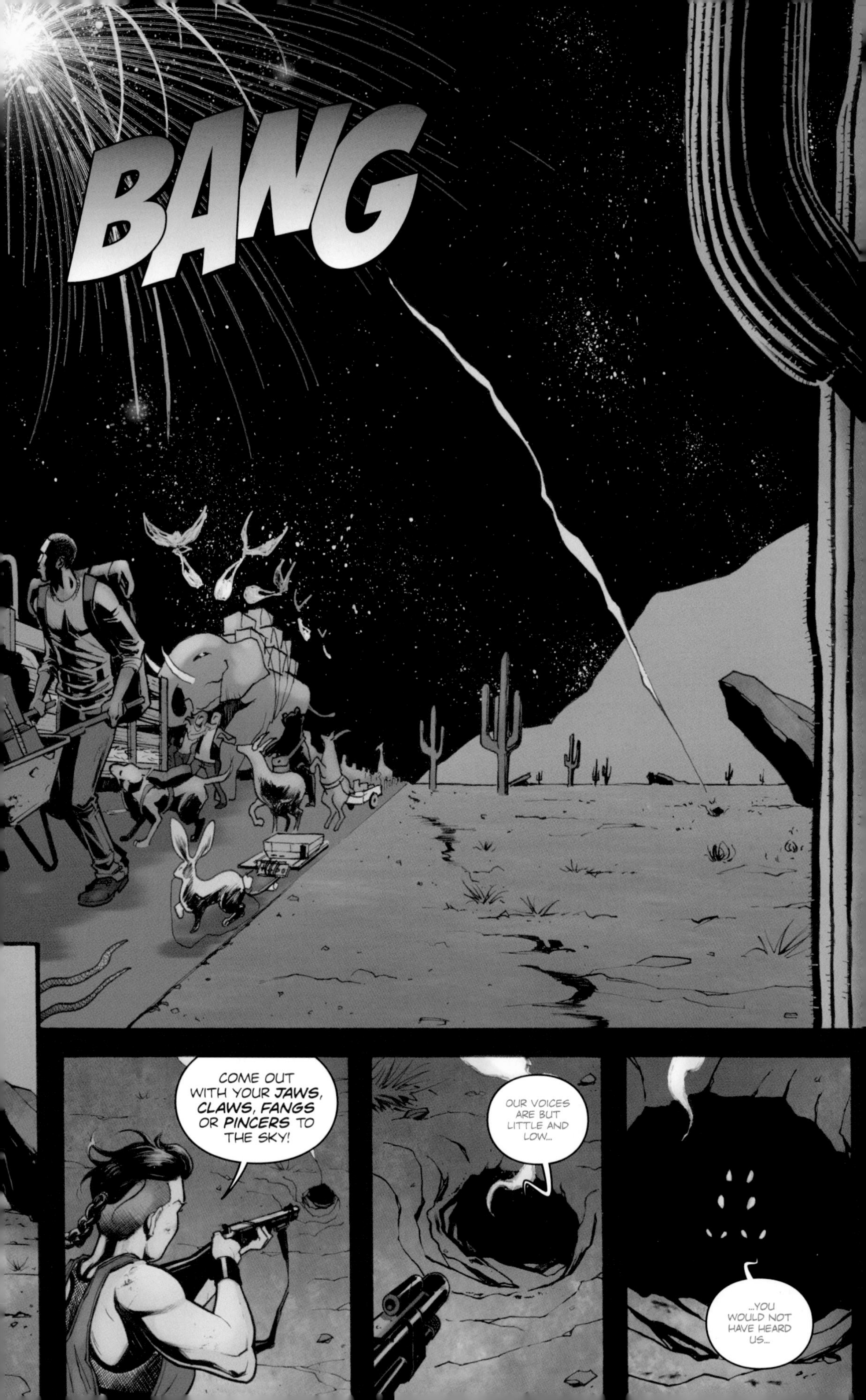
BANG
COME OUT WITH YOUR JAWS, CLAWS, FANGS OR PINCERS TO THE SKY!
OUR VOICES ARE BUT LITTLE AND LOW...
...YOU WOULD NOT HAVE HEARD US...

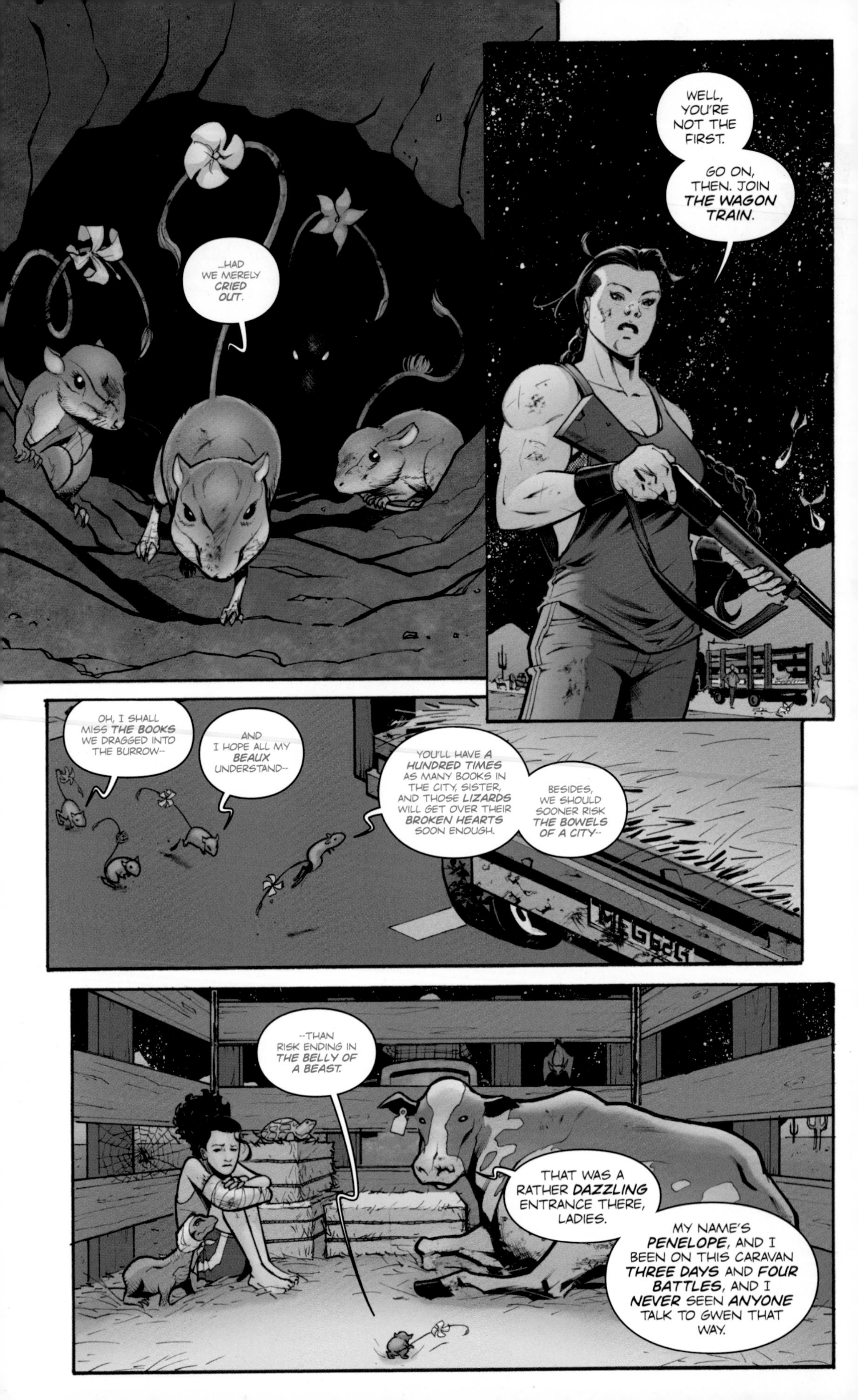
...HAD WE MERELY CRIED OUT.
WELL, YOU'RE NOT THE FIRST.
GO ON, THEN. JOIN THE WAGON TRAIN.
OH, I SHALL MISS THE BOOKS WE DRAGGED INTO THE BURROW--
AND I HOPE ALL MY BEAUX UNDERSTAND--
YOU'LL HAVE A HUNDRED TIMES AS MANY BOOKS IN THE CITY, SISTER, AND THOSE LIZARDS WILL GET OVER THEIR BROKEN HEARTS SOON ENOUGH.
BESIDES, WE SHOULD SOONER RISK THE BOWELS OF A CITY--
--THAN RISK ENDING IN THE BELLY OF A BEAST.
THAT WAS A RATHER DAZZLING ENTRANCE THERE, LADIES.
MY NAME'S PENELOPE, AND I BEEN ON THIS CARAVAN THREE DAYS AND FOUR BATTLES, AND I NEVER SEEN ANYONE TALK TO GWEN THAT WAY.

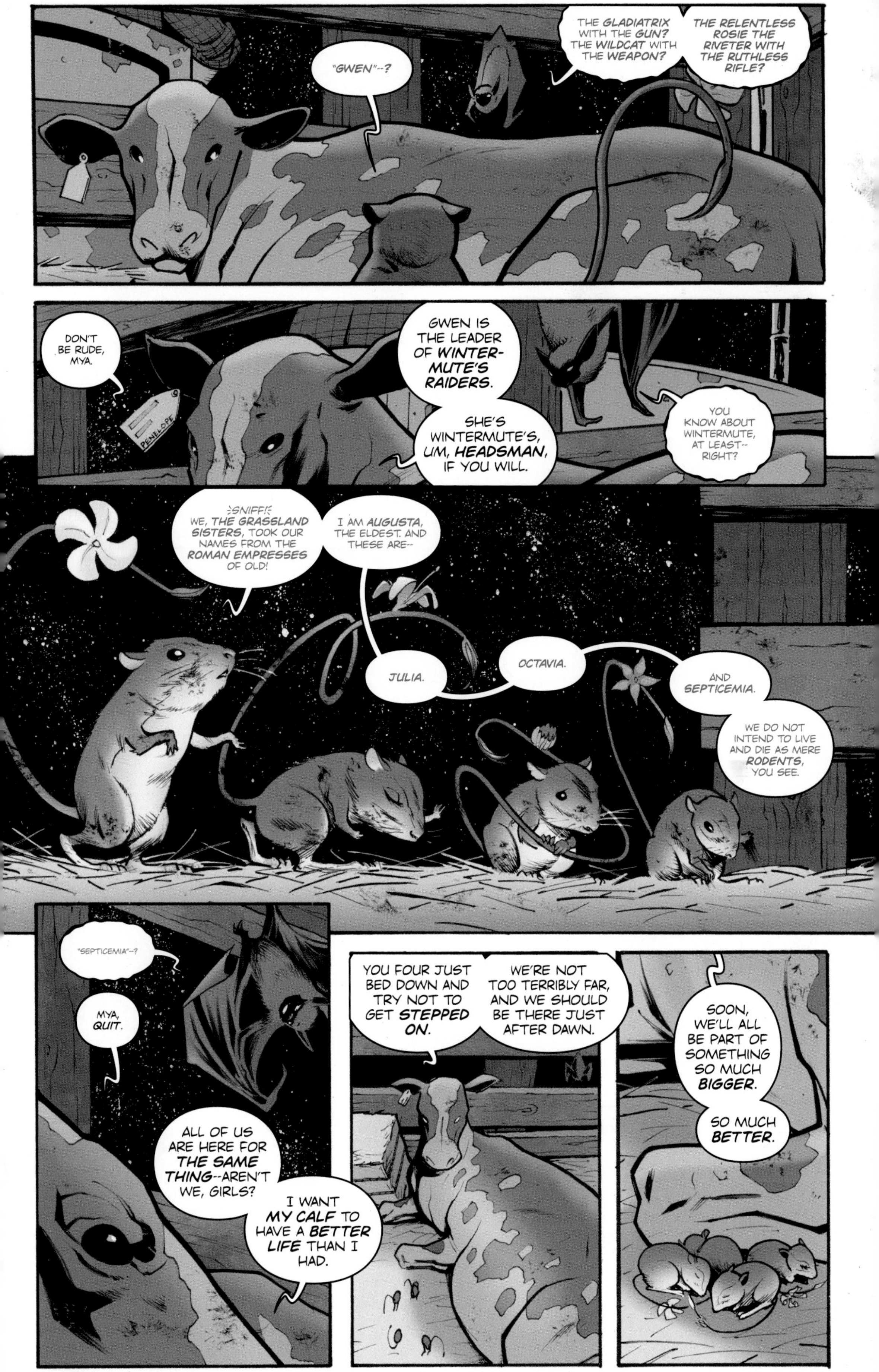
"GWEN"--?
THE GLADIATRIX WITH THE GUN? THE WILDCAT WITH THE WEAPON?
THE RELENTLESS ROSIE THE RIVETER WITH THE RUTHLESS RIFLE?
DON'T BE RUDE, MYA.
PENELOPE
GWEN IS THE LEADER OF WINTERMUTE'S RAIDERS.
SHE'S WINTERMUTE'S, UM, HEADSMAN, IF YOU WILL.
YOU KNOW ABOUT WINTERMUTE, AT LEAST-- RIGHT?
SNIFF! WE, THE GRASSLAND SISTERS, TOOK OUR NAMES FROM THE ROMAN EMPRESSES OF OLD!
I AM AUGUSTA, THE ELDEST. AND THESE ARE--
JULIA.
OCTAVIA.
AND SEPTICEMIA.
WE DO NOT INTEND TO LIVE AND DIE AS MERE RODENTS, YOU SEE.
"SEPTICEMIA"--?
MYA, QUIT.
ALL OF US ARE HERE FOR THE SAME THING--AREN'T WE, GIRLS?
I WANT MY CALF TO HAVE A BETTER LIFE THAN I HAD.
YOU FOUR JUST BED DOWN AND TRY NOT TO GET STEPPED ON.
WE'RE NOT TOO TERRIBLY FAR, AND WE SHOULD BE THERE JUST AFTER DAWN.
SOON, WE'LL ALL BE PART OF SOMETHING SO MUCH BIGGER.
SO MUCH BETTER.

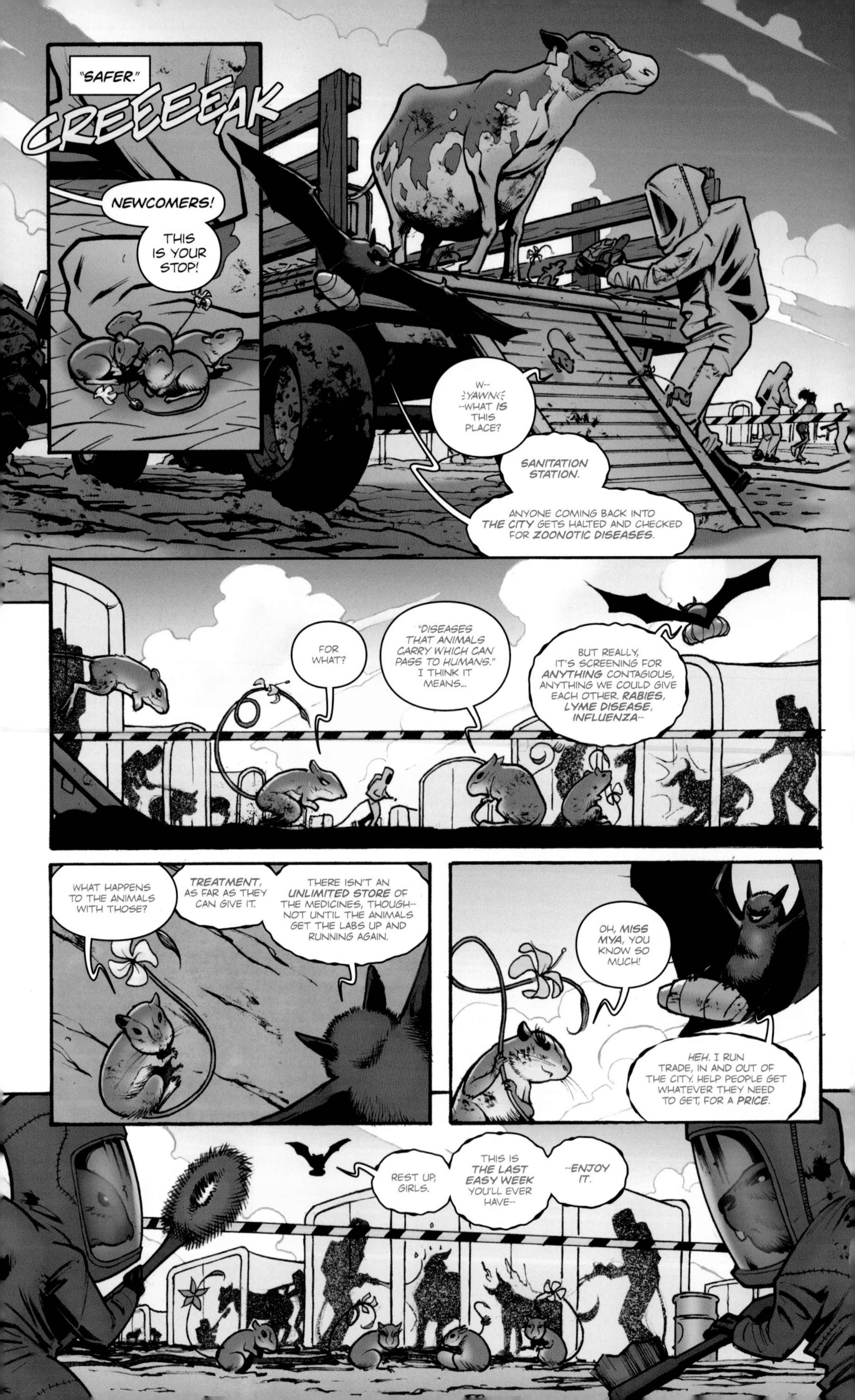
"SAFER."
CREEEEEAK
NEWCOMERS!
THIS IS YOUR STOP!
W-- YAWN --WHAT IS THIS PLACE?
SANITATION STATION.
ANYONE COMING BACK INTO THE CITY GETS HALTED AND CHECKED FOR ZOONOTIC DISEASES.
FOR WHAT?
"DISEASES THAT ANIMALS CARRY WHICH CAN PASS TO HUMANS." I THINK IT MEANS...
BUT REALLY, IT'S SCREENING FOR ANYTHING CONTAGIOUS, ANYTHING WE COULD GIVE EACH OTHER. RABIES, LYME DISEASE, INFLUENZA--
WHAT HAPPENS TO THE ANIMALS WITH THOSE?
TREATMENT, AS FAR AS THEY CAN GIVE IT.
THERE ISN'T AN UNLIMITED STORE OF THE MEDICINES, THOUGH-- NOT UNTIL THE ANIMALS GET THE LABS UP AND RUNNING AGAIN.
OH, MISS MYA, YOU KNOW SO MUCH!
HEH. I RUN TRADE, IN AND OUT OF THE CITY. HELP PEOPLE GET WHATEVER THEY NEED TO GET, FOR A PRICE.
REST UP, GIRLS.
THIS IS THE LAST EASY WEEK YOU'LL EVER HAVE--
--ENJOY IT.

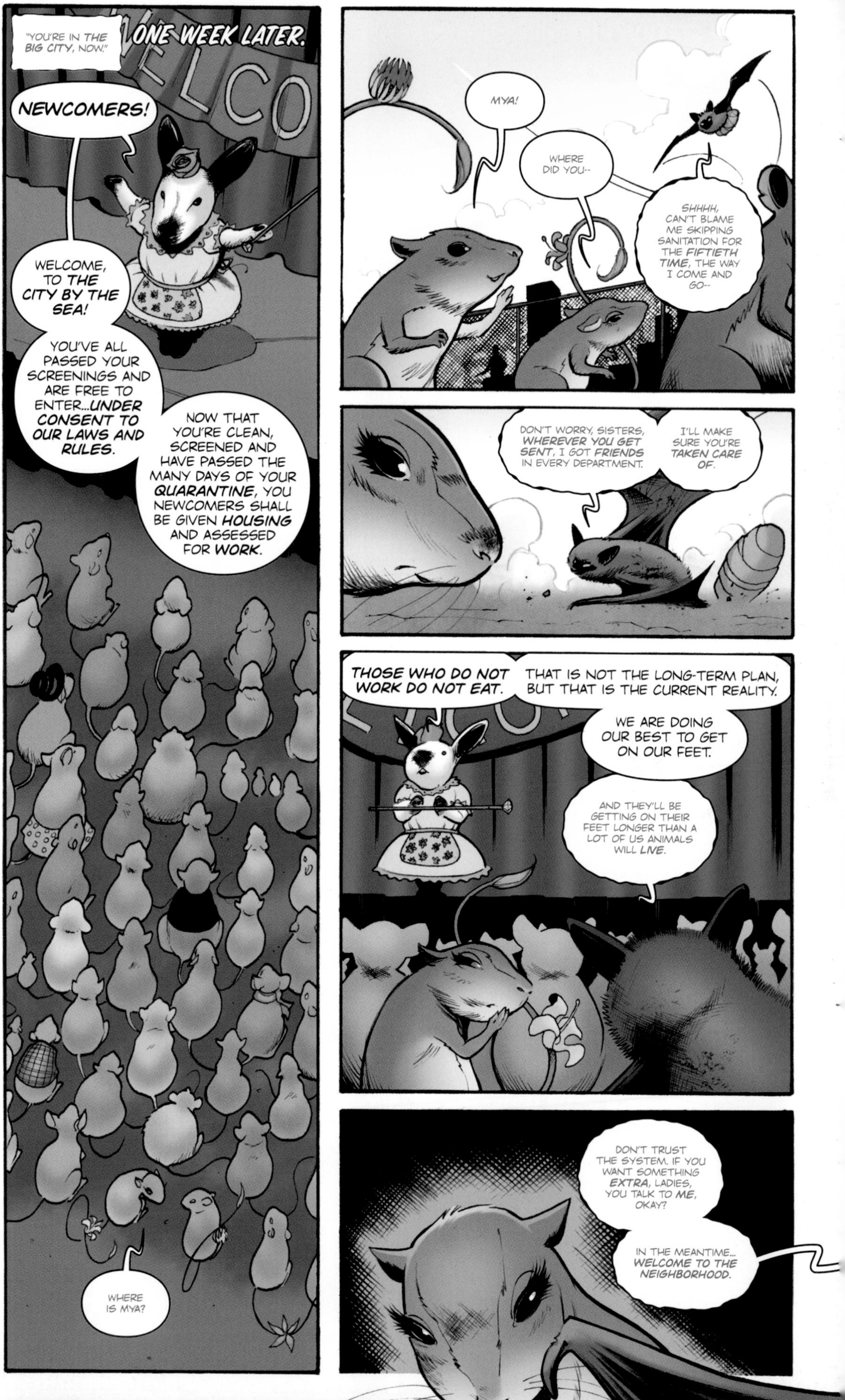
"YOU'RE IN THE BIG CITY, NOW."
ONE WEEK LATER.
NEWCOMERS!
WELCOME, TO THE CITY BY THE SEA!
YOU'VE ALL PASSED YOUR SCREENINGS AND ARE FREE TO ENTER...UNDER CONSENT TO OUR LAWS AND RULES.
NOW THAT YOU'RE CLEAN, SCREENED AND HAVE PASSED THE MANY DAYS OF YOUR QUARANTINE, YOU NEWCOMERS SHALL BE GIVEN HOUSING AND ASSESSED FOR WORK.
WHERE IS MYA?
MYA!
WHERE DID YOU--
SHHHH, CAN'T BLAME ME SKIPPING SANITATION FOR THE FIFTIETH TIME, THE WAY I COME AND GO--
DON'T WORRY, SISTERS, WHEREVER YOU GET SENT, I GOT FRIENDS IN EVERY DEPARTMENT.
I'LL MAKE SURE YOU'RE TAKEN CARE OF.
THOSE WHO DO NOT WORK DO NOT EAT.
THAT IS NOT THE LONG-TERM PLAN, BUT THAT IS THE CURRENT REALITY.
WE ARE DOING OUR BEST TO GET ON OUR FEET.
AND THEY'LL BE GETTING ON THEIR FEET LONGER THAN A LOT OF US ANIMALS WILL LIVE.
DON'T TRUST THE SYSTEM. IF YOU WANT SOMETHING EXTRA, LADIES, YOU TALK TO ME, OKAY?
IN THE MEANTIME... WELCOME TO THE NEIGHBORHOOD.

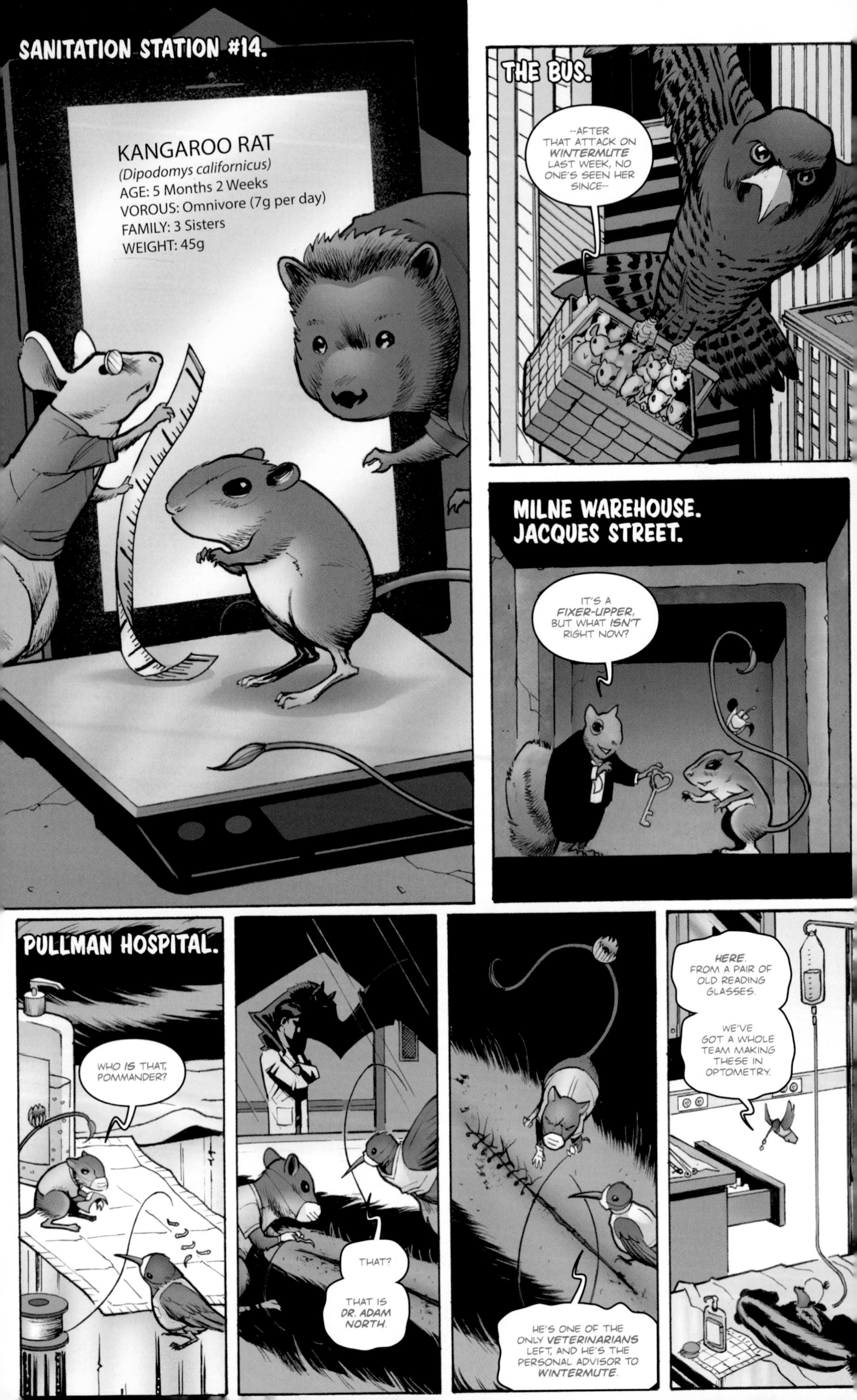
SANITATION STATION #14.
KANGAROO RAT
(Dipodomys californicus)
AGE: 5 Months 2 Weeks
VOROUS: Omnivore (7g per day)
FAMILY: 3 Sisters
WEIGHT: 45g
THE BUS.
--AFTER THAT ATTACK ON WINTERMUTE LAST WEEK, NO ONE'S SEEN HER SINCE--
MILNE WAREHOUSE. JACQUES STREET.
IT'S A FIXER-UPPER, BUT WHAT ISN'T RIGHT NOW?
PULLMAN HOSPITAL.
WHO IS THAT, POMMANDER?
THAT?
THAT IS DR. ADAM NORTH.
HE'S ONE OF THE ONLY VETERINARIANS LEFT, AND HE'S THE PERSONAL ADVISOR TO WINTERMUTE.
HERE. FROM A PAIR OF OLD READING GLASSES.
WE'VE GOT A WHOLE TEAM MAKING THESE IN OPTOMETRY.

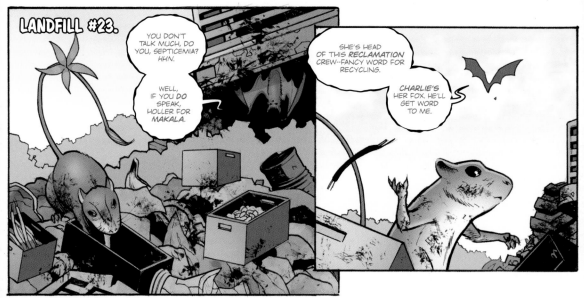

LANDFILL #23.

YOU DON'T TALK MUCH, DO YOU, SEPTICEMIA? HHN.

WELL, IF YOU *DO* SPEAK, HOLLER FOR *MAKALA.*

SHE'S HEAD OF THIS *RECLAMATION* CREW--FANCY WORD FOR RECYCLING.

CHARLIE'S HER FOX. HE'LL GET WORD TO ME.

FOOD DEPOSITORY.

--NEVER ENOUGH TO EAT--

HART, RAM & WOLF. LAW OFFICES.

DO WE MOVE THE CREATURES WITH THE *SHORTEST LIFE EXPECTANCIES* TO THE FRONT OF THE LINE FOR TREATMENT?

YOU'RE LUCKY TO WORK FOR IRENE.

IRENE'S A *LAWMAKER.* IT'S A WHOLE NEW WORLD WE'RE BUILDING...

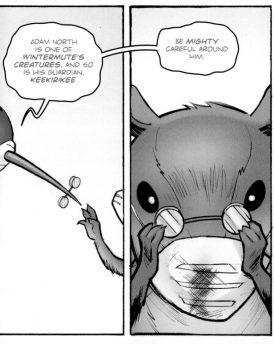

ADAM NORTH IS ONE OF *WINTERMUTE'S CREATURES,* AND SO IS HIS GUARDIAN, *KEEKIRIKEE.*

BE *MIGHTY* CAREFUL AROUND HIM.

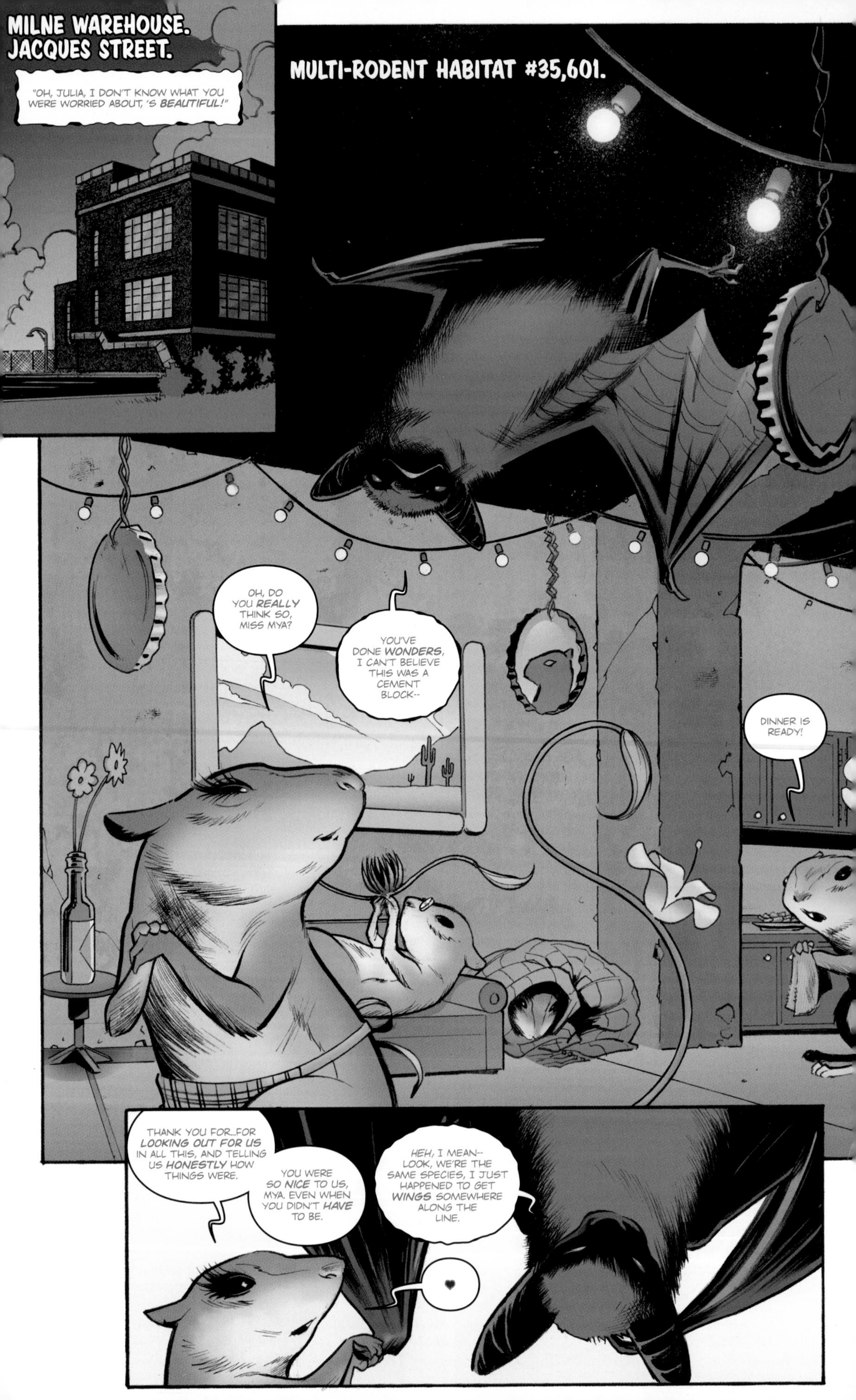
MILNE WAREHOUSE.
JACQUES STREET.
"OH, JULIA, I DON'T KNOW WHAT YOU WERE WORRIED ABOUT, 'S BEAUTIFUL!"
MULTI-RODENT HABITAT #35,601.
OH, DO YOU REALLY THINK SO, MISS MYA?
YOU'VE DONE WONDERS, I CAN'T BELIEVE THIS WAS A CEMENT BLOCK--
DINNER IS READY!
THANK YOU FOR...FOR LOOKING OUT FOR US IN ALL THIS, AND TELLING US HONESTLY HOW THINGS WERE.
YOU WERE SO NICE TO US, MYA. EVEN WHEN YOU DIDN'T HAVE TO BE.
HEH, I MEAN-- LOOK, WE'RE THE SAME SPECIES, I JUST HAPPENED TO GET WINGS SOMEWHERE ALONG THE LINE.

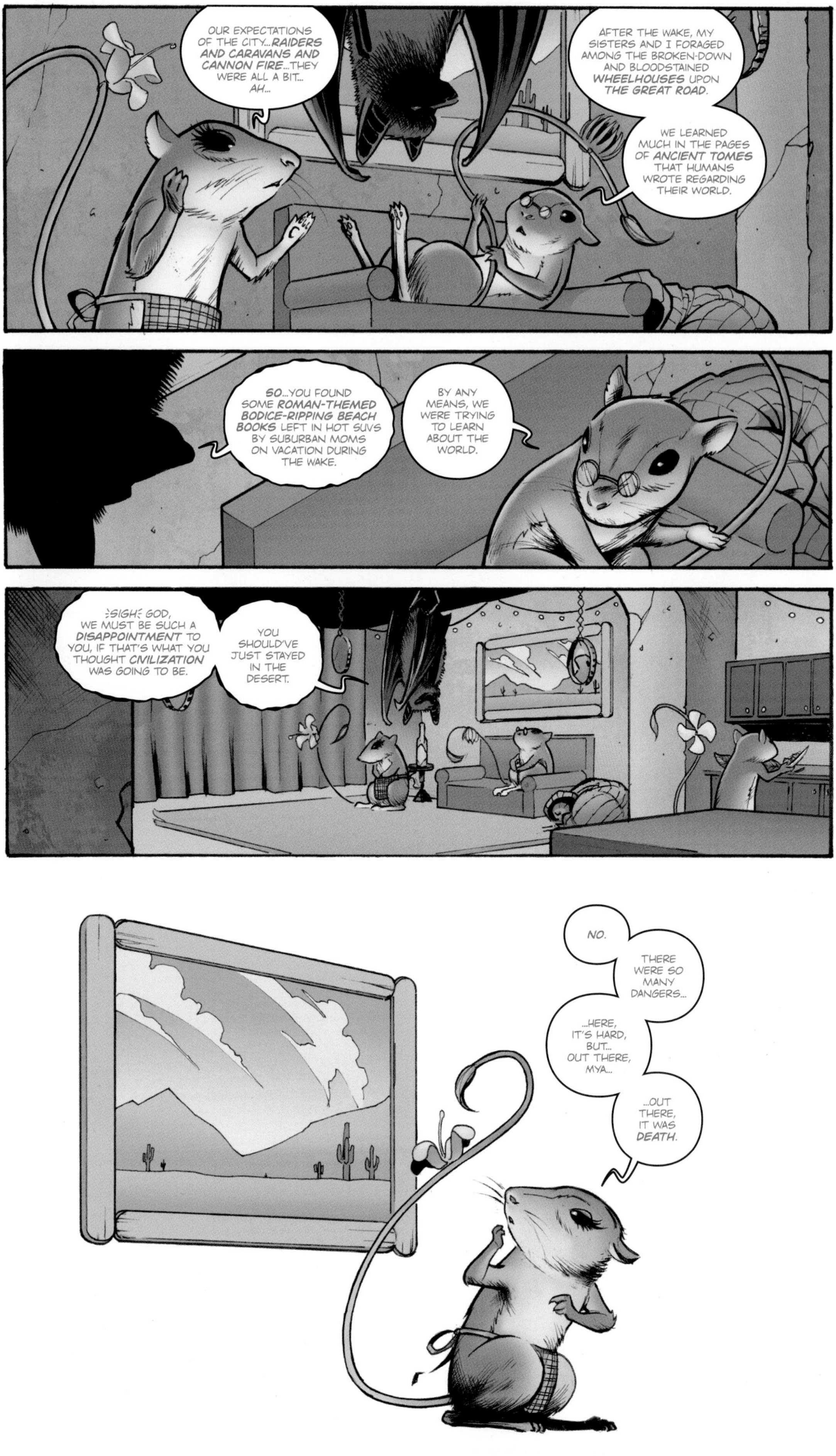
OUR EXPECTATIONS OF THE CITY... RAIDERS AND CARAVANS AND CANNON FIRE... THEY WERE ALL A BIT... AH...
AFTER THE WAKE, MY SISTERS AND I FORAGED AMONG THE BROKEN-DOWN AND BLOODSTAINED WHEELHOUSES UPON THE GREAT ROAD.
WE LEARNED MUCH IN THE PAGES OF ANCIENT TOMES THAT HUMANS WROTE REGARDING THEIR WORLD.
SO... YOU FOUND SOME ROMAN-THEMED BODICE-RIPPING BEACH BOOKS LEFT IN HOT SUVS BY SUBURBAN MOMS ON VACATION DURING THE WAKE.
BY ANY MEANS, WE WERE TRYING TO LEARN ABOUT THE WORLD.
SIGH GOD, WE MUST BE SUCH A DISAPPOINTMENT TO YOU, IF THAT'S WHAT YOU THOUGHT CIVILIZATION WAS GOING TO BE.
YOU SHOULD'VE JUST STAYED IN THE DESERT.
NO.
THERE WERE SO MANY DANGERS...
...HERE, IT'S HARD, BUT... OUT THERE, MYA...
...OUT THERE, IT WAS DEATH.

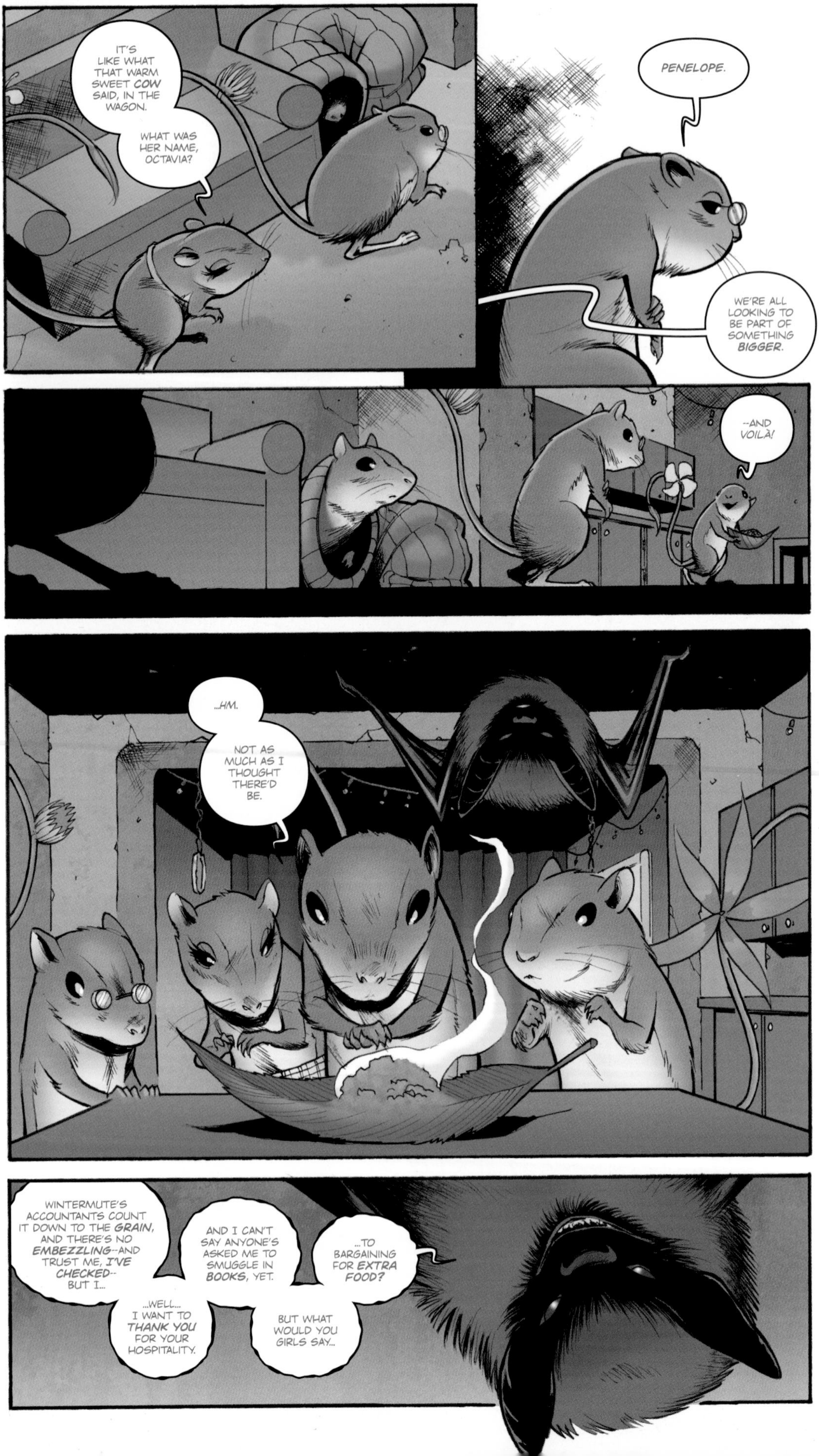
IT'S LIKE WHAT THAT WARM SWEET COW SAID, IN THE WAGON.
WHAT WAS HER NAME, OCTAVIA?
PENELOPE.
WE'RE ALL LOOKING TO BE PART OF SOMETHING BIGGER.
--AND VOILÀ!
...HM.
NOT AS MUCH AS I THOUGHT THERE'D BE.
WINTERMUTE'S ACCOUNTANTS COUNT IT DOWN TO THE GRAIN, AND THERE'S NO EMBEZZLING--AND TRUST ME, I'VE CHECKED-- BUT I...
...WELL... I WANT TO THANK YOU FOR YOUR HOSPITALITY.
AND I CAN'T SAY ANYONE'S ASKED ME TO SMUGGLE IN BOOKS, YET.
BUT WHAT WOULD YOU GIRLS SAY...
...TO BARGAINING FOR EXTRA FOOD?

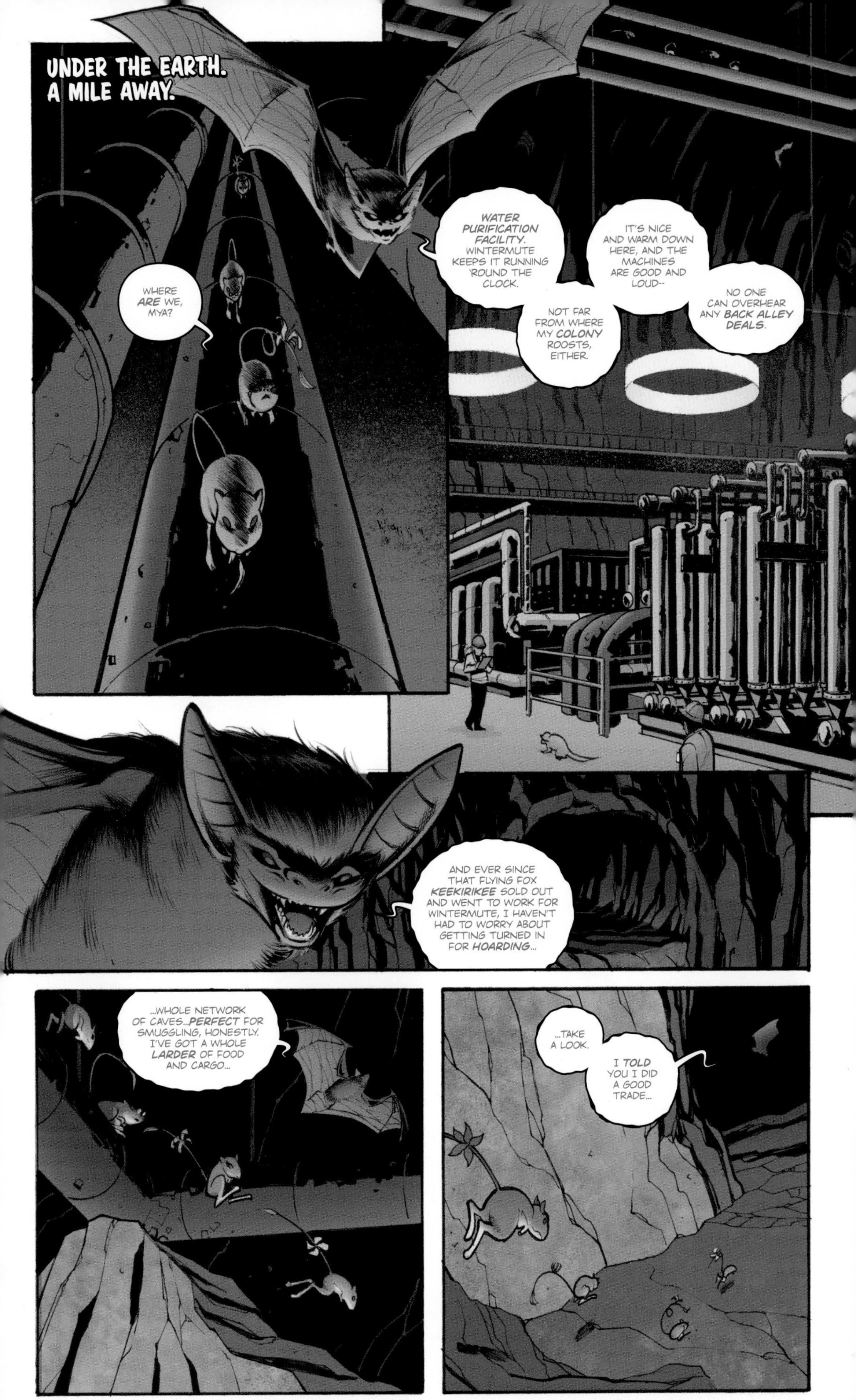
UNDER THE EARTH. A MILE AWAY.
WHERE ARE WE, MYA?
WATER PURIFICATION FACILITY. WINTERMUTE KEEPS IT RUNNING 'ROUND THE CLOCK.
NOT FAR FROM WHERE MY COLONY ROOSTS, EITHER.
IT'S NICE AND WARM DOWN HERE, AND THE MACHINES ARE GOOD AND LOUD--
NO ONE CAN OVERHEAR ANY BACK ALLEY DEALS.
AND EVER SINCE THAT FLYING FOX KEEKIRIKEE SOLD OUT AND WENT TO WORK FOR WINTERMUTE, I HAVEN'T HAD TO WORRY ABOUT GETTING TURNED IN FOR HOARDING...
...WHOLE NETWORK OF CAVES...PERFECT FOR SMUGGLING, HONESTLY. I'VE GOT A WHOLE LARDER OF FOOD AND CARGO...
...TAKE A LOOK.
I TOLD YOU I DID A GOOD TRADE...

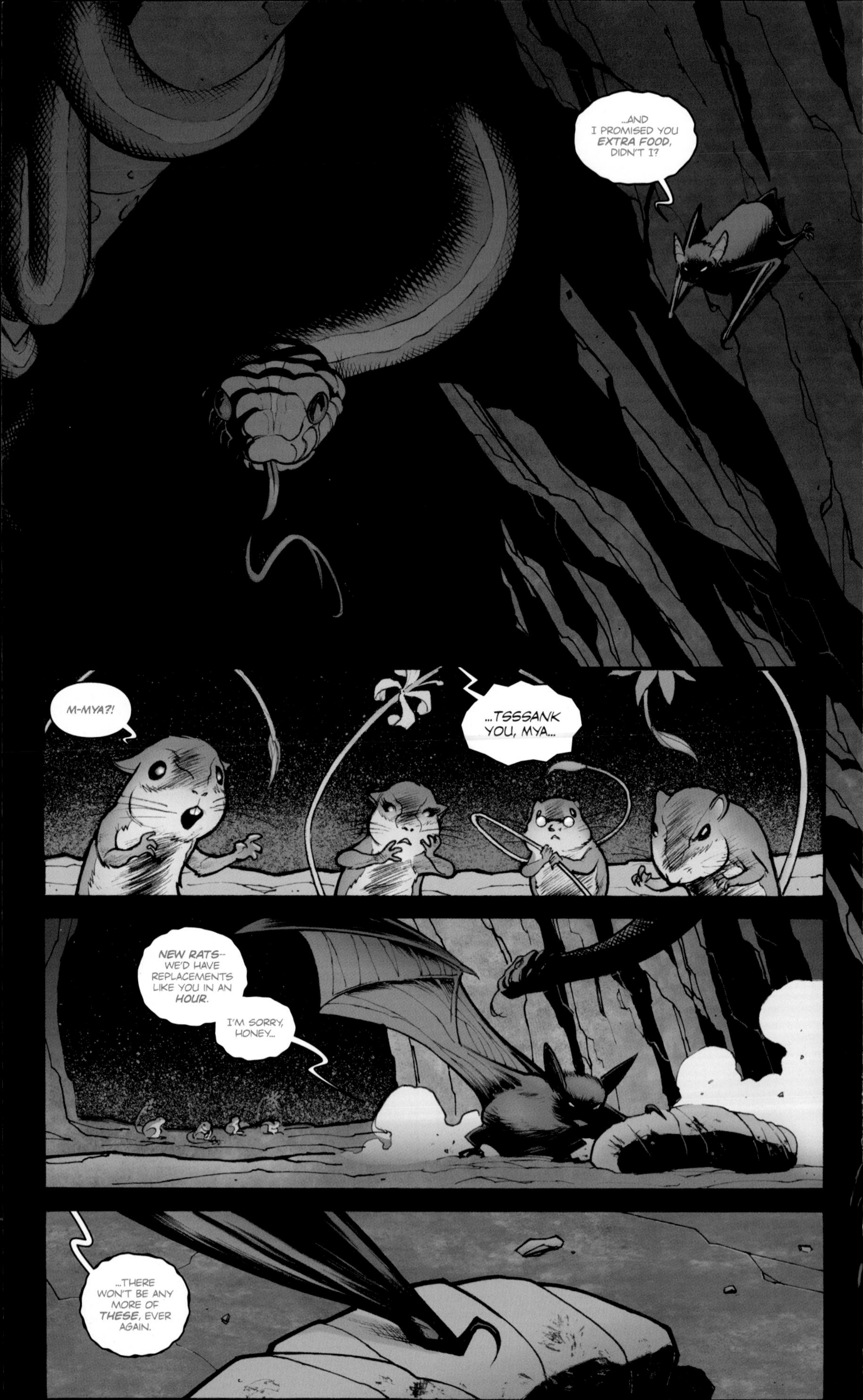
...AND I PROMISED YOU EXTRA FOOD, DIDN'T I?
M-MYA?!
...TSSSANK YOU, MYA...
NEW RATS-- WE'D HAVE REPLACEMENTS LIKE YOU IN AN HOUR.
I'M SORRY, HONEY...
...THERE WON'T BE ANY MORE OF THESE, EVER AGAIN.

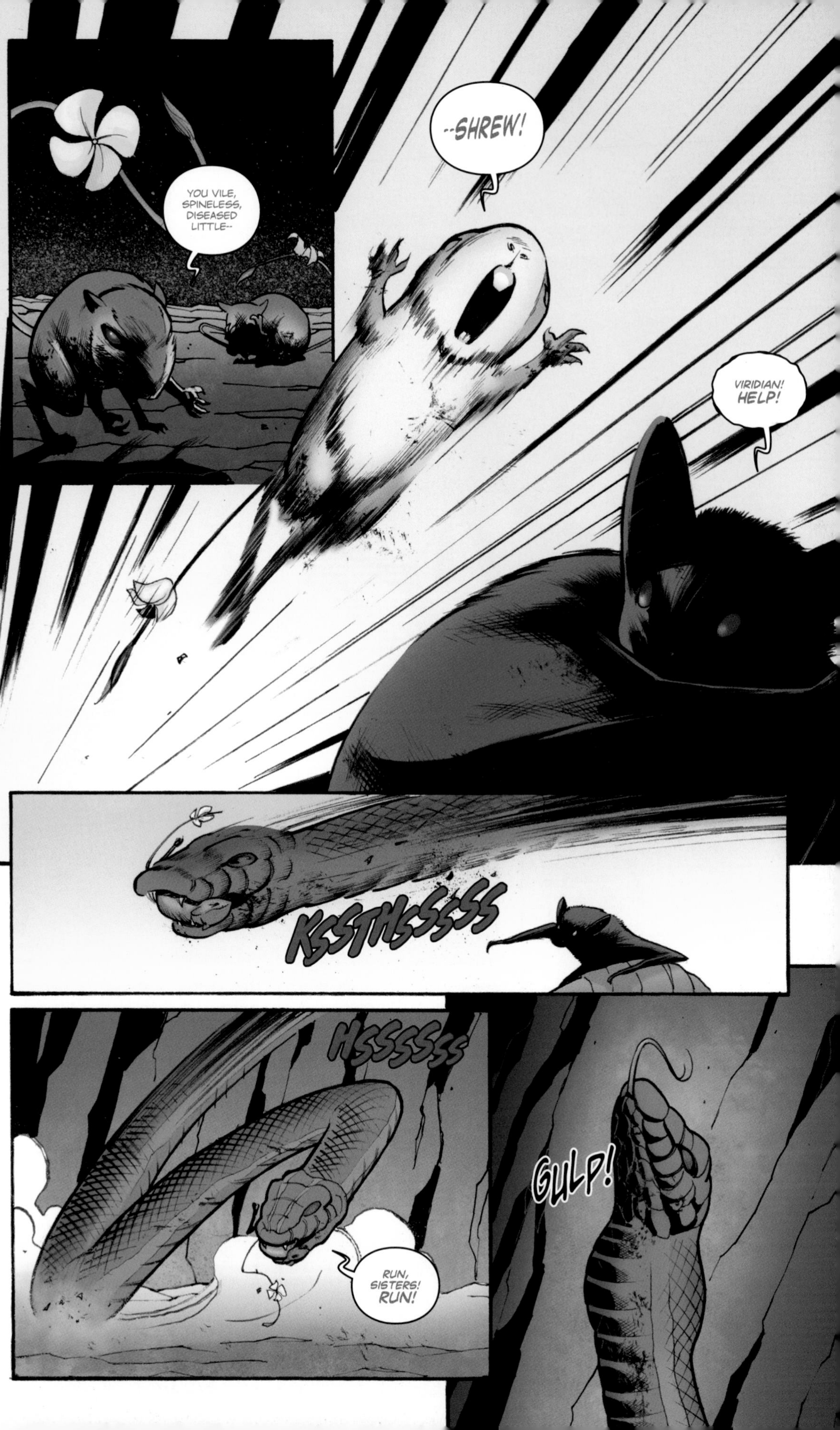

YOU VILE, SPINELESS, DISEASED LITTLE--
--SHREW!
VIRIDIAN! HELP!
KSSTHSSSSS
HSSSSSS
RUN, SISTERS! RUN!
GULP!

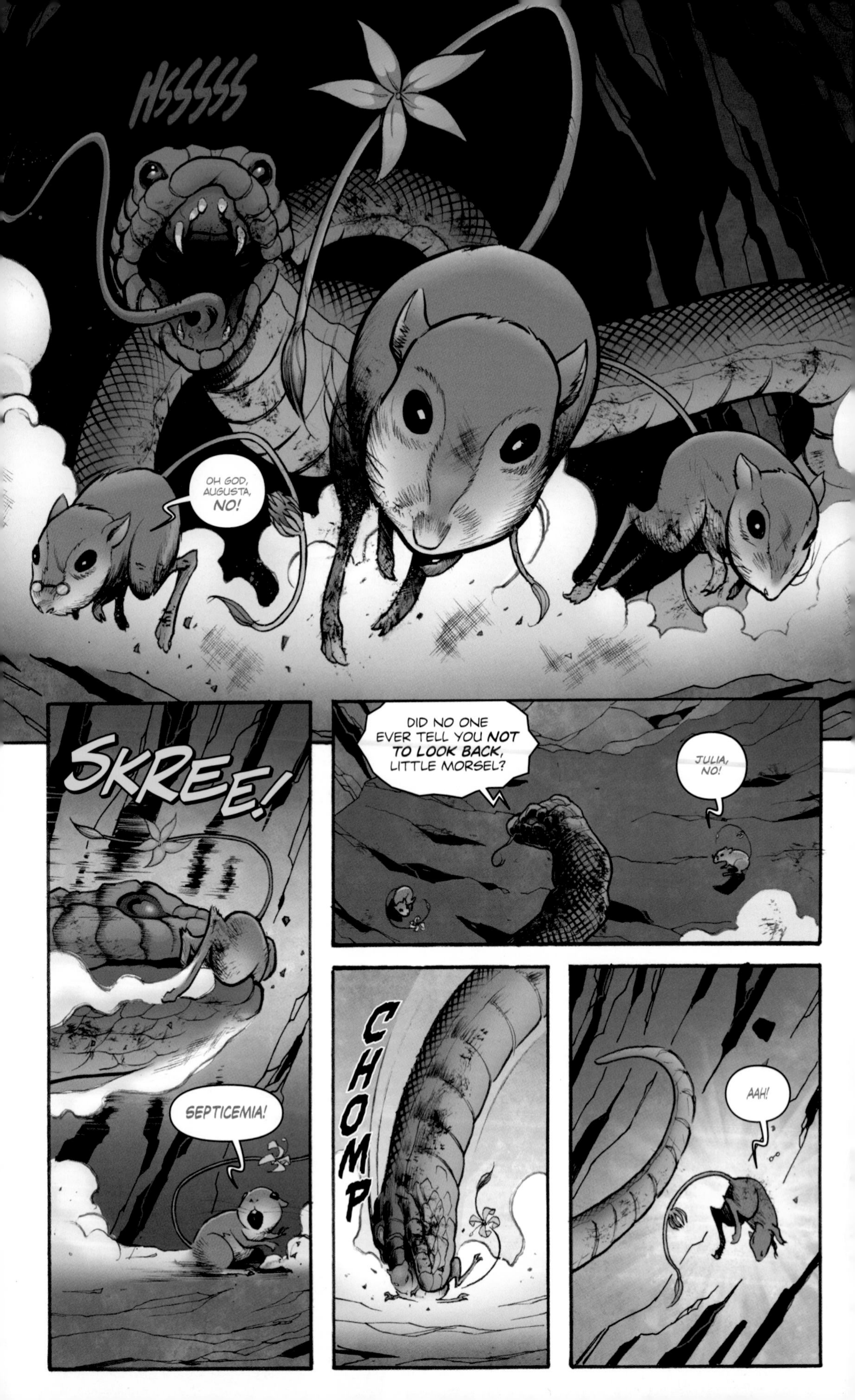
HSSSSS
OH GOD, AUGUSTA, NO!
SKREE!
SEPTICEMIA!
DID NO ONE EVER TELL YOU NOT TO LOOK BACK, LITTLE MORSEL?
JULIA, NO!
CHOMP
AAH!

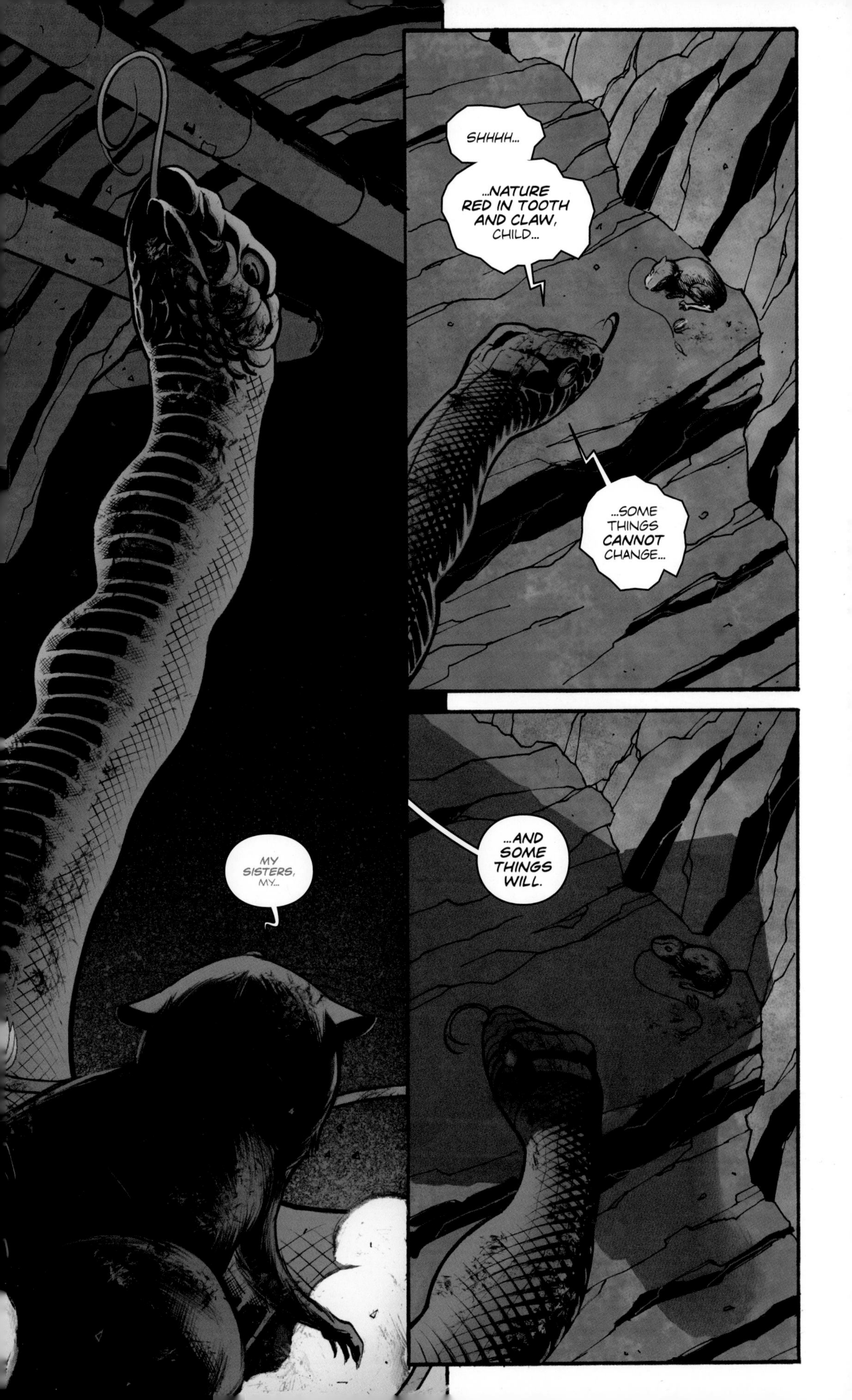
SHHHH...
...NATURE RED IN TOOTH AND CLAW, CHILD...
...SOME THINGS CANNOT CHANGE...
...AND SOME THINGS WILL.
MY SISTERS, MY...

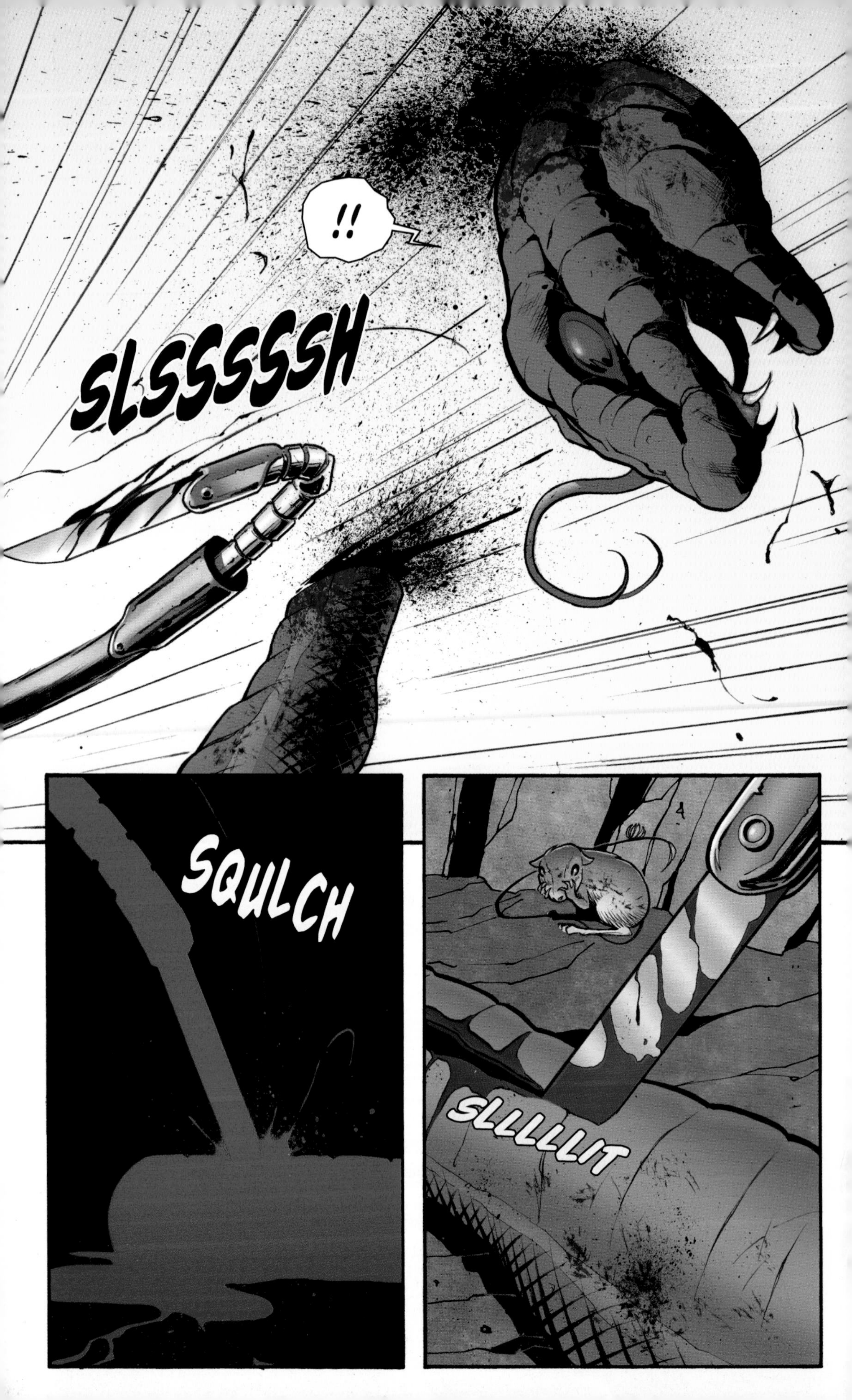
!!
SLSSSSSH
SQULCH
SLLLLLIT

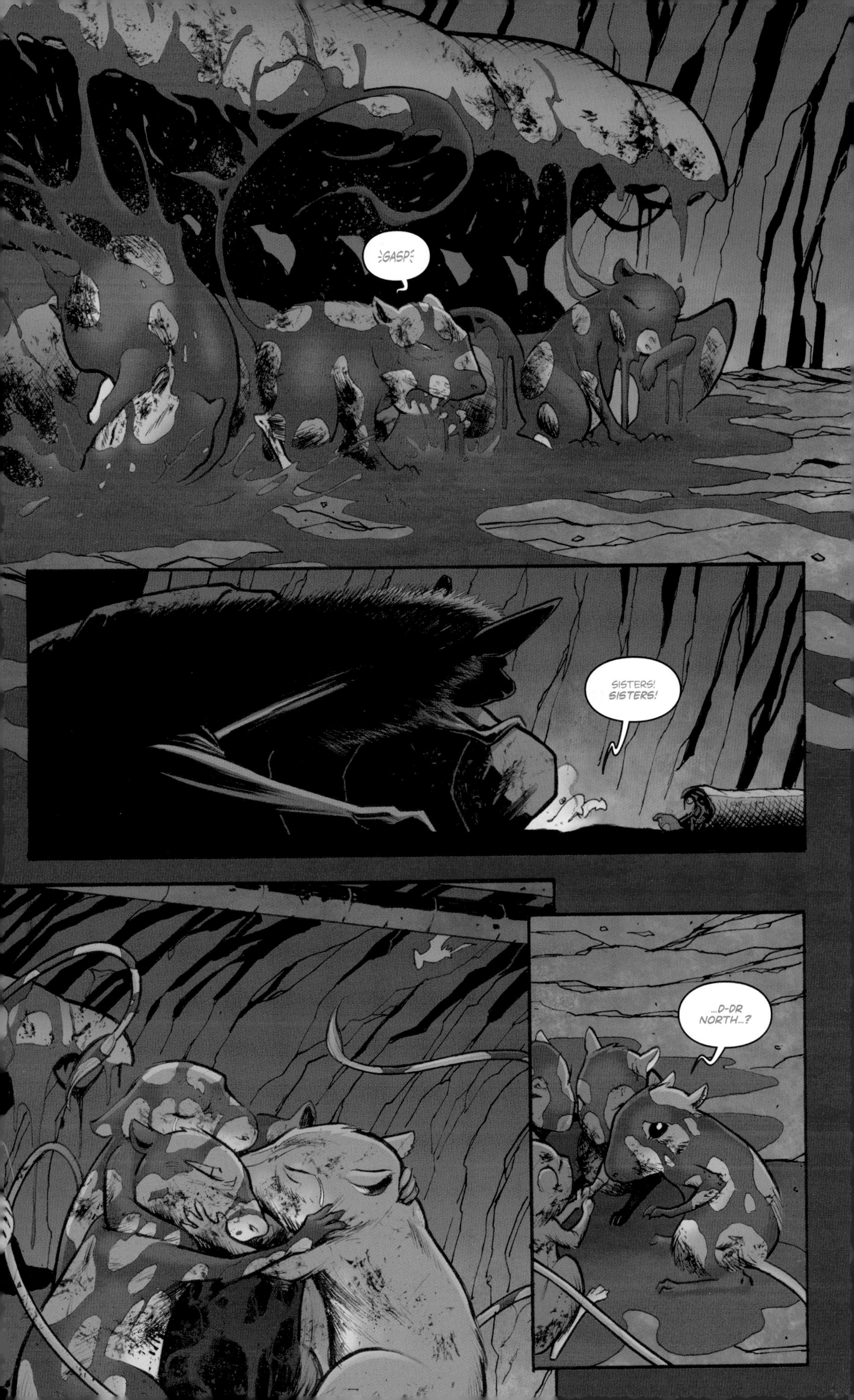
GASP
SISTERS! SISTERS!
...D-DR NORTH...?

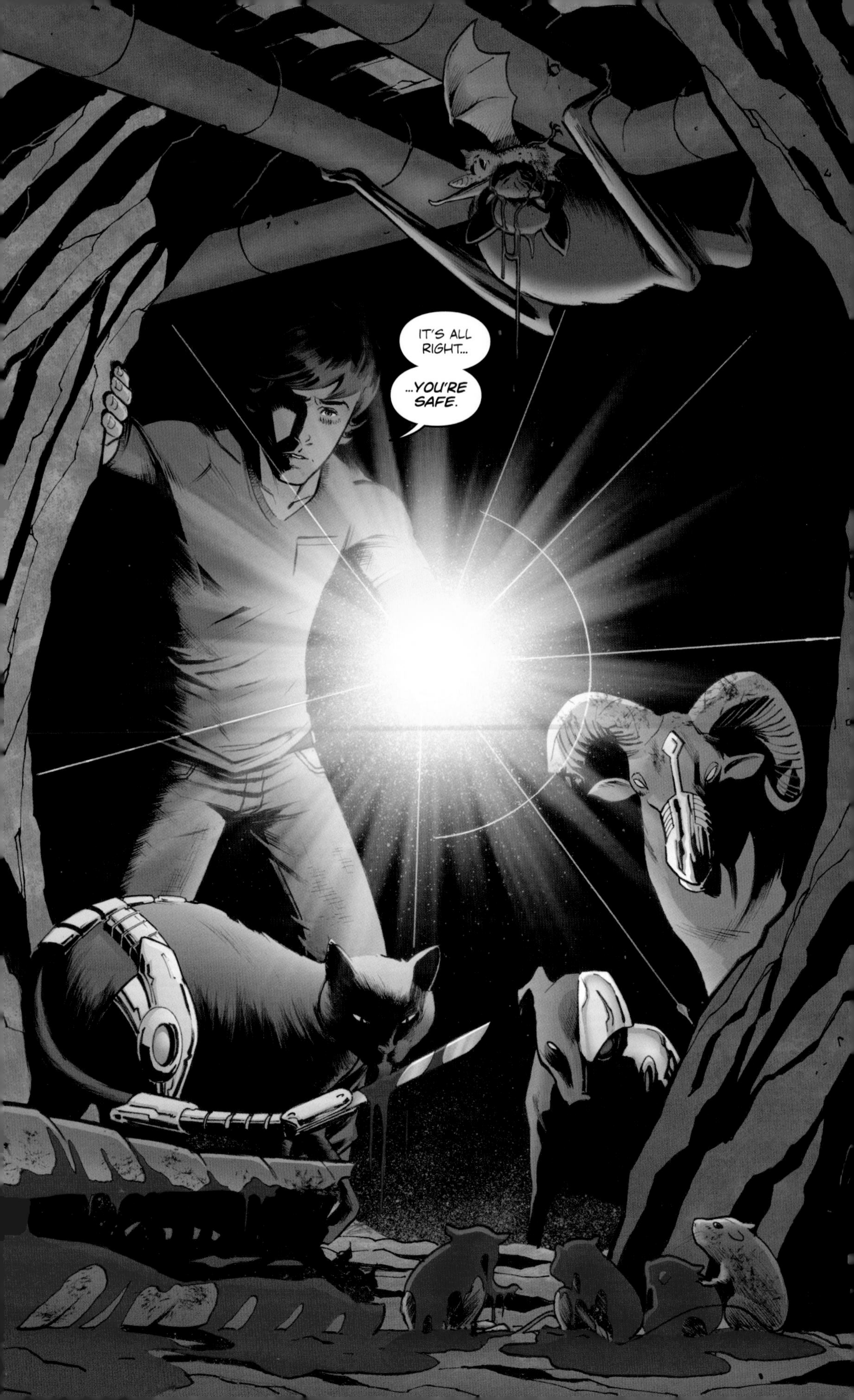
IT'S ALL RIGHT...
...YOU'RE SAFE.

3

"LEX ANIMATA: PART 1"

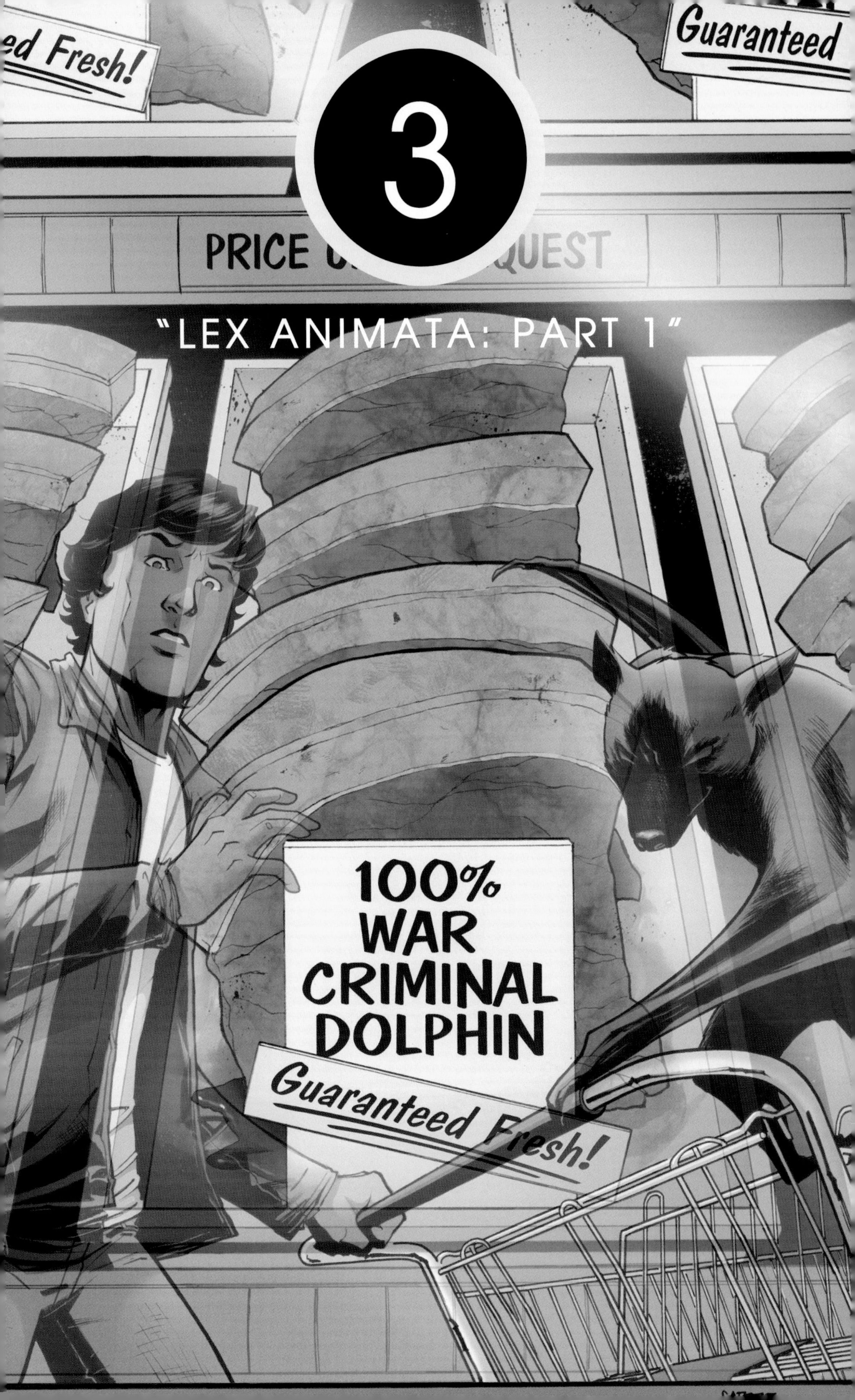
Guaranteed
100% WAR CRIMINAL DOLPHIN
Guaranteed Fresh!

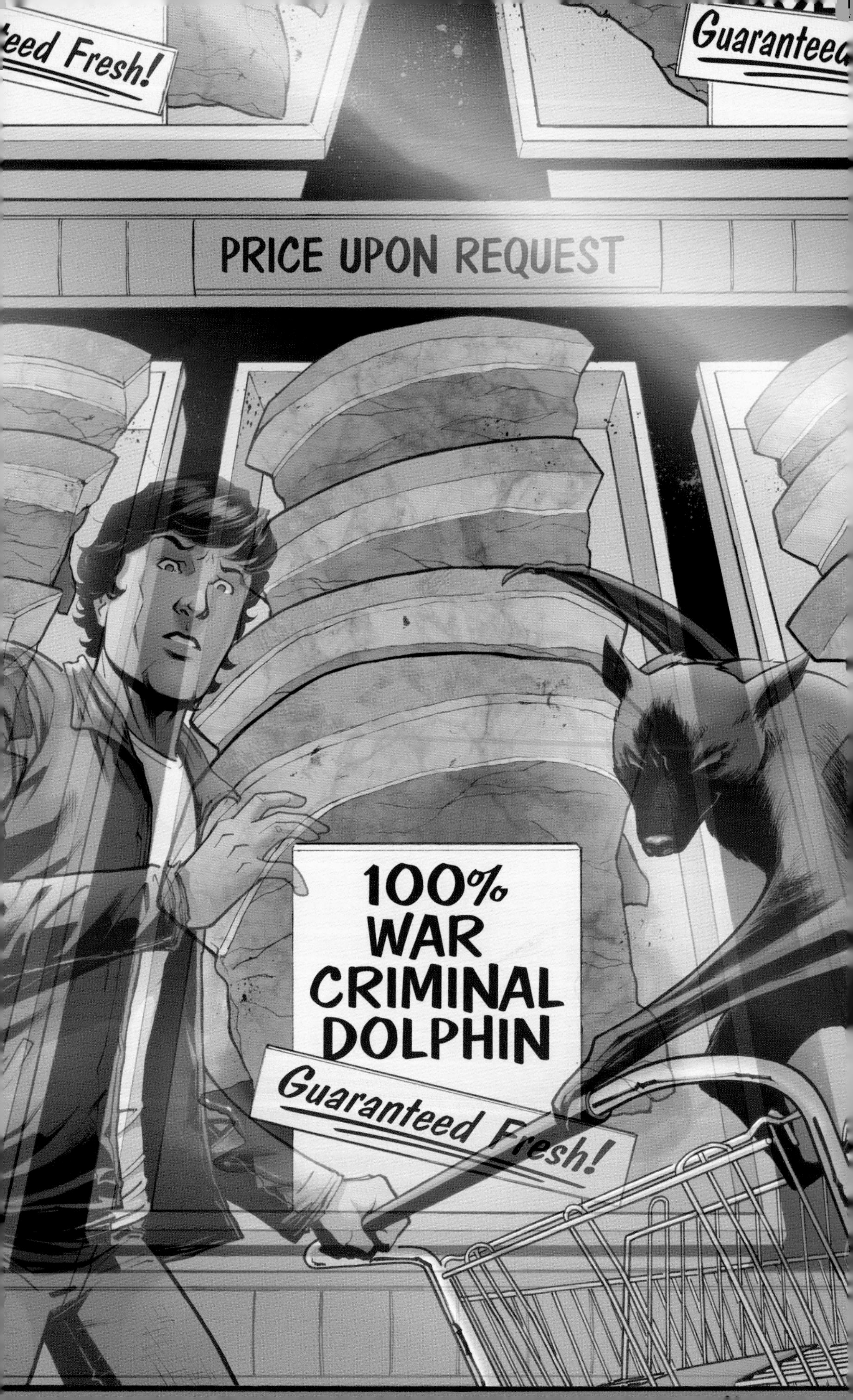
eed Fresh!
Guarantee
PRICE UPON REQUEST
100%
WAR
CRIMINAL
DOLPHIN
Guaranteed Fresh!

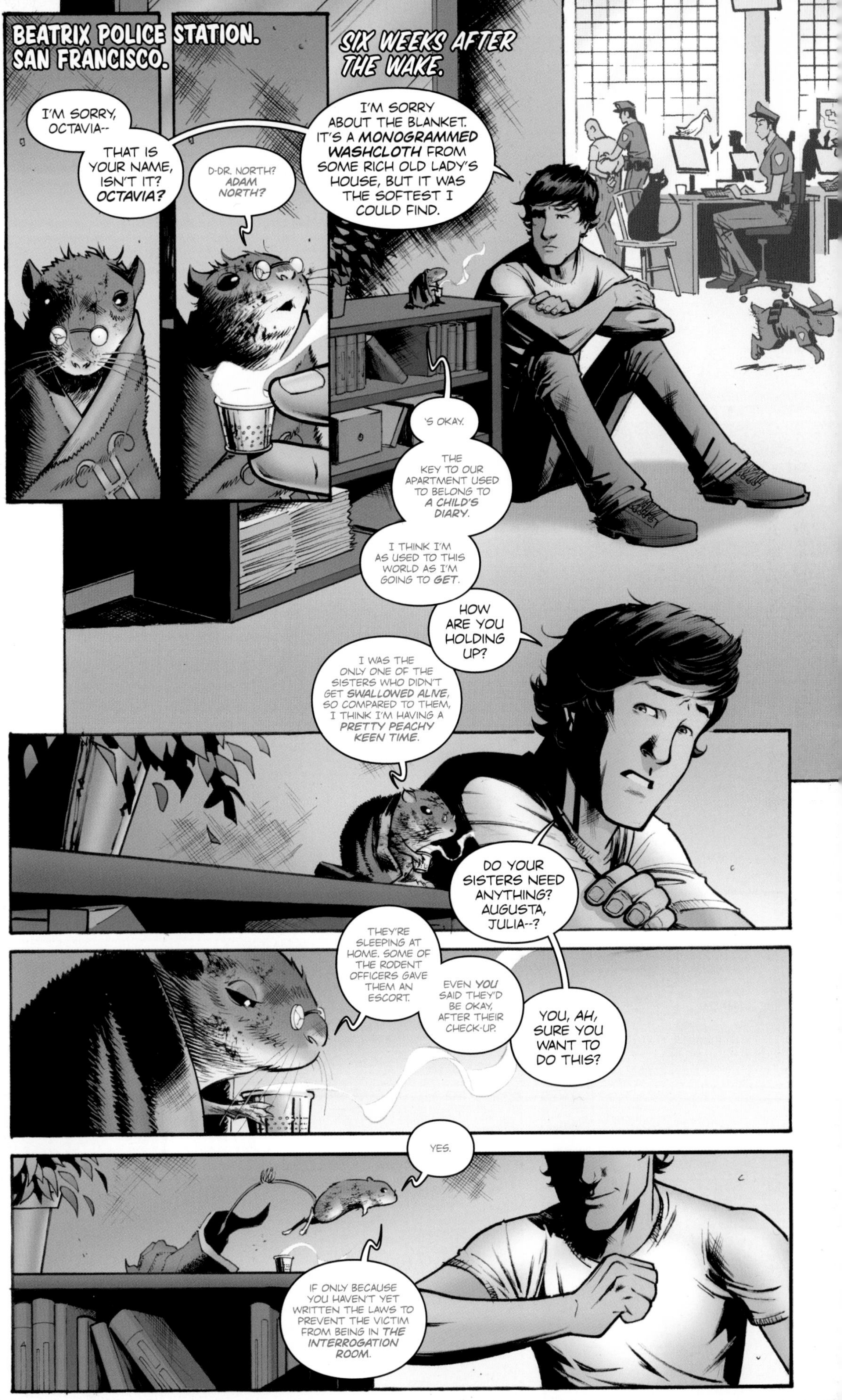
BEATRIX POLICE STATION. SAN FRANCISCO.
SIX WEEKS AFTER THE WAKE.
I'M SORRY, OCTAVIA--
THAT IS YOUR NAME, ISN'T IT? OCTAVIA?
D-DR. NORTH? ADAM NORTH?
I'M SORRY ABOUT THE BLANKET. IT'S A MONOGRAMMED WASHCLOTH FROM SOME RICH OLD LADY'S HOUSE, BUT IT WAS THE SOFTEST I COULD FIND.
'S OKAY.
THE KEY TO OUR APARTMENT USED TO BELONG TO A CHILD'S DIARY.
I THINK I'M AS USED TO THIS WORLD AS I'M GOING TO GET.
HOW ARE YOU HOLDING UP?
I WAS THE ONLY ONE OF THE SISTERS WHO DIDN'T GET SWALLOWED ALIVE, SO COMPARED TO THEM, I THINK I'M HAVING A PRETTY PEACHY KEEN TIME.
DO YOUR SISTERS NEED ANYTHING? AUGUSTA, JULIA--?
THEY'RE SLEEPING AT HOME. SOME OF THE RODENT OFFICERS GAVE THEM AN ESCORT.
EVEN YOU SAID THEY'D BE OKAY, AFTER THEIR CHECK-UP.
YOU, AH, SURE YOU WANT TO DO THIS?
YES.
IF ONLY BECAUSE YOU HAVEN'T YET WRITTEN THE LAWS TO PREVENT THE VICTIM FROM BEING IN THE INTERROGATION ROOM.

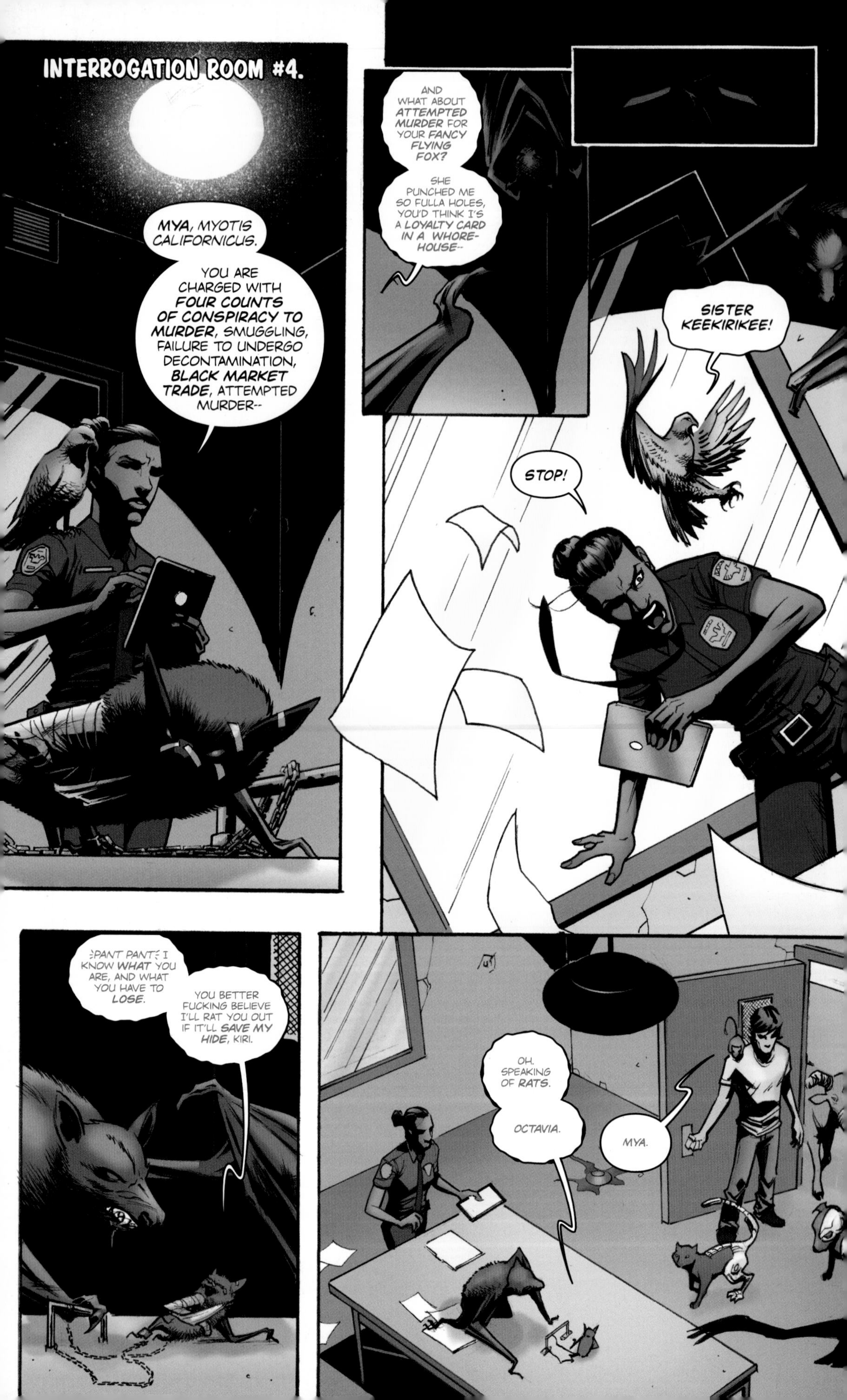
INTERROGATION ROOM #4.
MYA, MYOTIS CALIFORNICUS.
YOU ARE CHARGED WITH FOUR COUNTS OF CONSPIRACY TO MURDER, SMUGGLING, FAILURE TO UNDERGO DECONTAMINATION, BLACK MARKET TRADE, ATTEMPTED MURDER--
AND WHAT ABOUT ATTEMPTED MURDER FOR YOUR FANCY FLYING FOX?
SHE PUNCHED ME SO FULLA HOLES, YOU'D THINK I'S A LOYALTY CARD IN A WHORE-HOUSE--
SISTER KEEKIRIKEE!
STOP!
PANT PANT I KNOW WHAT YOU ARE, AND WHAT YOU HAVE TO LOSE.
YOU BETTER FUCKING BELIEVE I'LL RAT YOU OUT IF IT'LL SAVE MY HIDE, KIRI.
OH. SPEAKING OF RATS.
OCTAVIA.
MYA.

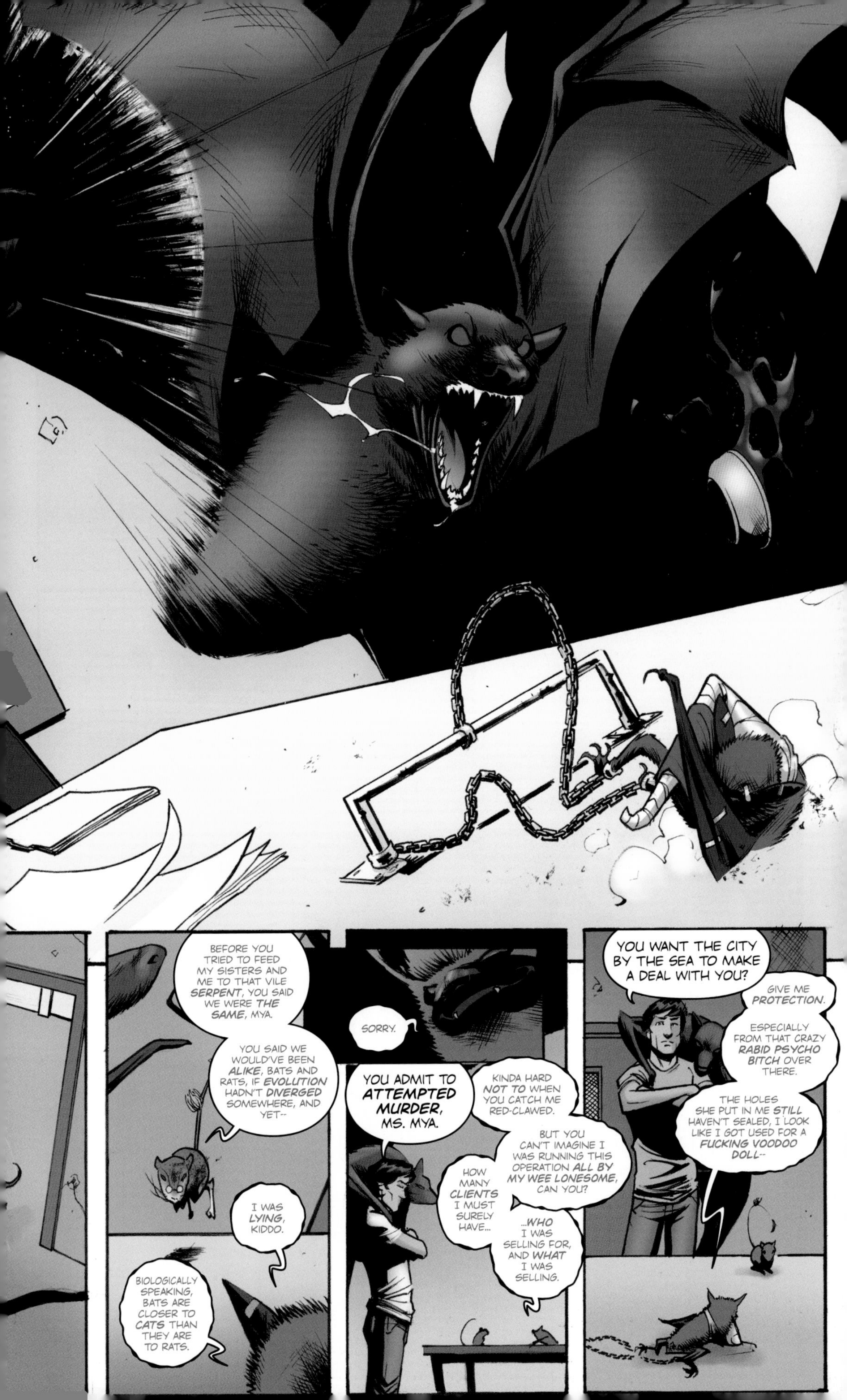
BEFORE YOU TRIED TO FEED MY SISTERS AND ME TO THAT VILE SERPENT, YOU SAID WE WERE THE SAME, MYA.
YOU SAID WE WOULD'VE BEEN ALIKE, BATS AND RATS, IF EVOLUTION HADN'T DIVERGED SOMEWHERE, AND YET--
I WAS LYING, KIDDO.
BIOLOGICALLY SPEAKING, BATS ARE CLOSER TO CATS THAN THEY ARE TO RATS.
SORRY.
YOU ADMIT TO ATTEMPTED MURDER, MS. MYA.
KINDA HARD NOT TO WHEN YOU CATCH ME RED-CLAWED.
BUT YOU CAN'T IMAGINE I WAS RUNNING THIS OPERATION ALL BY MY WEE LONESOME, CAN YOU?
HOW MANY CLIENTS I MUST SURELY HAVE...
...WHO I WAS SELLING FOR, AND WHAT I WAS SELLING.
YOU WANT THE CITY BY THE SEA TO MAKE A DEAL WITH YOU?
GIVE ME PROTECTION.
ESPECIALLY FROM THAT CRAZY RABID PSYCHO BITCH OVER THERE.
THE HOLES SHE PUT IN ME STILL HAVEN'T SEALED, I LOOK LIKE I GOT USED FOR A FUCKING VOODOO DOLL--

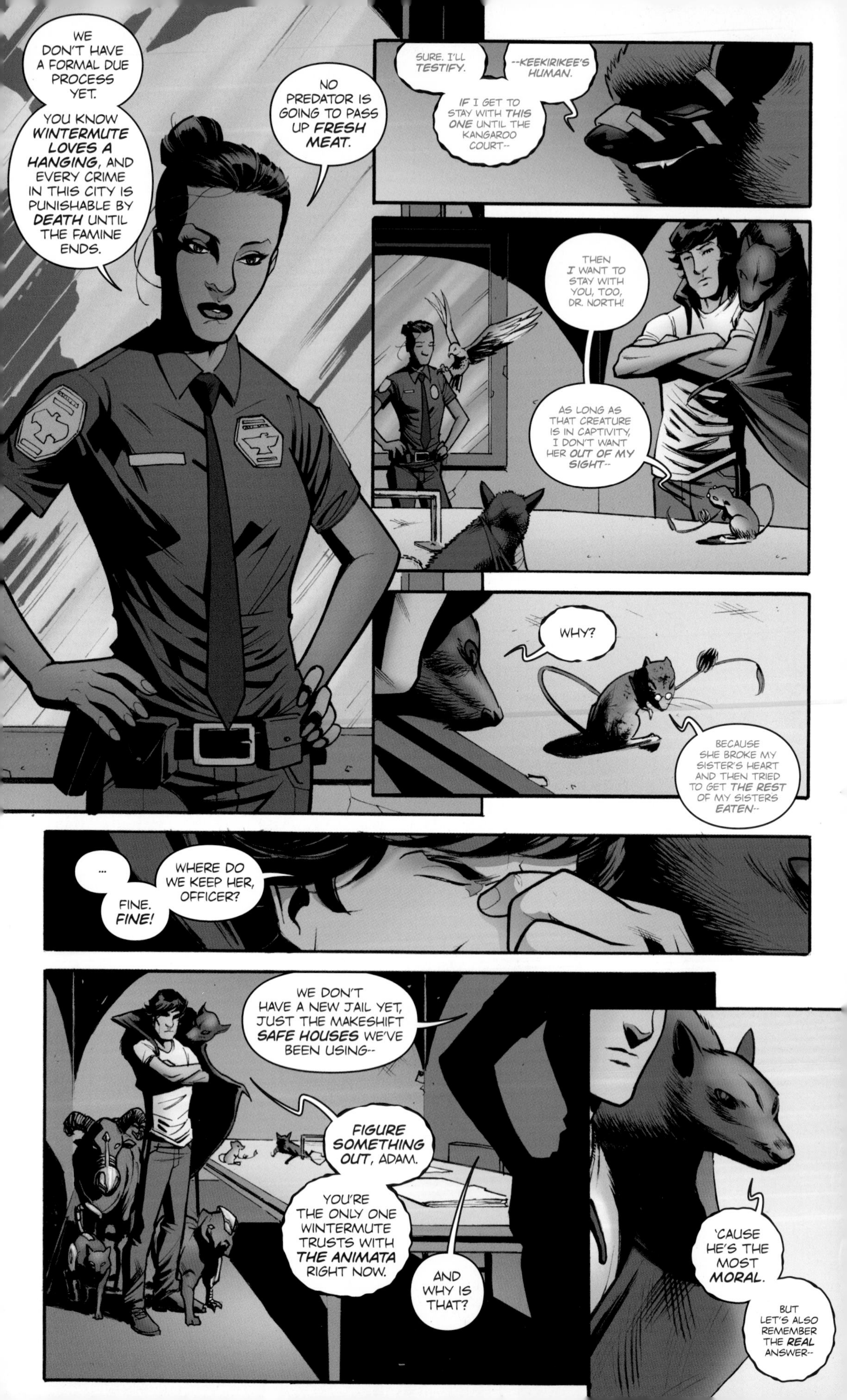
WE DON'T HAVE A FORMAL DUE PROCESS YET.
YOU KNOW WINTERMUTE LOVES A HANGING, AND EVERY CRIME IN THIS CITY IS PUNISHABLE BY DEATH UNTIL THE FAMINE ENDS.
NO PREDATOR IS GOING TO PASS UP FRESH MEAT.
SURE. I'LL TESTIFY.
--KEEKIRIKEE'S HUMAN.
IF I GET TO STAY WITH THIS ONE UNTIL THE KANGAROO COURT--
THEN I WANT TO STAY WITH YOU, TOO, DR. NORTH!
AS LONG AS THAT CREATURE IS IN CAPTIVITY, I DON'T WANT HER OUT OF MY SIGHT--
WHY?
BECAUSE SHE BROKE MY SISTER'S HEART AND THEN TRIED TO GET THE REST OF MY SISTERS EATEN--
...
FINE. FINE!
WHERE DO WE KEEP HER, OFFICER?
WE DON'T HAVE A NEW JAIL YET, JUST THE MAKESHIFT SAFE HOUSES WE'VE BEEN USING--
FIGURE SOMETHING OUT, ADAM.
YOU'RE THE ONLY ONE WINTERMUTE TRUSTS WITH THE ANIMATA RIGHT NOW.
AND WHY IS THAT?
'CAUSE HE'S THE MOST MORAL.
BUT LET'S ALSO REMEMBER THE REAL ANSWER--

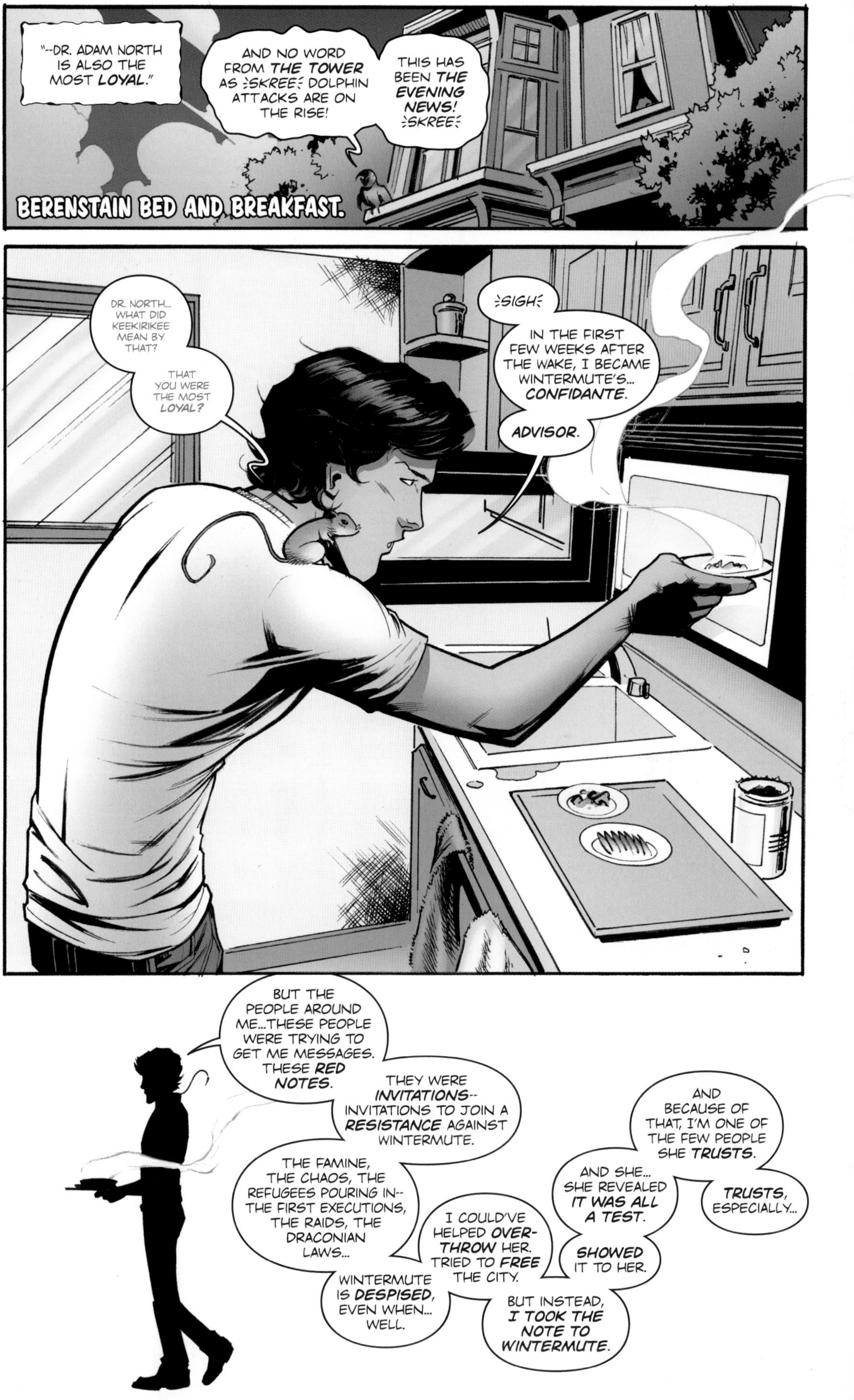
"--DR. ADAM NORTH IS ALSO THE MOST LOYAL."
AND NO WORD FROM THE TOWER AS SKREE DOLPHIN ATTACKS ARE ON THE RISE!
THIS HAS BEEN THE EVENING NEWS! SKREE
BERENSTAIN BED AND BREAKFAST.
DR. NORTH... WHAT DID KEEKIRIKEE MEAN BY THAT?
THAT YOU WERE THE MOST LOYAL?
SIGH
IN THE FIRST FEW WEEKS AFTER THE WAKE, I BECAME WINTERMUTE'S... CONFIDANTE.
ADVISOR.
BUT THE PEOPLE AROUND ME...THESE PEOPLE WERE TRYING TO GET ME MESSAGES. THESE RED NOTES.
THEY WERE INVITATIONS-- INVITATIONS TO JOIN A RESISTANCE AGAINST WINTERMUTE.
THE FAMINE, THE CHAOS, THE REFUGEES POURING IN-- THE FIRST EXECUTIONS, THE RAIDS, THE DRACONIAN LAWS...
WINTERMUTE IS DESPISED, EVEN WHEN... WELL.
I COULD'VE HELPED OVER-THROW HER. TRIED TO FREE THE CITY.
BUT INSTEAD, I TOOK THE NOTE TO WINTERMUTE.
SHOWED IT TO HER.
AND SHE... SHE REVEALED IT WAS ALL A TEST.
AND BECAUSE OF THAT, I'M ONE OF THE FEW PEOPLE SHE TRUSTS.
TRUSTS, ESPECIALLY...

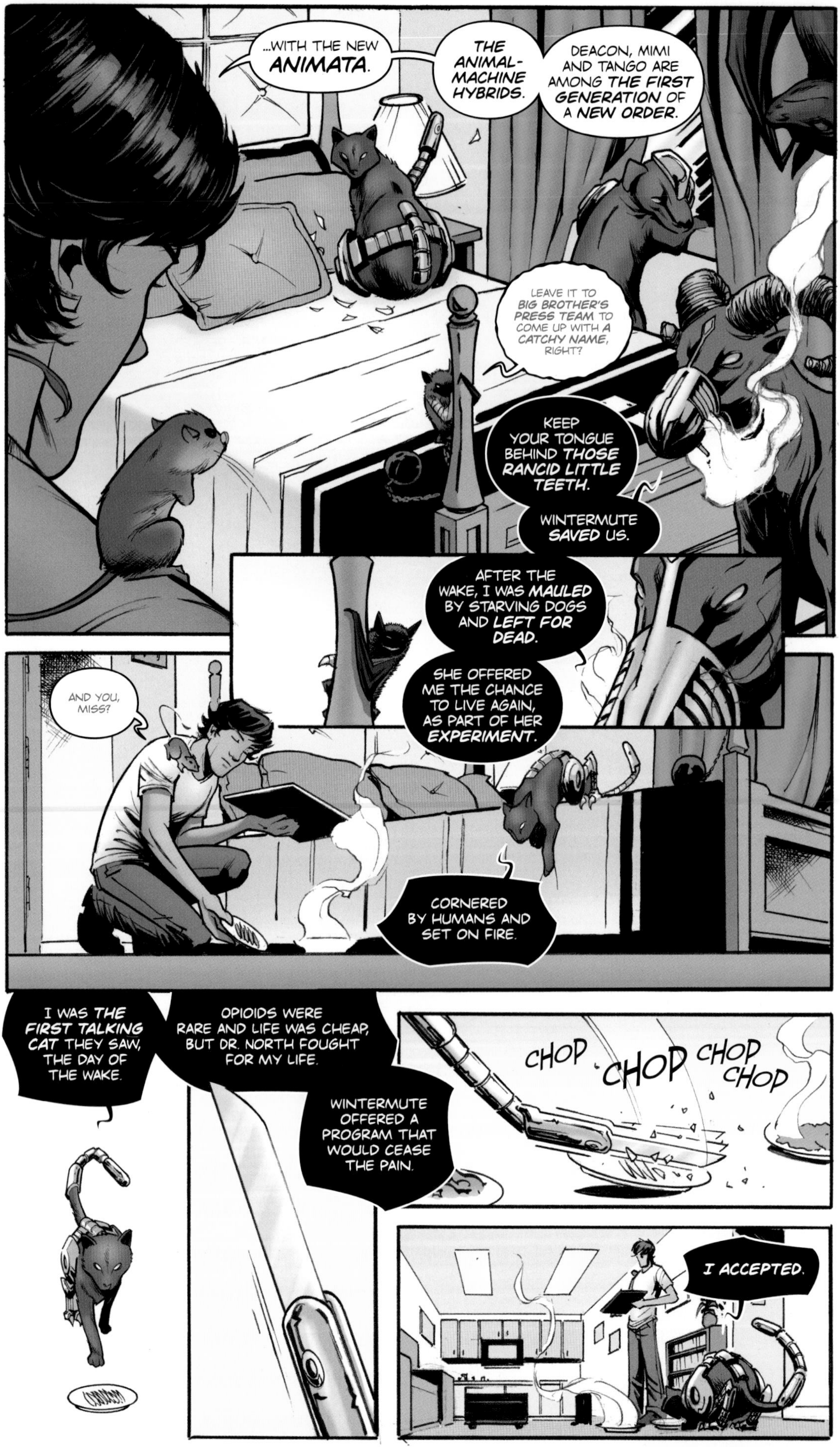
...WITH THE NEW ANIMATA.
THE ANIMAL-MACHINE HYBRIDS.
DEACON, MIMI AND TANGO ARE AMONG THE FIRST GENERATION OF A NEW ORDER.
LEAVE IT TO BIG BROTHER'S PRESS TEAM TO COME UP WITH A CATCHY NAME, RIGHT?
KEEP YOUR TONGUE BEHIND THOSE RANCID LITTLE TEETH.
WINTERMUTE SAVED US.
AFTER THE WAKE, I WAS MAULED BY STARVING DOGS AND LEFT FOR DEAD.
SHE OFFERED ME THE CHANCE TO LIVE AGAIN, AS PART OF HER EXPERIMENT.
AND YOU, MISS?
CORNERED BY HUMANS AND SET ON FIRE.
I WAS THE FIRST TALKING CAT THEY SAW, THE DAY OF THE WAKE.
OPIOIDS WERE RARE AND LIFE WAS CHEAP, BUT DR. NORTH FOUGHT FOR MY LIFE.
WINTERMUTE OFFERED A PROGRAM THAT WOULD CEASE THE PAIN.
CHOP CHOP CHOP CHOP
I ACCEPTED.

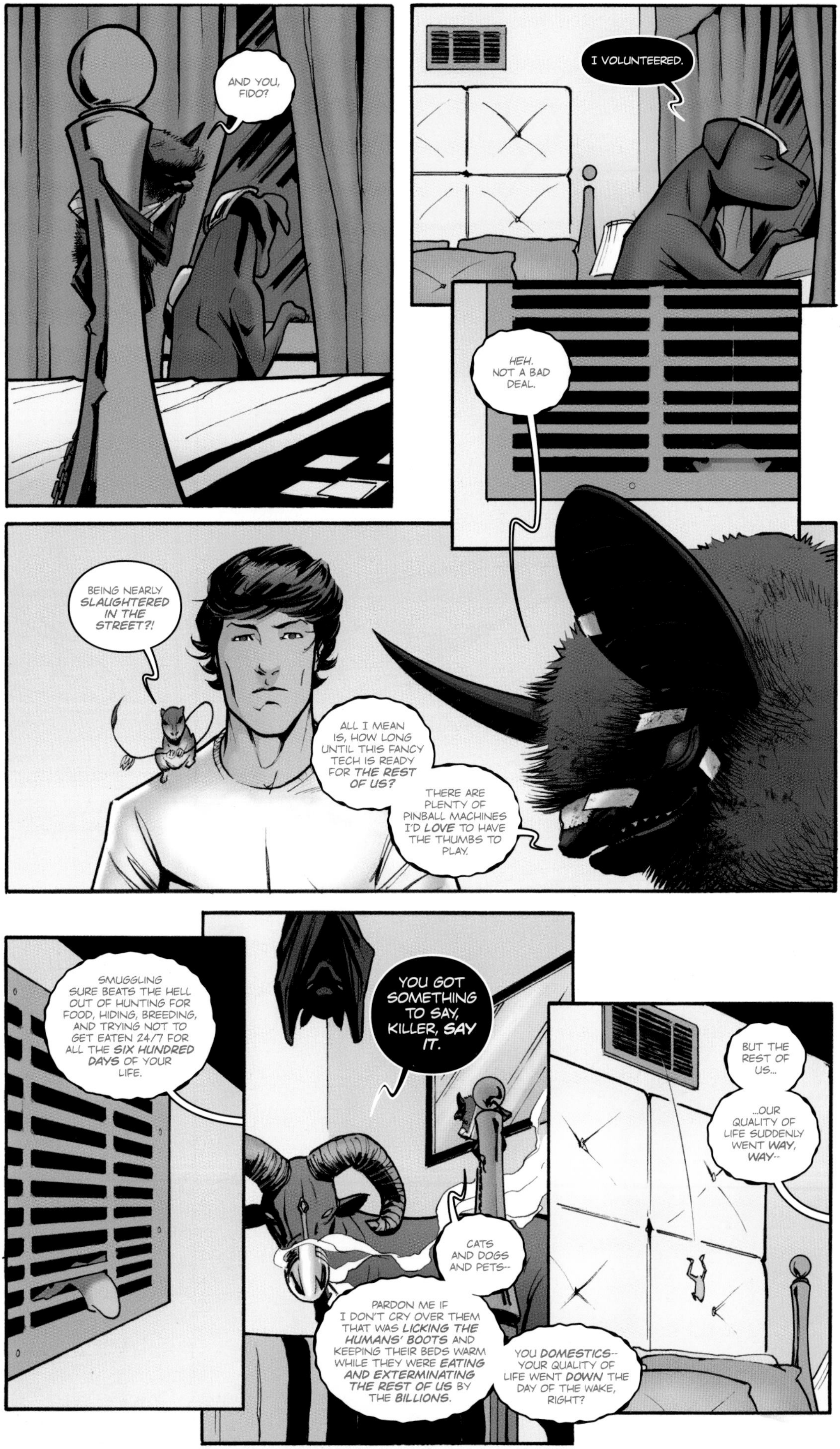
AND YOU, FIDO?
I VOLUNTEERED.
HEH. NOT A BAD DEAL.
BEING NEARLY SLAUGHTERED IN THE STREET?!
ALL I MEAN IS, HOW LONG UNTIL THIS FANCY TECH IS READY FOR THE REST OF US?
THERE ARE PLENTY OF PINBALL MACHINES I'D LOVE TO HAVE THE THUMBS TO PLAY.
SMUGGLING SURE BEATS THE HELL OUT OF HUNTING FOR FOOD, HIDING, BREEDING, AND TRYING NOT TO GET EATEN 24/7 FOR ALL THE SIX HUNDRED DAYS OF YOUR LIFE.
YOU GOT SOMETHING TO SAY, KILLER, SAY IT.
CATS AND DOGS AND PETS--
PARDON ME IF I DON'T CRY OVER THEM THAT WAS LICKING THE HUMANS' BOOTS AND KEEPING THEIR BEDS WARM WHILE THEY WERE EATING AND EXTERMINATING THE REST OF US BY THE BILLIONS.
YOU DOMESTICS-- YOUR QUALITY OF LIFE WENT DOWN THE DAY OF THE WAKE, RIGHT?
BUT THE REST OF US...
...OUR QUALITY OF LIFE SUDDENLY WENT WAY, WAY--

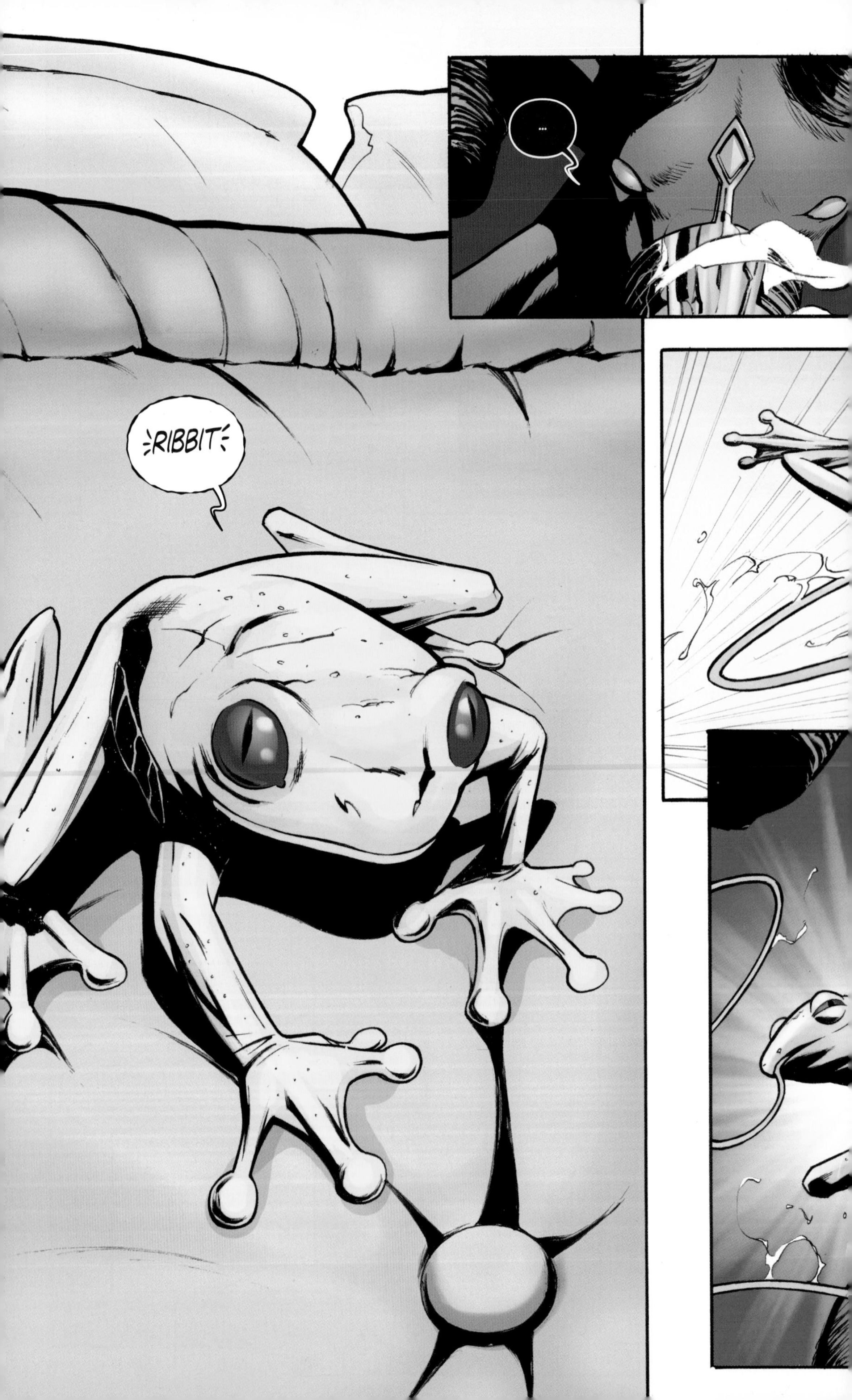
...
RIBBIT

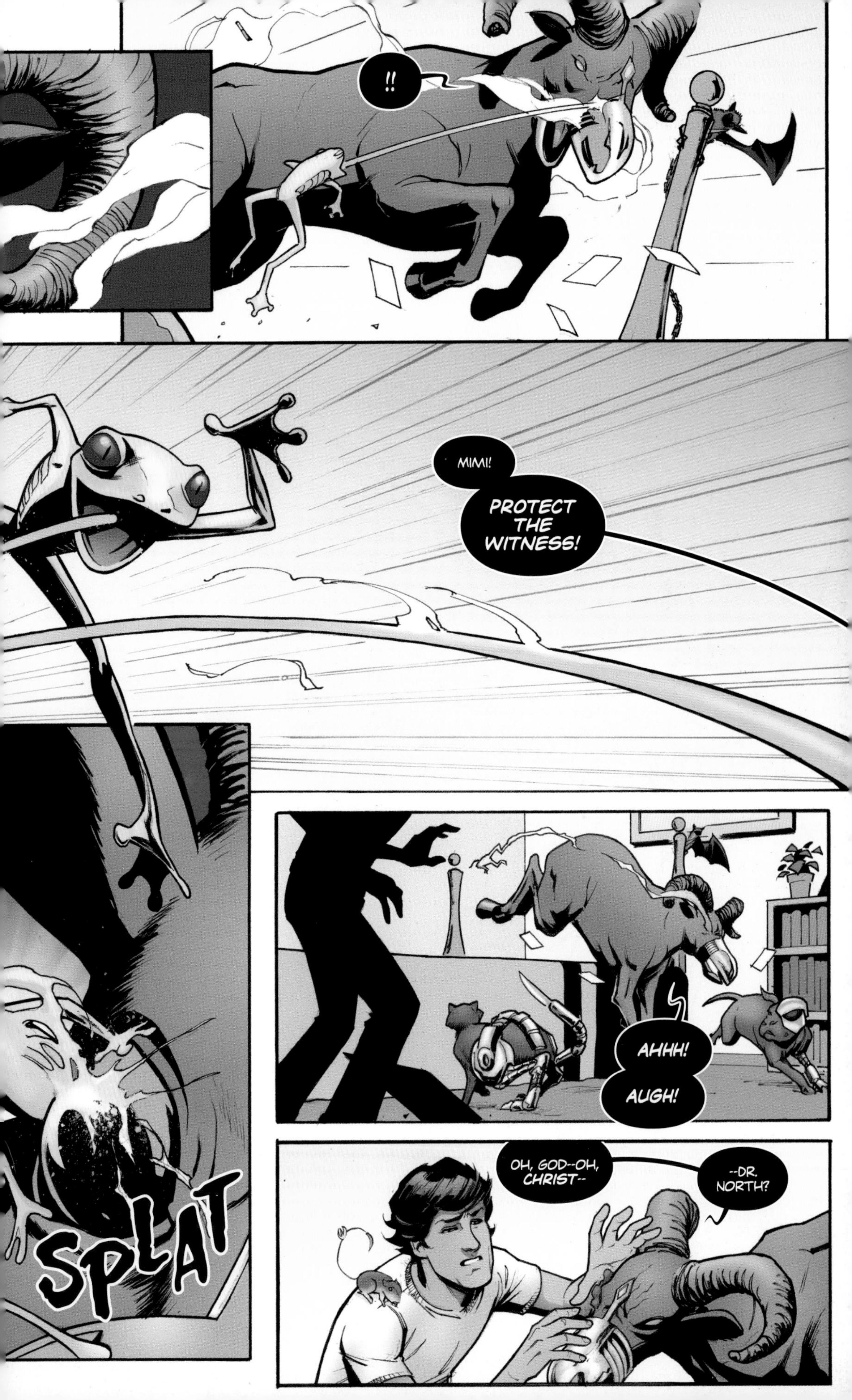
!!
MIMI!
PROTECT THE WITNESS!
SPLAT
AHHH!
AUGH!
OH, GOD--OH, CHRIST--
--DR. NORTH?

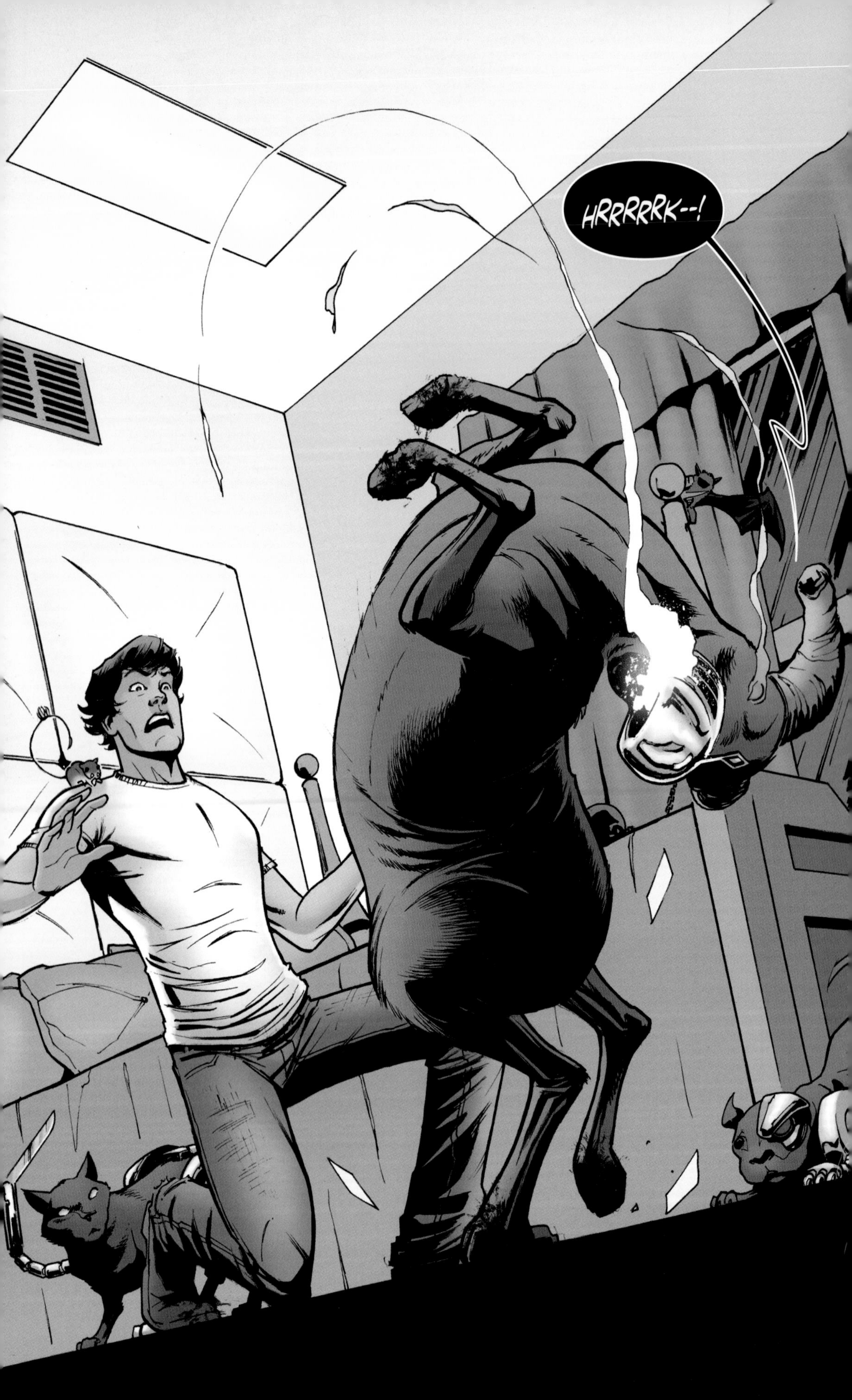
HRRRRRK--!

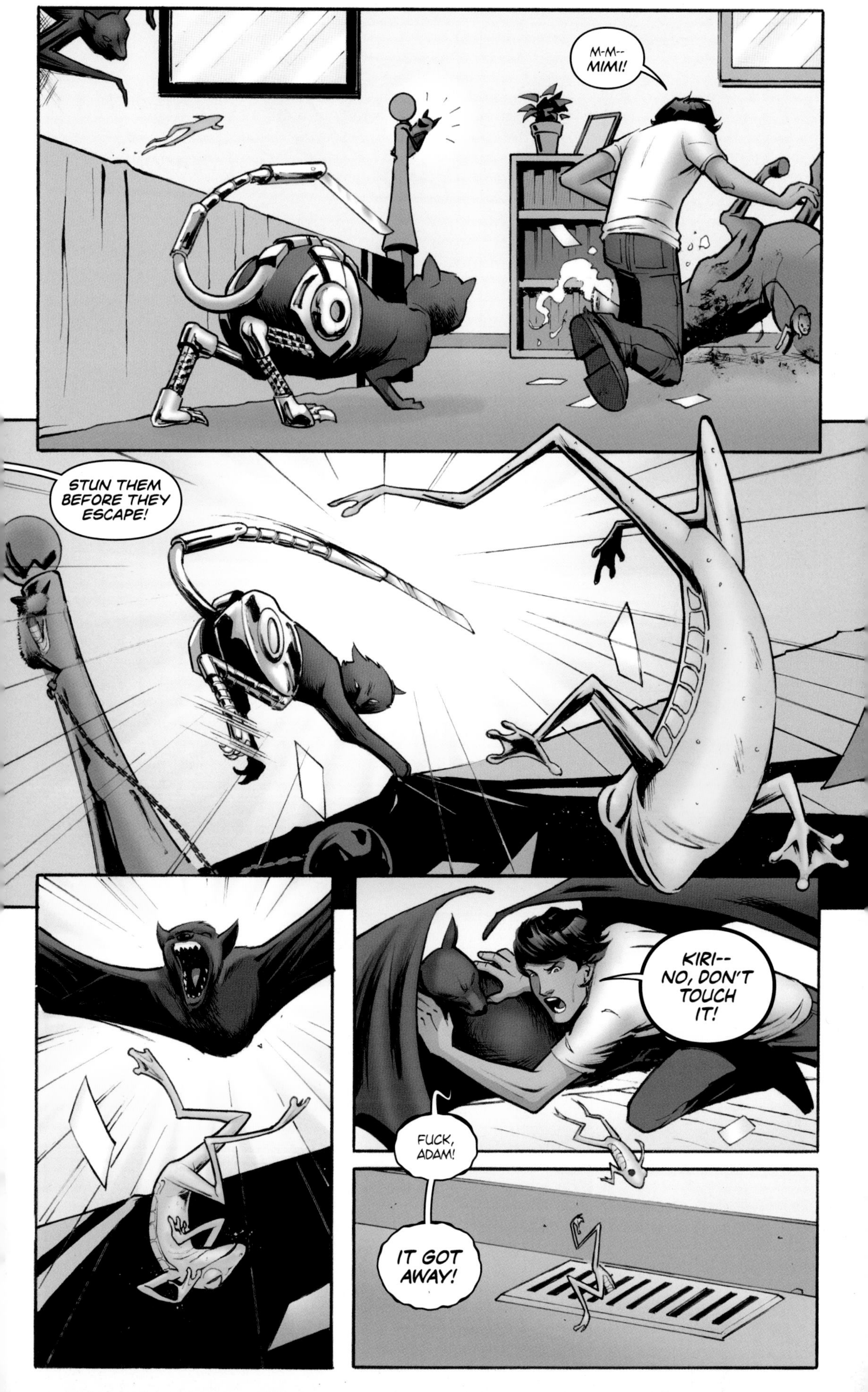
M-M--
MIMI!
STUN THEM BEFORE THEY ESCAPE!
KIRI--
NO, DON'T TOUCH IT!
FUCK, ADAM!
IT GOT AWAY!

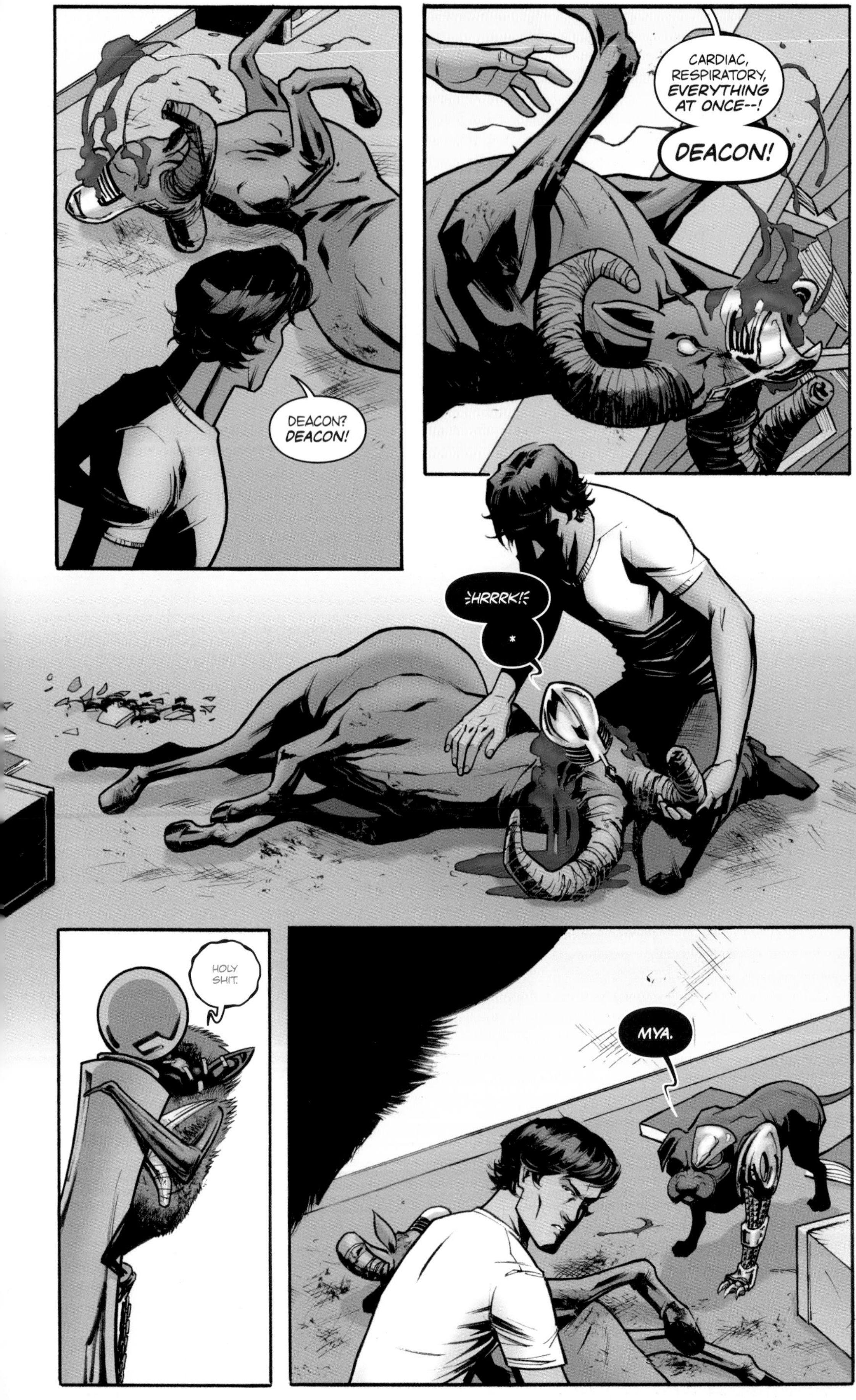
DEACON?
DEACON!
CARDIAC, RESPIRATORY, EVERYTHING AT ONCE--!
DEACON!
HRRRK!
*
HOLY SHIT.
MYA.

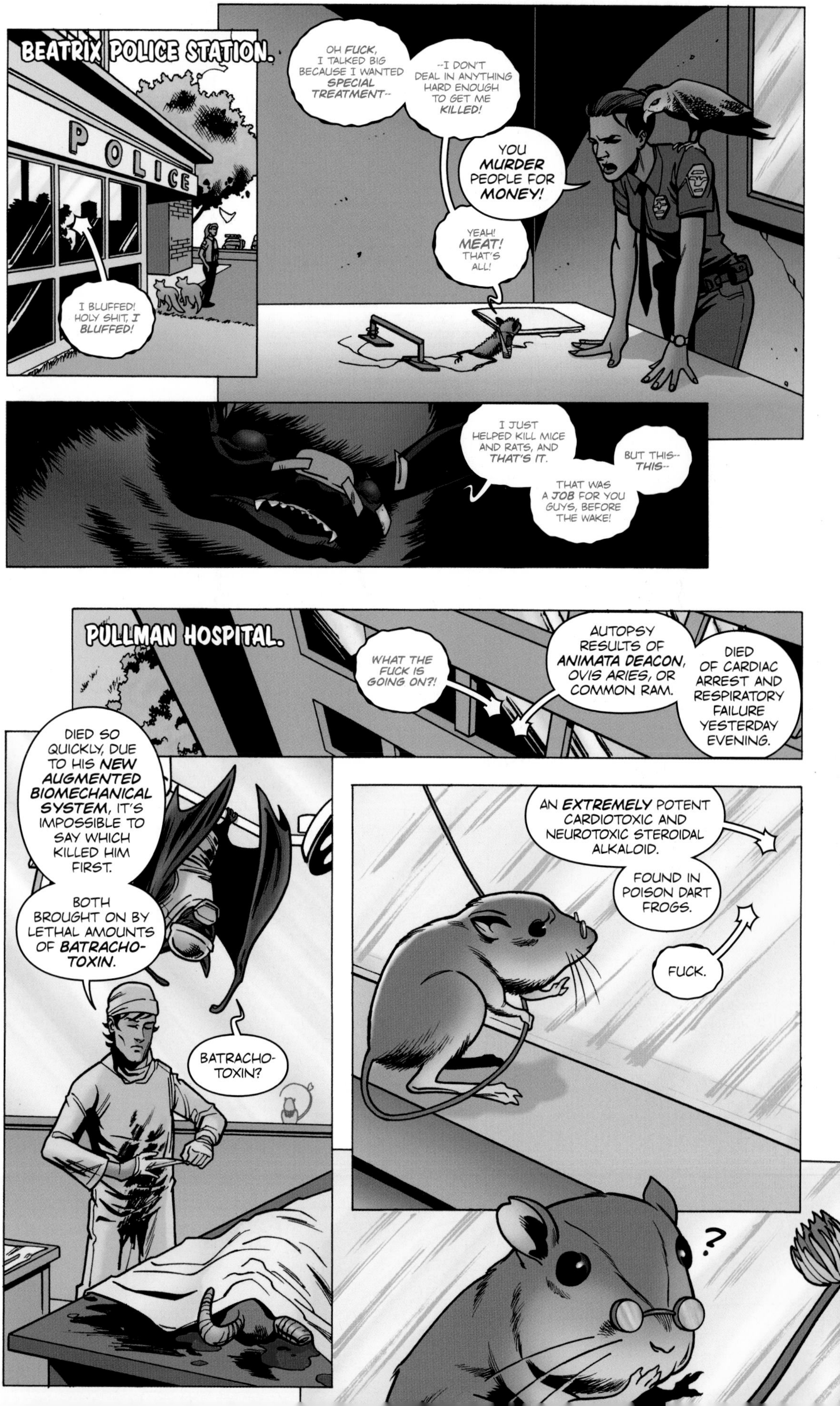
BEATRIX POLICE STATION.
I BLUFFED! HOLY SHIT, I BLUFFED!
OH FUCK, I TALKED BIG BECAUSE I WANTED SPECIAL TREATMENT--
--I DON'T DEAL IN ANYTHING HARD ENOUGH TO GET ME KILLED!
YOU MURDER PEOPLE FOR MONEY!
YEAH! MEAT! THAT'S ALL!
I JUST HELPED KILL MICE AND RATS, AND THAT'S IT.
BUT THIS-- THIS--
THAT WAS A JOB FOR YOU GUYS, BEFORE THE WAKE!
PULLMAN HOSPITAL.
WHAT THE FUCK IS GOING ON?!
AUTOPSY RESULTS OF ANIMATA DEACON, OVIS ARIES, OR COMMON RAM.
DIED OF CARDIAC ARREST AND RESPIRATORY FAILURE YESTERDAY EVENING.
DIED SO QUICKLY, DUE TO HIS NEW AUGMENTED BIOMECHANICAL SYSTEM, IT'S IMPOSSIBLE TO SAY WHICH KILLED HIM FIRST.
BOTH BROUGHT ON BY LETHAL AMOUNTS OF BATRACHO-TOXIN.
BATRACHO-TOXIN?
AN EXTREMELY POTENT CARDIOTOXIC AND NEUROTOXIC STEROIDAL ALKALOID.
FOUND IN POISON DART FROGS.
FUCK.
?

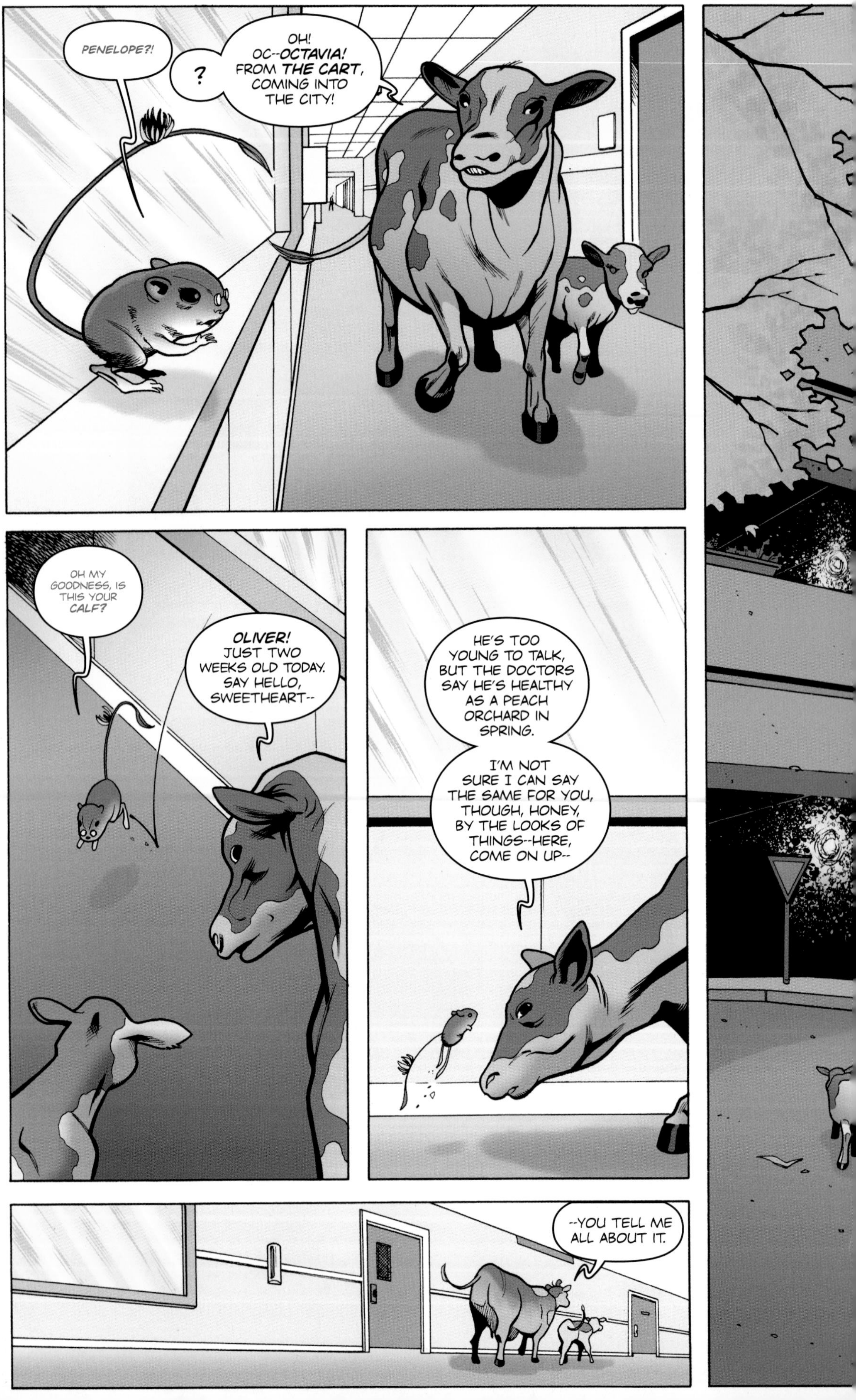
PENELOPE?!
?
OH! OC--OCTAVIA! FROM THE CART, COMING INTO THE CITY!
OH MY GOODNESS, IS THIS YOUR CALF?
OLIVER! JUST TWO WEEKS OLD TODAY. SAY HELLO, SWEETHEART--
HE'S TOO YOUNG TO TALK, BUT THE DOCTORS SAY HE'S HEALTHY AS A PEACH ORCHARD IN SPRING.
I'M NOT SURE I CAN SAY THE SAME FOR YOU, THOUGH, HONEY, BY THE LOOKS OF THINGS--HERE, COME ON UP--
--YOU TELL ME ALL ABOUT IT.

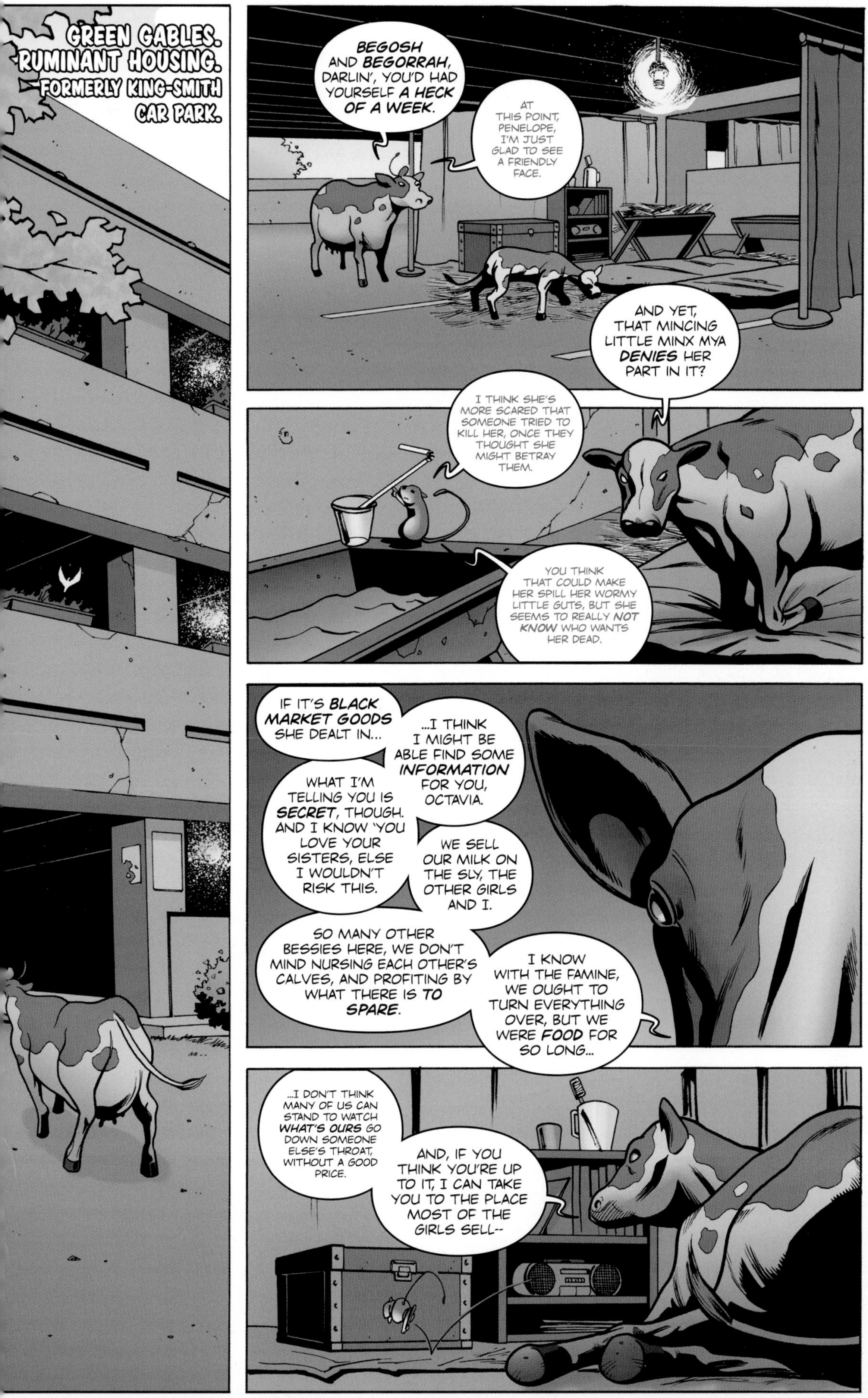
GREEN GABLES. RUMINANT HOUSING. FORMERLY KING-SMITH CAR PARK.
BEGOSH AND BEGORRAH, DARLIN', YOU'D HAD YOURSELF A HECK OF A WEEK.
AT THIS POINT, PENELOPE, I'M JUST GLAD TO SEE A FRIENDLY FACE.
AND YET, THAT MINCING LITTLE MINX MYA DENIES HER PART IN IT?
I THINK SHE'S MORE SCARED THAT SOMEONE TRIED TO KILL HER, ONCE THEY THOUGHT SHE MIGHT BETRAY THEM.
YOU THINK THAT COULD MAKE HER SPILL HER WORMY LITTLE GUTS, BUT SHE SEEMS TO REALLY NOT KNOW WHO WANTS HER DEAD.
IF IT'S BLACK MARKET GOODS SHE DEALT IN...
...I THINK I MIGHT BE ABLE FIND SOME INFORMATION FOR YOU, OCTAVIA.
WHAT I'M TELLING YOU IS SECRET, THOUGH. AND I KNOW 'YOU LOVE YOUR SISTERS, ELSE I WOULDN'T RISK THIS.
WE SELL OUR MILK ON THE SLY, THE OTHER GIRLS AND I.
SO MANY OTHER BESSIES HERE, WE DON'T MIND NURSING EACH OTHER'S CALVES, AND PROFITING BY WHAT THERE IS TO SPARE.
I KNOW WITH THE FAMINE, WE OUGHT TO TURN EVERYTHING OVER, BUT WE WERE FOOD FOR SO LONG...
...I DON'T THINK MANY OF US CAN STAND TO WATCH WHAT'S OURS GO DOWN SOMEONE ELSE'S THROAT, WITHOUT A GOOD PRICE.
AND, IF YOU THINK YOU'RE UP TO IT, I CAN TAKE YOU TO THE PLACE MOST OF THE GIRLS SELL--

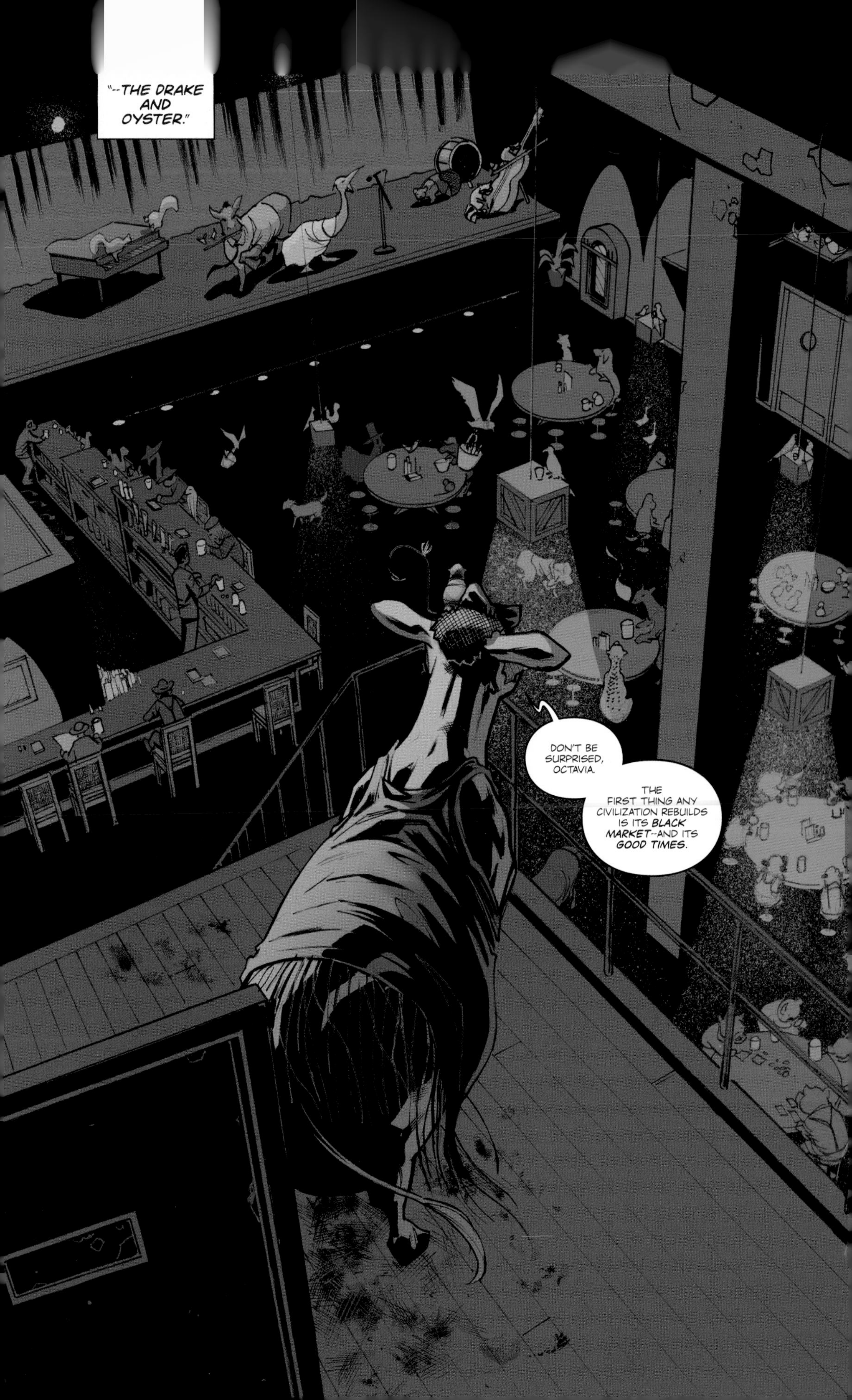
"--THE DRAKE AND OYSTER."
DON'T BE SURPRISED, OCTAVIA.
THE FIRST THING ANY CIVILIZATION REBUILDS IS ITS *BLACK MARKET*--AND ITS *GOOD TIMES.*

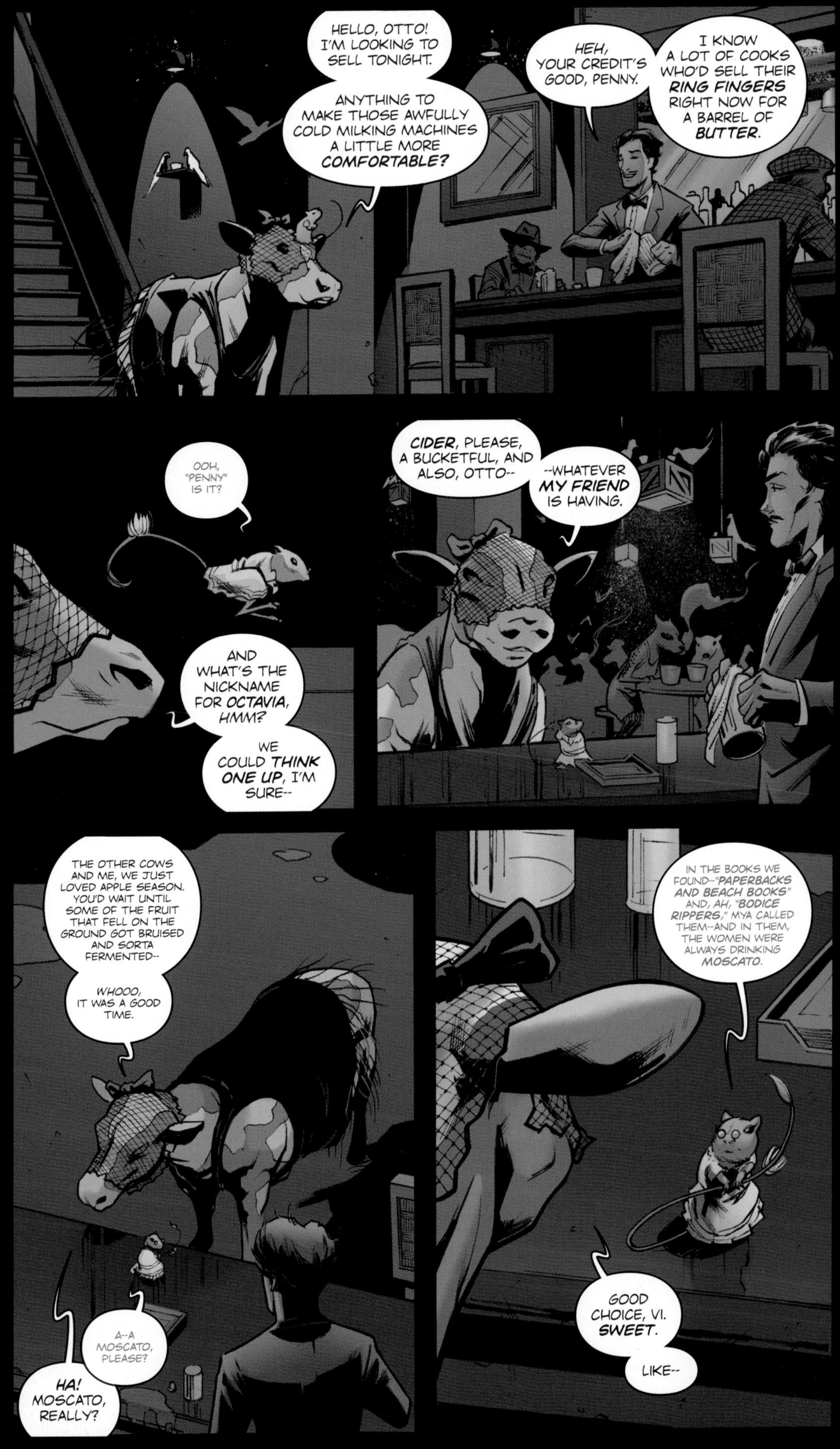
HELLO, OTTO! I'M LOOKING TO SELL TONIGHT.
ANYTHING TO MAKE THOSE AWFULLY COLD MILKING MACHINES A LITTLE MORE **COMFORTABLE?**
HEH, YOUR CREDIT'S GOOD, PENNY.
I KNOW A LOT OF COOKS WHO'D SELL THEIR ***RING FINGERS*** RIGHT NOW FOR A BARREL OF ***BUTTER***.
OOH, "PENNY" IS IT?
AND WHAT'S THE NICKNAME FOR *OCTAVIA*, HMM?
WE COULD ***THINK ONE UP***, I'M SURE--
CIDER, PLEASE, A BUCKETFUL, AND ALSO, OTTO--
--WHATEVER ***MY FRIEND*** IS HAVING.
THE OTHER COWS AND ME, WE JUST LOVED APPLE SEASON. YOU'D WAIT UNTIL SOME OF THE FRUIT THAT FELL ON THE GROUND GOT BRUISED AND SORTA FERMENTED--
WHOOO, IT WAS A GOOD TIME.
A--A MOSCATO, PLEASE?
HA! MOSCATO, REALLY?
IN THE BOOKS WE FOUND--"***PAPERBACKS AND BEACH BOOKS***" AND, AH, "***BODICE RIPPERS,***" MYA CALLED THEM--AND IN THEM, THE WOMEN WERE ALWAYS DRINKING ***MOSCATO***.
GOOD CHOICE, VI. **SWEET**.
LIKE--

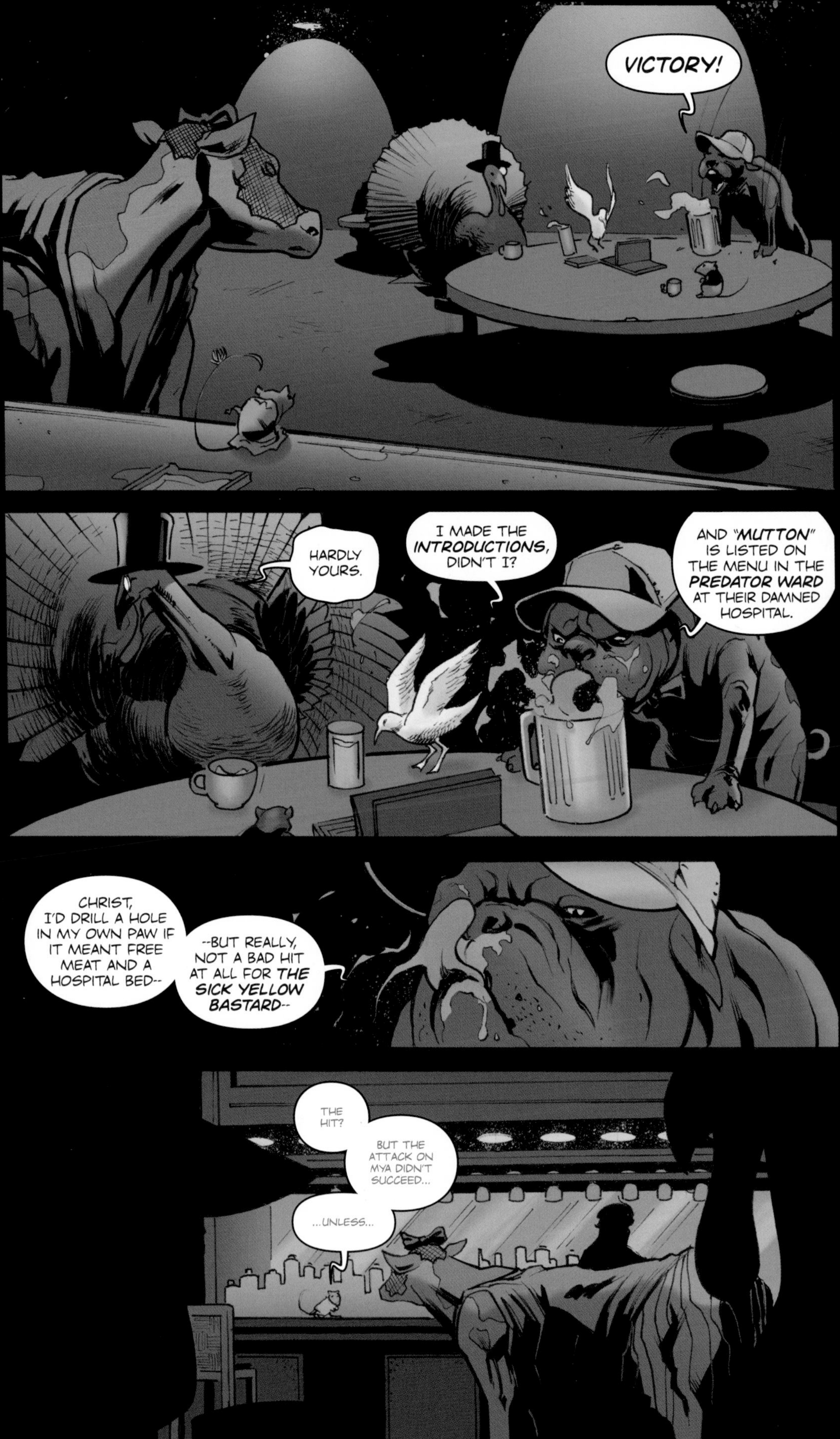
VICTORY!
HARDLY YOURS.
I MADE THE INTRODUCTIONS, DIDN'T I?
AND "MUTTON" IS LISTED ON THE MENU IN THE PREDATOR WARD AT THEIR DAMNED HOSPITAL.
CHRIST, I'D DRILL A HOLE IN MY OWN PAW IF IT MEANT FREE MEAT AND A HOSPITAL BED--
--BUT REALLY, NOT A BAD HIT AT ALL FOR THE SICK YELLOW BASTARD--
THE HIT?
BUT THE ATTACK ON MYA DIDN'T SUCCEED...
...UNLESS...

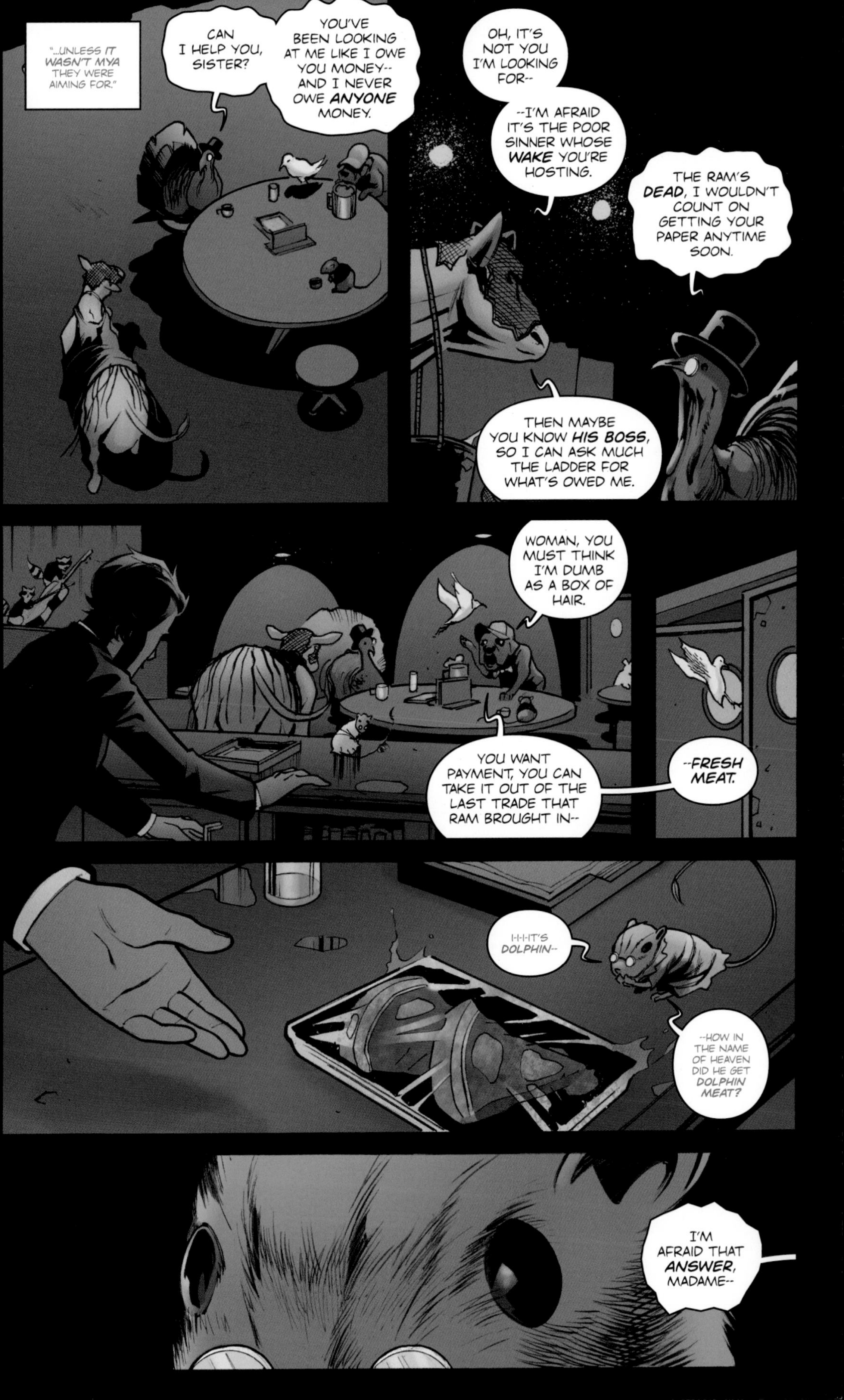
"...UNLESS IT WASN'T MYA THEY WERE AIMING FOR."
CAN I HELP YOU, SISTER?
YOU'VE BEEN LOOKING AT ME LIKE I OWE YOU MONEY-- AND I NEVER OWE ANYONE MONEY.
OH, IT'S NOT YOU I'M LOOKING FOR--
--I'M AFRAID IT'S THE POOR SINNER WHOSE WAKE YOU'RE HOSTING.
THE RAM'S DEAD, I WOULDN'T COUNT ON GETTING YOUR PAPER ANYTIME SOON.
THEN MAYBE YOU KNOW HIS BOSS, SO I CAN ASK MUCH THE LADDER FOR WHAT'S OWED ME.
WOMAN, YOU MUST THINK I'M DUMB AS A BOX OF HAIR.
YOU WANT PAYMENT, YOU CAN TAKE IT OUT OF THE LAST TRADE THAT RAM BROUGHT IN--
--FRESH MEAT.
I-I-I-IT'S DOLPHIN--
--HOW IN THE NAME OF HEAVEN DID HE GET DOLPHIN MEAT?
I'M AFRAID THAT ANSWER, MADAME--

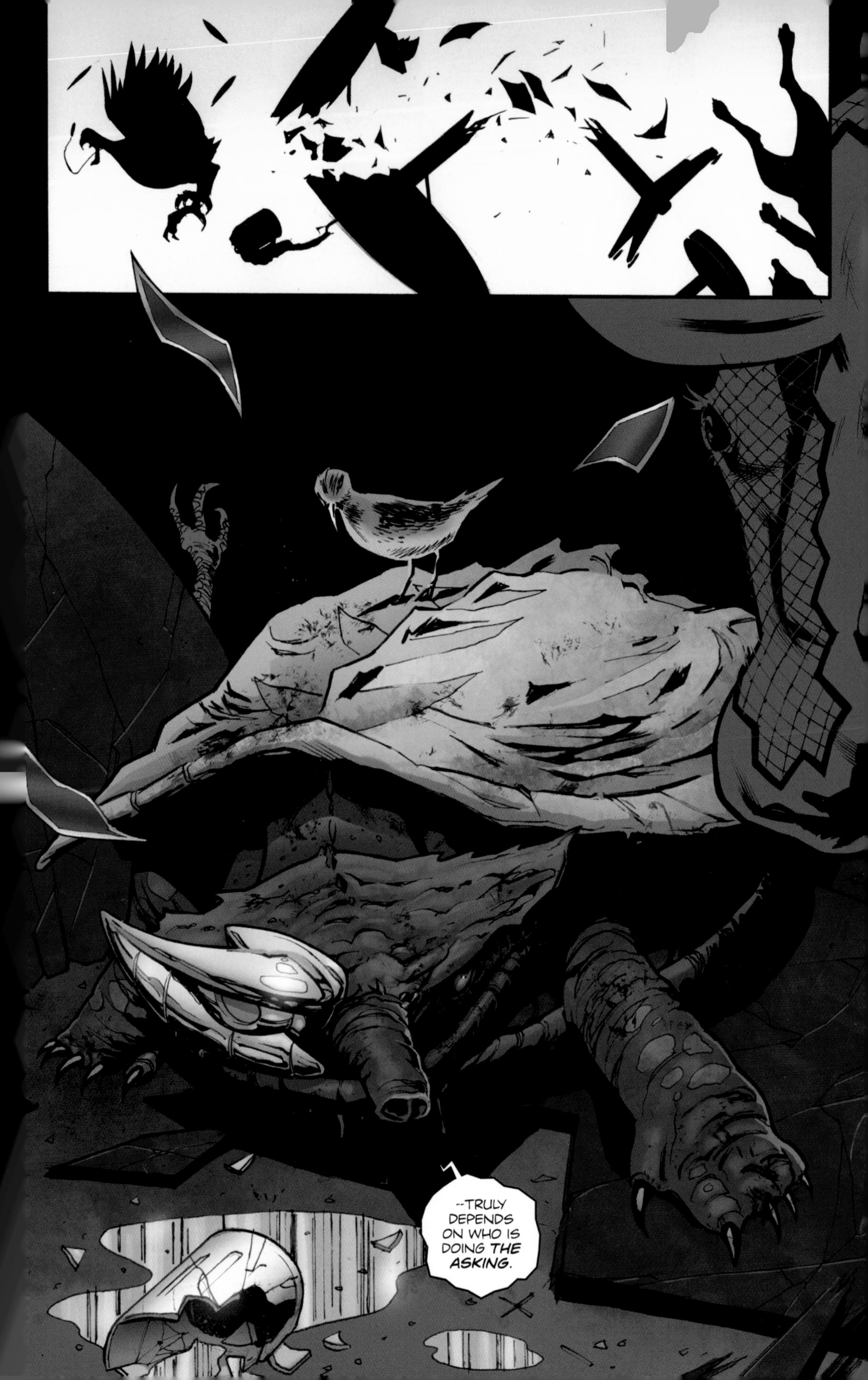
--TRULY DEPENDS ON WHO IS DOING THE ASKING.

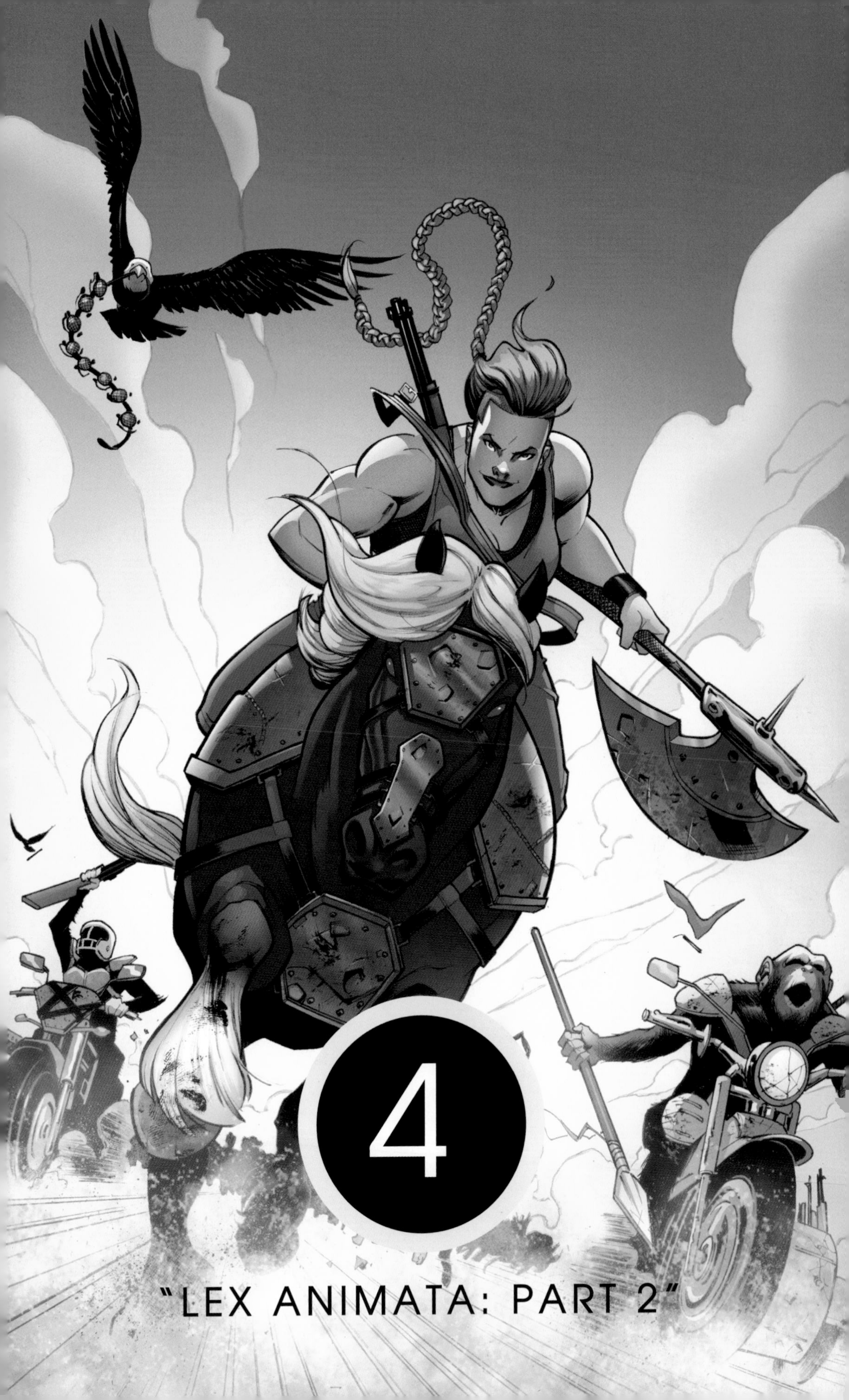

4

"LEX ANIMATA: PART 2"

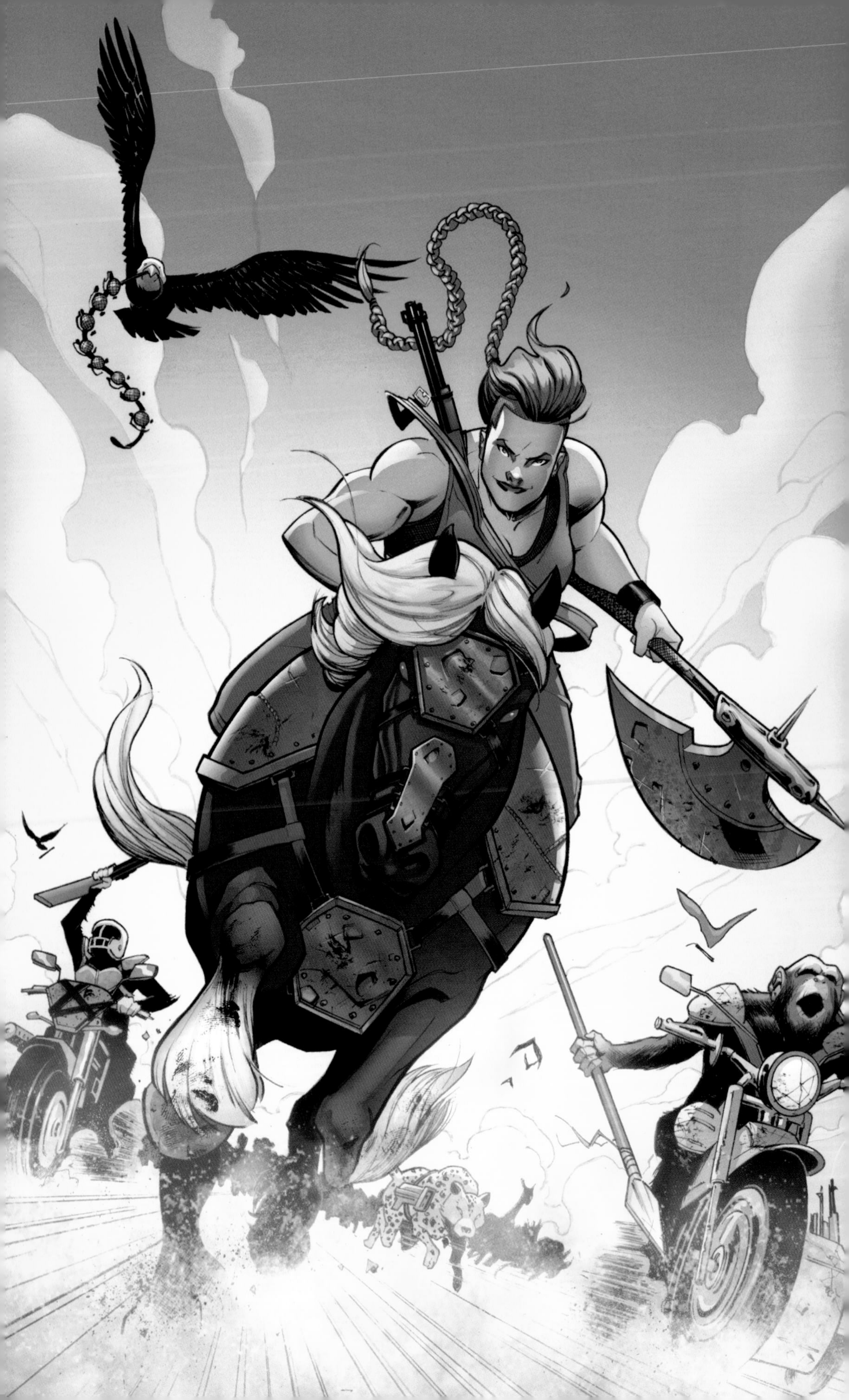

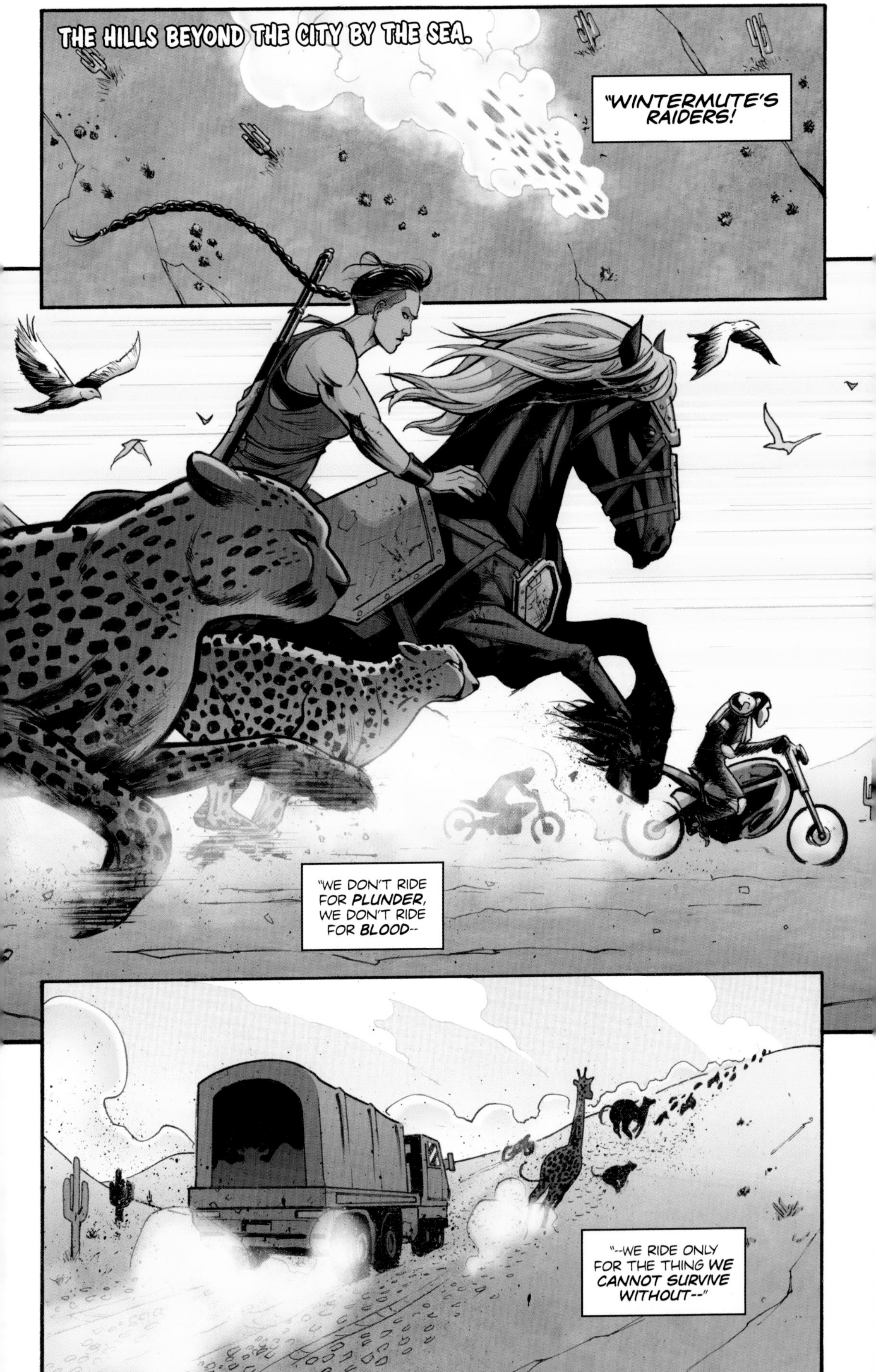
THE HILLS BEYOND THE CITY BY THE SEA.
"WINTERMUTE'S RAIDERS!
"WE DON'T RIDE FOR PLUNDER, WE DON'T RIDE FOR BLOOD--
"--WE RIDE ONLY FOR THE THING WE CANNOT SURVIVE WITHOUT--"

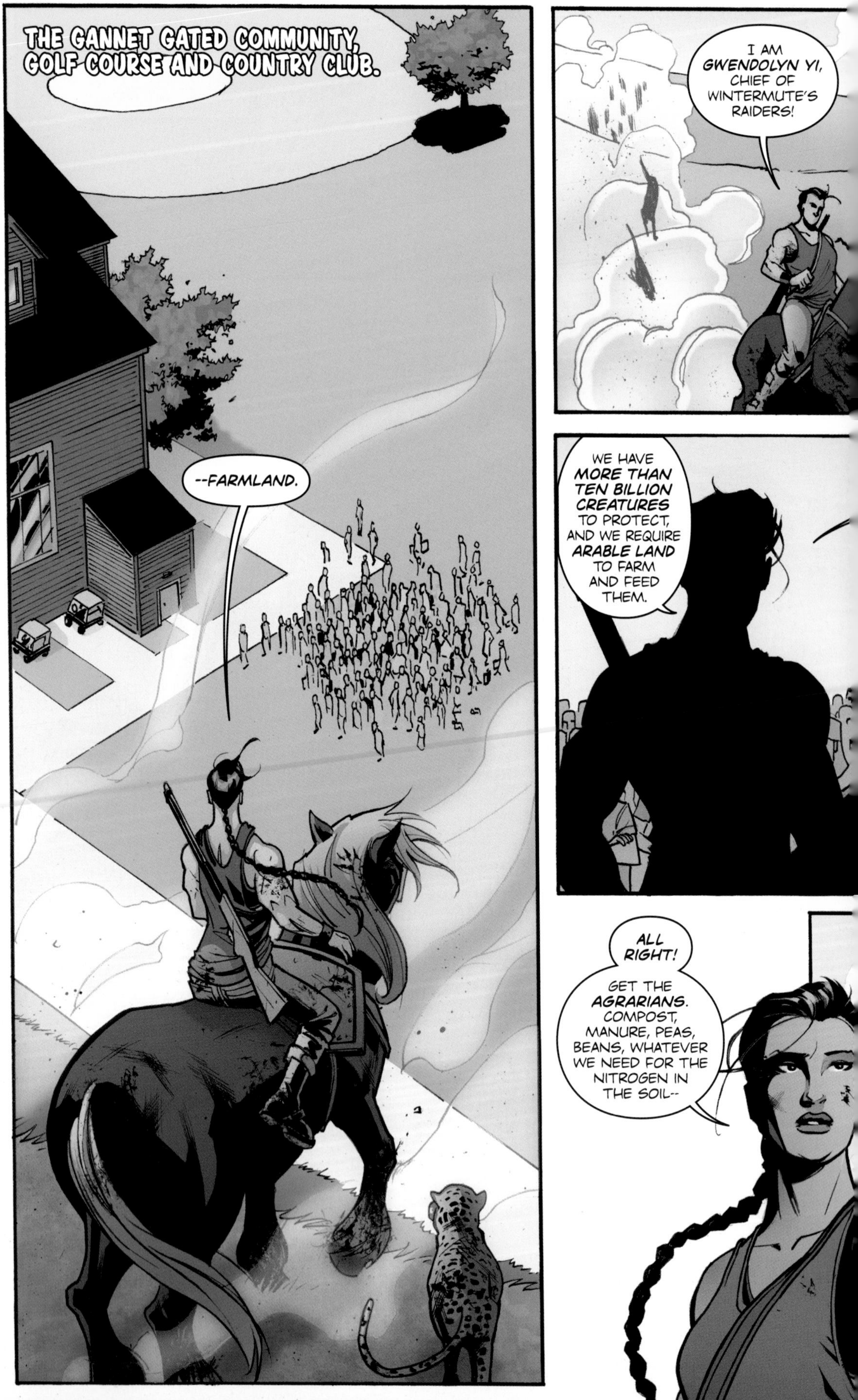
THE GANNET GATED COMMUNITY, GOLF COURSE AND COUNTRY CLUB.
--FARMLAND.
I AM GWENDOLYN YI, CHIEF OF WINTERMUTE'S RAIDERS!
WE HAVE MORE THAN TEN BILLION CREATURES TO PROTECT, AND WE REQUIRE ARABLE LAND TO FARM AND FEED THEM.
ALL RIGHT!
GET THE AGRARIANS. COMPOST, MANURE, PEAS, BEANS, WHATEVER WE NEED FOR THE NITROGEN IN THE SOIL--

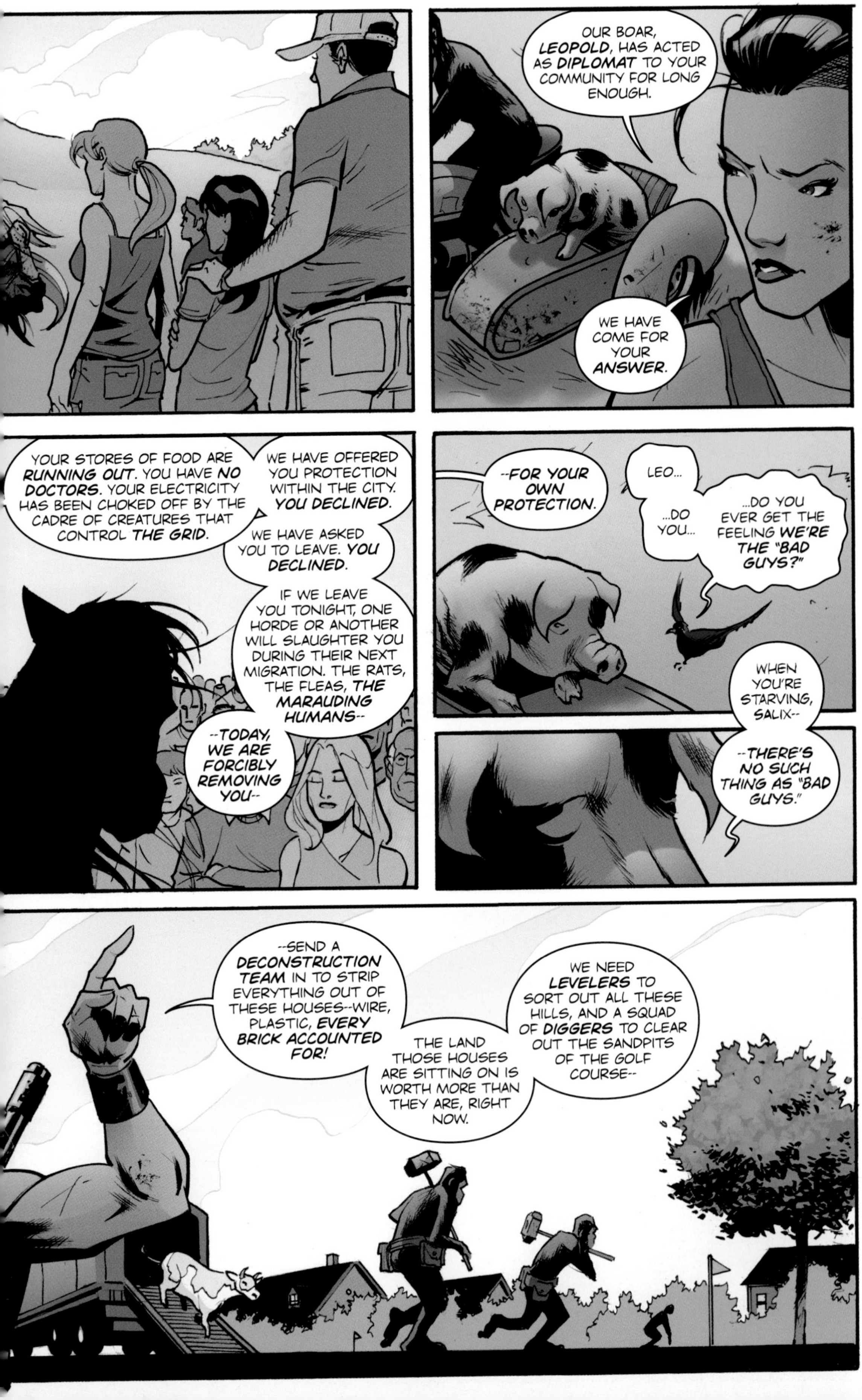
OUR BOAR, LEOPOLD, HAS ACTED AS DIPLOMAT TO YOUR COMMUNITY FOR LONG ENOUGH.
WE HAVE COME FOR YOUR ANSWER.
YOUR STORES OF FOOD ARE RUNNING OUT. YOU HAVE NO DOCTORS. YOUR ELECTRICITY HAS BEEN CHOKED OFF BY THE CADRE OF CREATURES THAT CONTROL THE GRID.
WE HAVE OFFERED YOU PROTECTION WITHIN THE CITY. YOU DECLINED.
WE HAVE ASKED YOU TO LEAVE. YOU DECLINED.
IF WE LEAVE YOU TONIGHT, ONE HORDE OR ANOTHER WILL SLAUGHTER YOU DURING THEIR NEXT MIGRATION. THE RATS, THE FLEAS, THE MARAUDING HUMANS--
--TODAY, WE ARE FORCIBLY REMOVING YOU--
--FOR YOUR OWN PROTECTION.
LEO...
...DO YOU...
...DO YOU EVER GET THE FEELING WE'RE THE "BAD GUYS?"
WHEN YOU'RE STARVING, SALIX--
--THERE'S NO SUCH THING AS "BAD GUYS."
--SEND A DECONSTRUCTION TEAM IN TO STRIP EVERYTHING OUT OF THESE HOUSES--WIRE, PLASTIC, EVERY BRICK ACCOUNTED FOR!
THE LAND THOSE HOUSES ARE SITTING ON IS WORTH MORE THAN THEY ARE, RIGHT NOW.
WE NEED LEVELERS TO SORT OUT ALL THESE HILLS, AND A SQUAD OF DIGGERS TO CLEAR OUT THE SANDPITS OF THE GOLF COURSE--

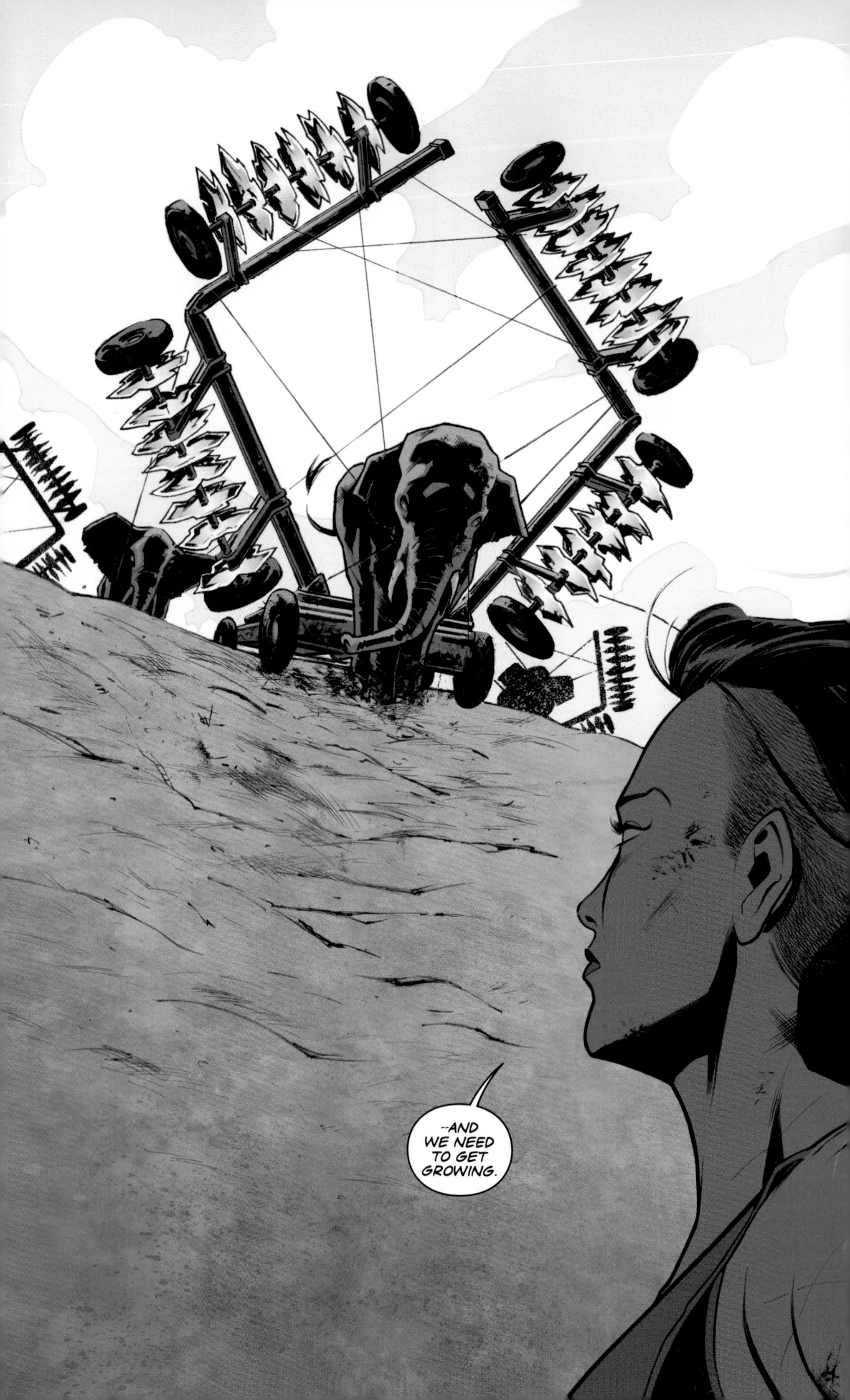
--AND WE NEED TO GET GROWING.

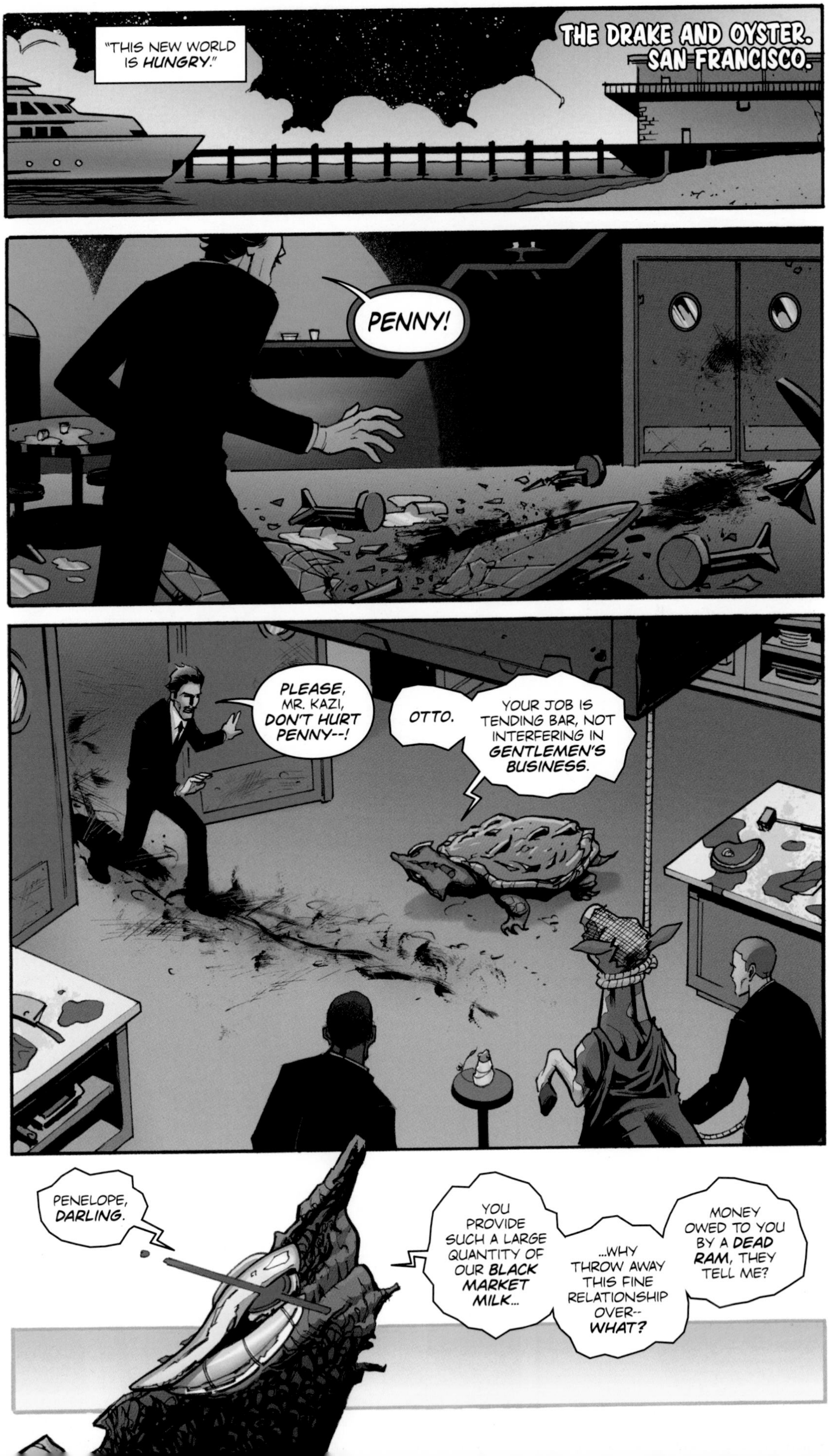
"THIS NEW WORLD IS HUNGRY."
THE DRAKE AND OYSTER. SAN FRANCISCO.
PENNY!
PLEASE, MR. KAZI, DON'T HURT PENNY--!
OTTO.
YOUR JOB IS TENDING BAR, NOT INTERFERING IN GENTLEMEN'S BUSINESS.
PENELOPE, DARLING.
YOU PROVIDE SUCH A LARGE QUANTITY OF OUR BLACK MARKET MILK...
...WHY THROW AWAY THIS FINE RELATIONSHIP OVER-- WHAT?
MONEY OWED TO YOU BY A DEAD RAM, THEY TELL ME?

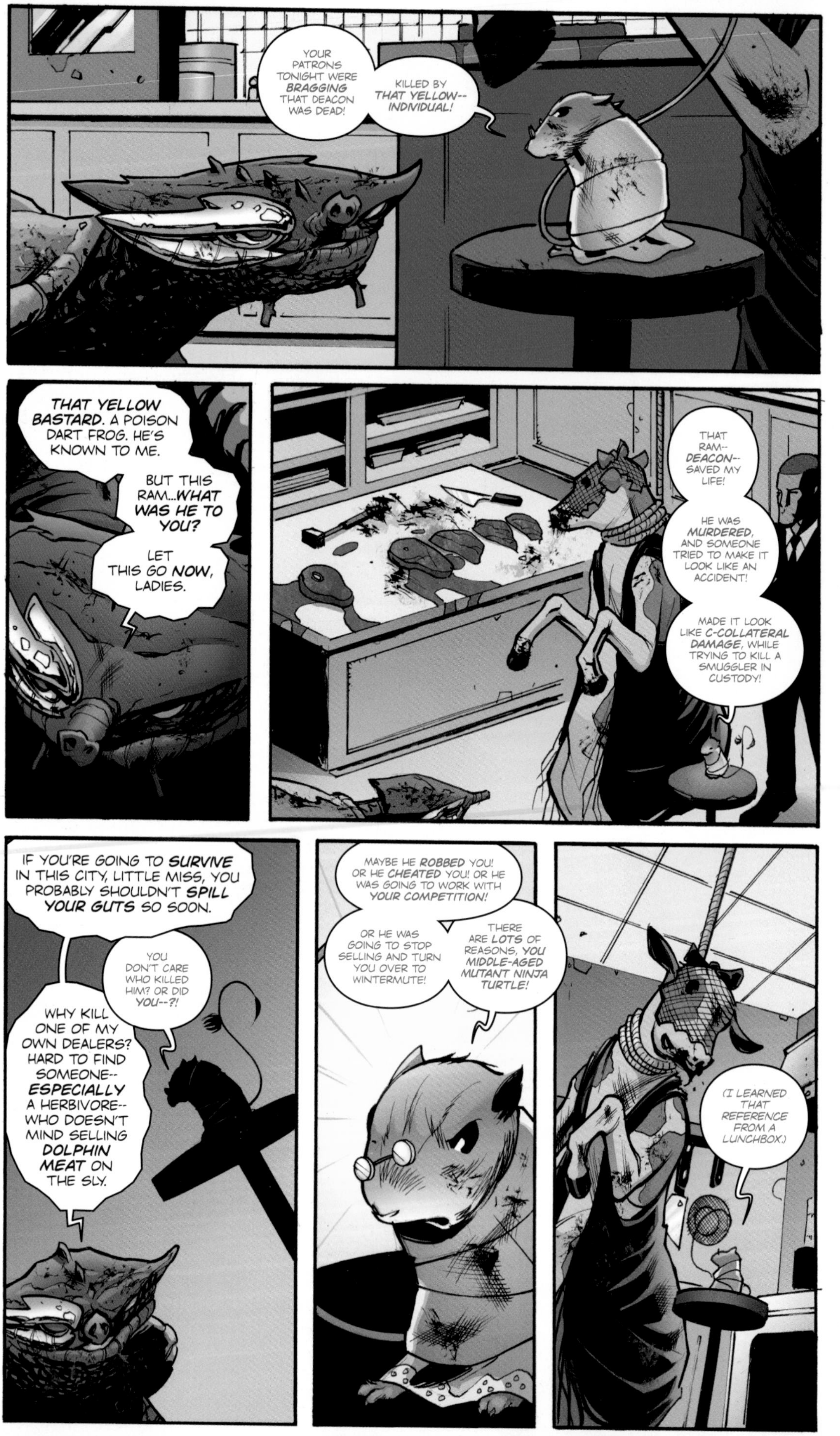
YOUR PATRONS TONIGHT WERE BRAGGING THAT DEACON WAS DEAD!
KILLED BY THAT YELLOW--INDIVIDUAL!
THAT YELLOW BASTARD. A POISON DART FROG. HE'S KNOWN TO ME.
BUT THIS RAM...WHAT WAS HE TO YOU?
LET THIS GO NOW, LADIES.
THAT RAM--DEACON--SAVED MY LIFE!
HE WAS MURDERED, AND SOMEONE TRIED TO MAKE IT LOOK LIKE AN ACCIDENT!
MADE IT LOOK LIKE C-COLLATERAL DAMAGE, WHILE TRYING TO KILL A SMUGGLER IN CUSTODY!
IF YOU'RE GOING TO SURVIVE IN THIS CITY, LITTLE MISS, YOU PROBABLY SHOULDN'T SPILL YOUR GUTS SO SOON.
YOU DON'T CARE WHO KILLED HIM? OR DID YOU--?!
WHY KILL ONE OF MY OWN DEALERS? HARD TO FIND SOMEONE--ESPECIALLY A HERBIVORE--WHO DOESN'T MIND SELLING DOLPHIN MEAT ON THE SLY.
MAYBE HE ROBBED YOU! OR HE CHEATED YOU! OR HE WAS GOING TO WORK WITH YOUR COMPETITION!
OR HE WAS GOING TO STOP SELLING AND TURN YOU OVER TO WINTERMUTE!
THERE ARE LOTS OF REASONS, YOU MIDDLE-AGED MUTANT NINJA TURTLE!
(I LEARNED THAT REFERENCE FROM A LUNCHBOX.)

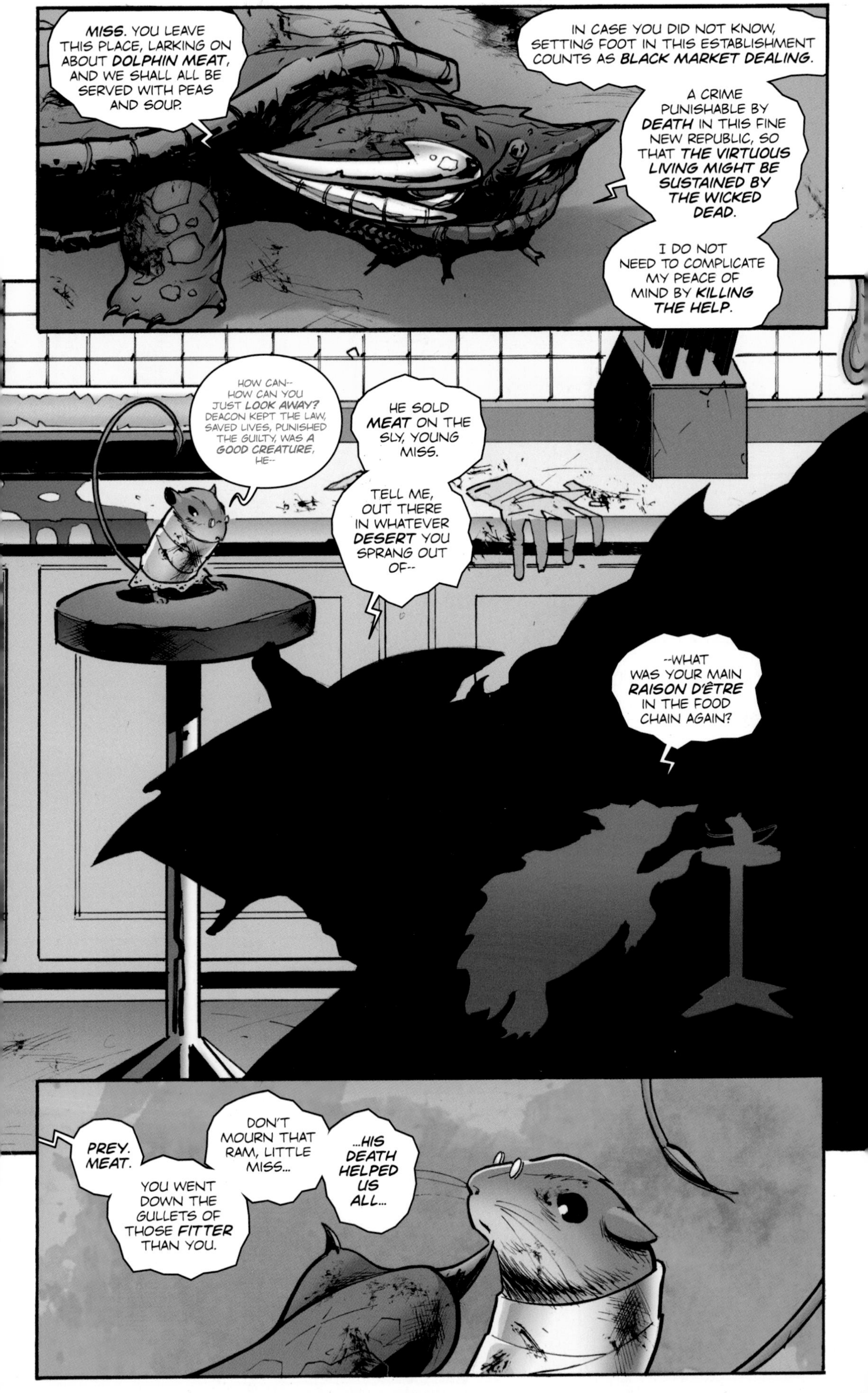
MISS. YOU LEAVE THIS PLACE, LARKING ON ABOUT DOLPHIN MEAT, AND WE SHALL ALL BE SERVED WITH PEAS AND SOUP.
IN CASE YOU DID NOT KNOW, SETTING FOOT IN THIS ESTABLISHMENT COUNTS AS BLACK MARKET DEALING.
A CRIME PUNISHABLE BY DEATH IN THIS FINE NEW REPUBLIC, SO THAT THE VIRTUOUS LIVING MIGHT BE SUSTAINED BY THE WICKED DEAD.
I DO NOT NEED TO COMPLICATE MY PEACE OF MIND BY KILLING THE HELP.
HOW CAN-- HOW CAN YOU JUST LOOK AWAY? DEACON KEPT THE LAW, SAVED LIVES, PUNISHED THE GUILTY, WAS A GOOD CREATURE, HE--
HE SOLD MEAT ON THE SLY, YOUNG MISS.
TELL ME, OUT THERE IN WHATEVER DESERT YOU SPRANG OUT OF--
--WHAT WAS YOUR MAIN RAISON D'ÊTRE IN THE FOOD CHAIN AGAIN?
PREY. MEAT.
YOU WENT DOWN THE GULLETS OF THOSE FITTER THAN YOU.
DON'T MOURN THAT RAM, LITTLE MISS...
...HIS DEATH HELPED US ALL...

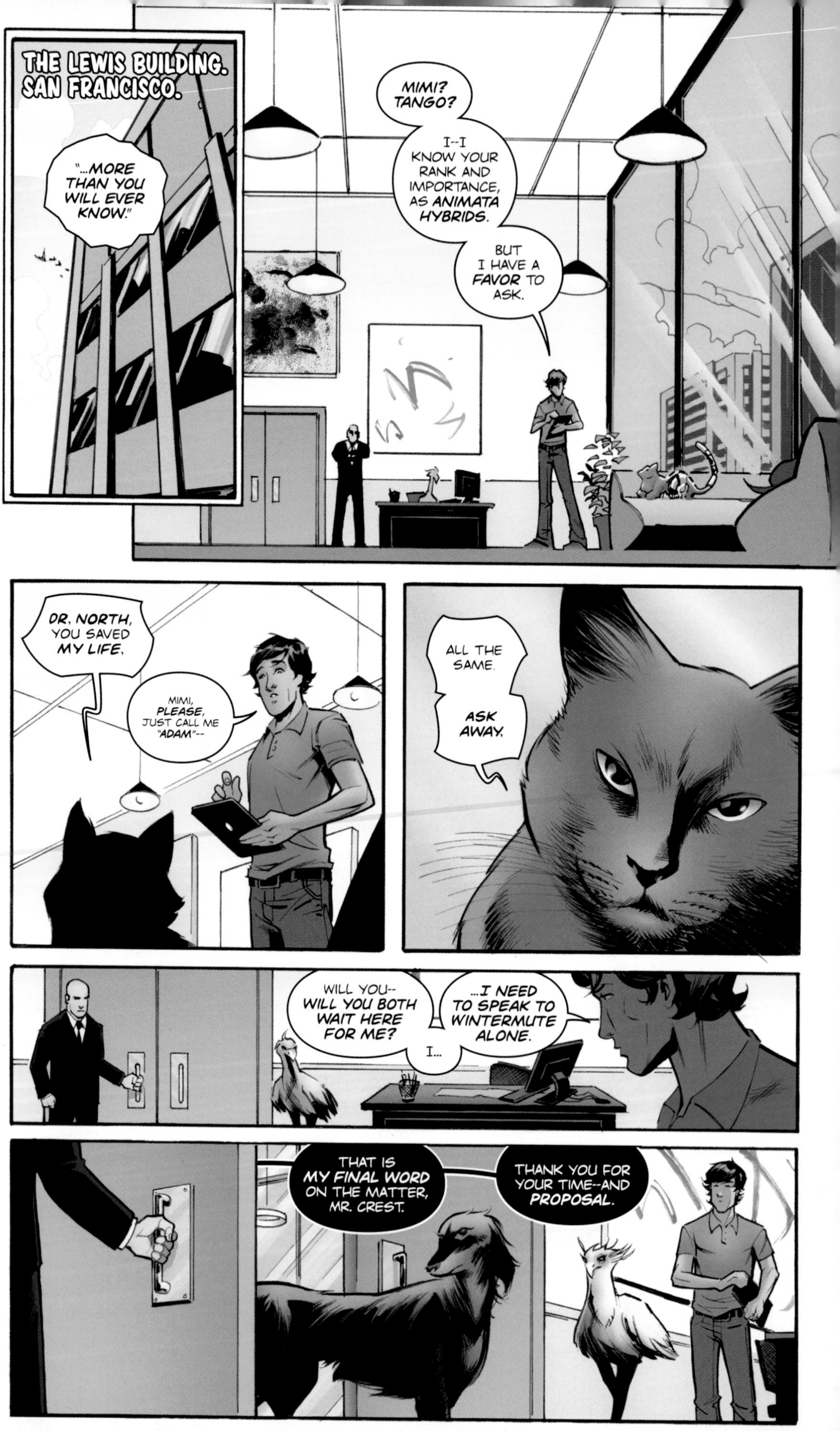
THE LEWIS BUILDING. SAN FRANCISCO.
"...MORE THAN YOU WILL EVER KNOW."
MIMI? TANGO?
I--I KNOW YOUR RANK AND IMPORTANCE, AS ANIMATA HYBRIDS.
BUT I HAVE A FAVOR TO ASK.
DR. NORTH, YOU SAVED MY LIFE.
MIMI, PLEASE, JUST CALL ME "ADAM"--
ALL THE SAME.
ASK AWAY.
WILL YOU-- WILL YOU BOTH WAIT HERE FOR ME?
I...
...I NEED TO SPEAK TO WINTERMUTE ALONE.
THAT IS MY FINAL WORD ON THE MATTER, MR. CREST.
THANK YOU FOR YOUR TIME--AND PROPOSAL.

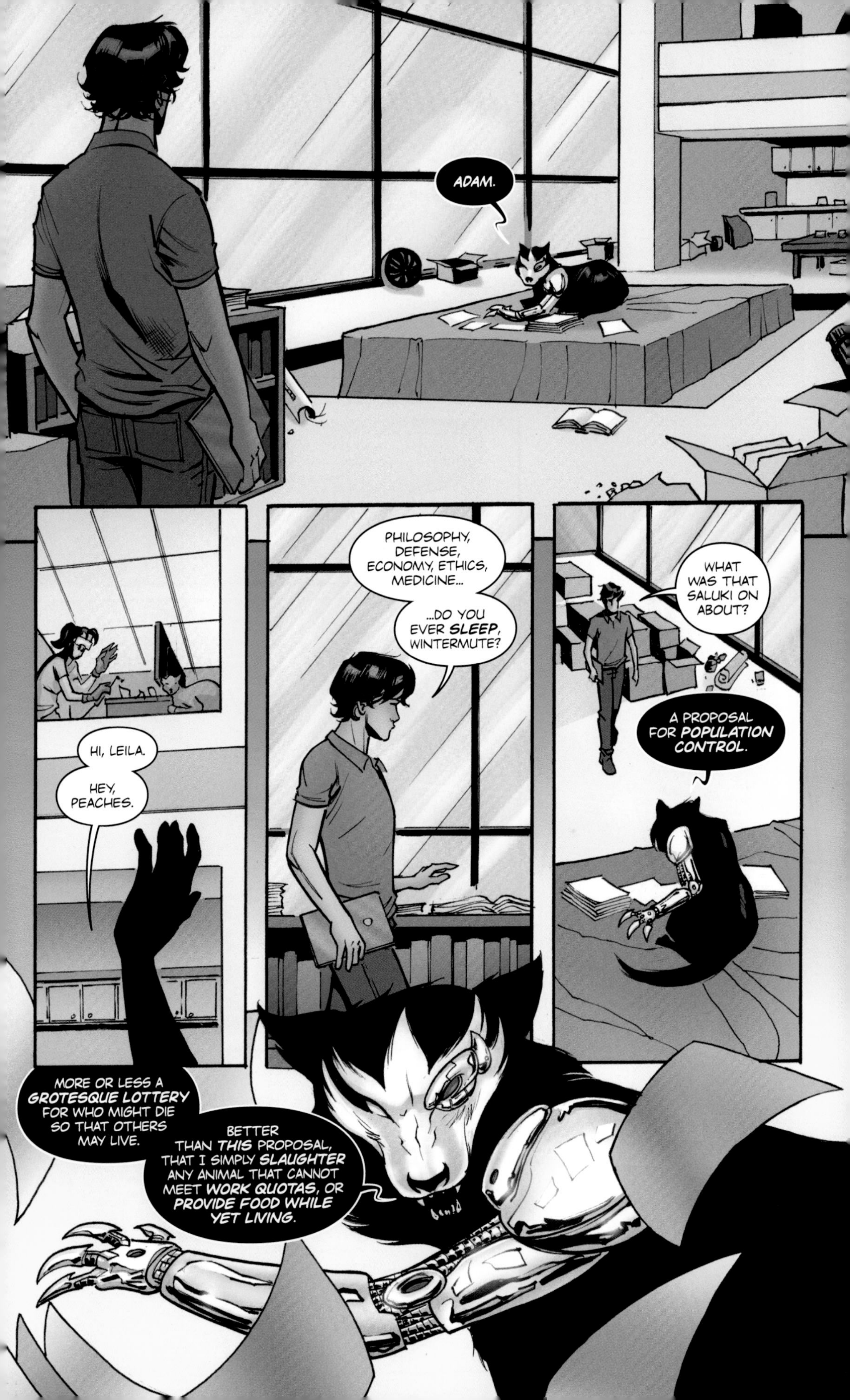
ADAM.
HI, LEILA.
HEY, PEACHES.
PHILOSOPHY, DEFENSE, ECONOMY, ETHICS, MEDICINE...
...DO YOU EVER SLEEP, WINTERMUTE?
WHAT WAS THAT SALUKI ON ABOUT?
A PROPOSAL FOR POPULATION CONTROL.
MORE OR LESS A GROTESQUE LOTTERY FOR WHO MIGHT DIE SO THAT OTHERS MAY LIVE.
BETTER THAN THIS PROPOSAL, THAT I SIMPLY SLAUGHTER ANY ANIMAL THAT CANNOT MEET WORK QUOTAS, OR PROVIDE FOOD WHILE YET LIVING.

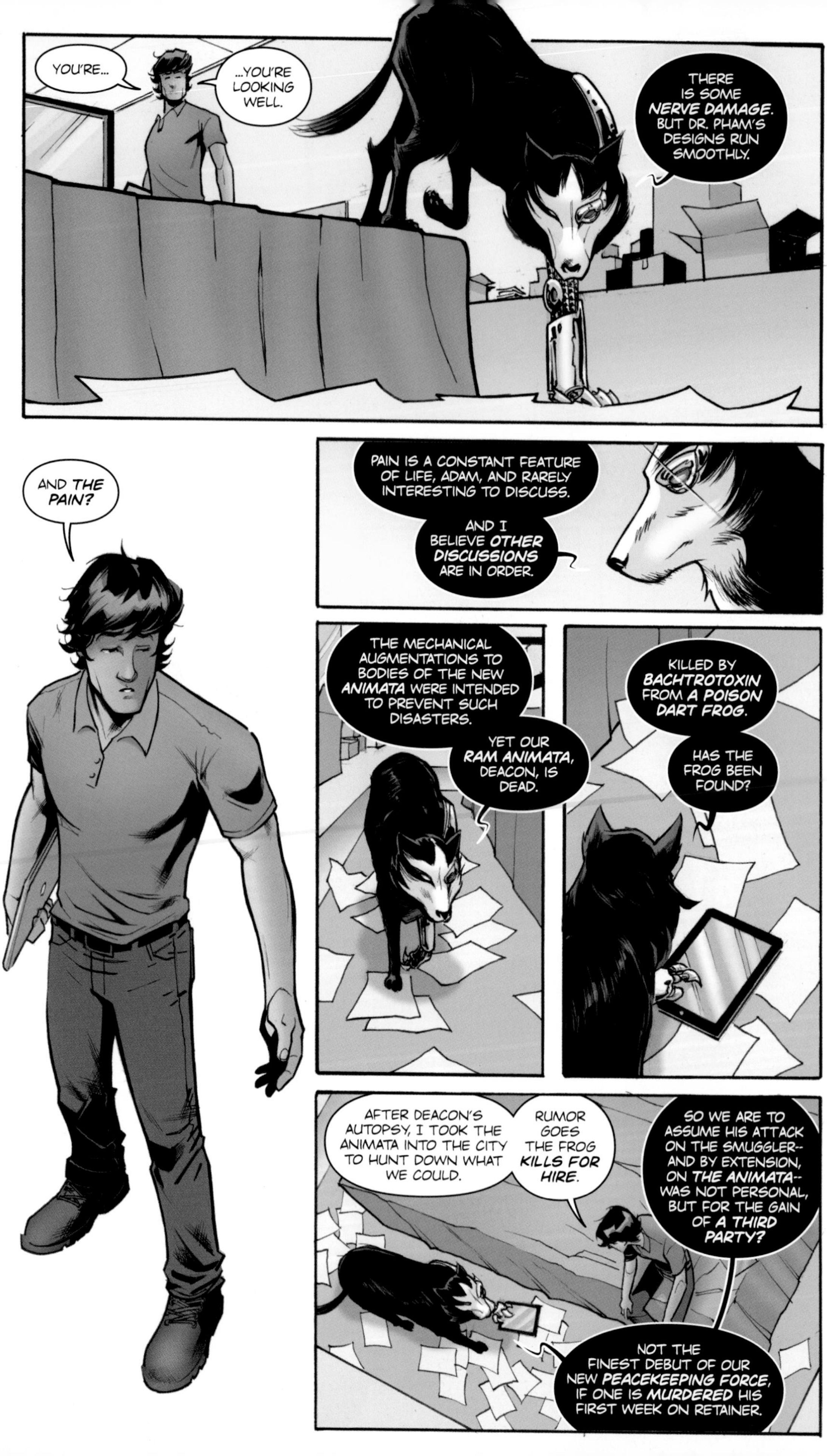

YOU'RE...
...YOU'RE LOOKING WELL.
THERE IS SOME NERVE DAMAGE. BUT DR. PHAM'S DESIGNS RUN SMOOTHLY.
AND THE PAIN?
PAIN IS A CONSTANT FEATURE OF LIFE, ADAM, AND RARELY INTERESTING TO DISCUSS.
AND I BELIEVE OTHER DISCUSSIONS ARE IN ORDER.
THE MECHANICAL AUGMENTATIONS TO BODIES OF THE NEW ANIMATA WERE INTENDED TO PREVENT SUCH DISASTERS.
YET OUR RAM ANIMATA, DEACON, IS DEAD.
KILLED BY BACHTROTOXIN FROM A POISON DART FROG.
HAS THE FROG BEEN FOUND?
AFTER DEACON'S AUTOPSY, I TOOK THE ANIMATA INTO THE CITY TO HUNT DOWN WHAT WE COULD.
RUMOR GOES THE FROG KILLS FOR HIRE.
SO WE ARE TO ASSUME HIS ATTACK ON THE SMUGGLER-- AND BY EXTENSION, ON THE ANIMATA-- WAS NOT PERSONAL, BUT FOR THE GAIN OF A THIRD PARTY?
NOT THE FINEST DEBUT OF OUR NEW PEACEKEEPING FORCE, IF ONE IS MURDERED HIS FIRST WEEK ON RETAINER.

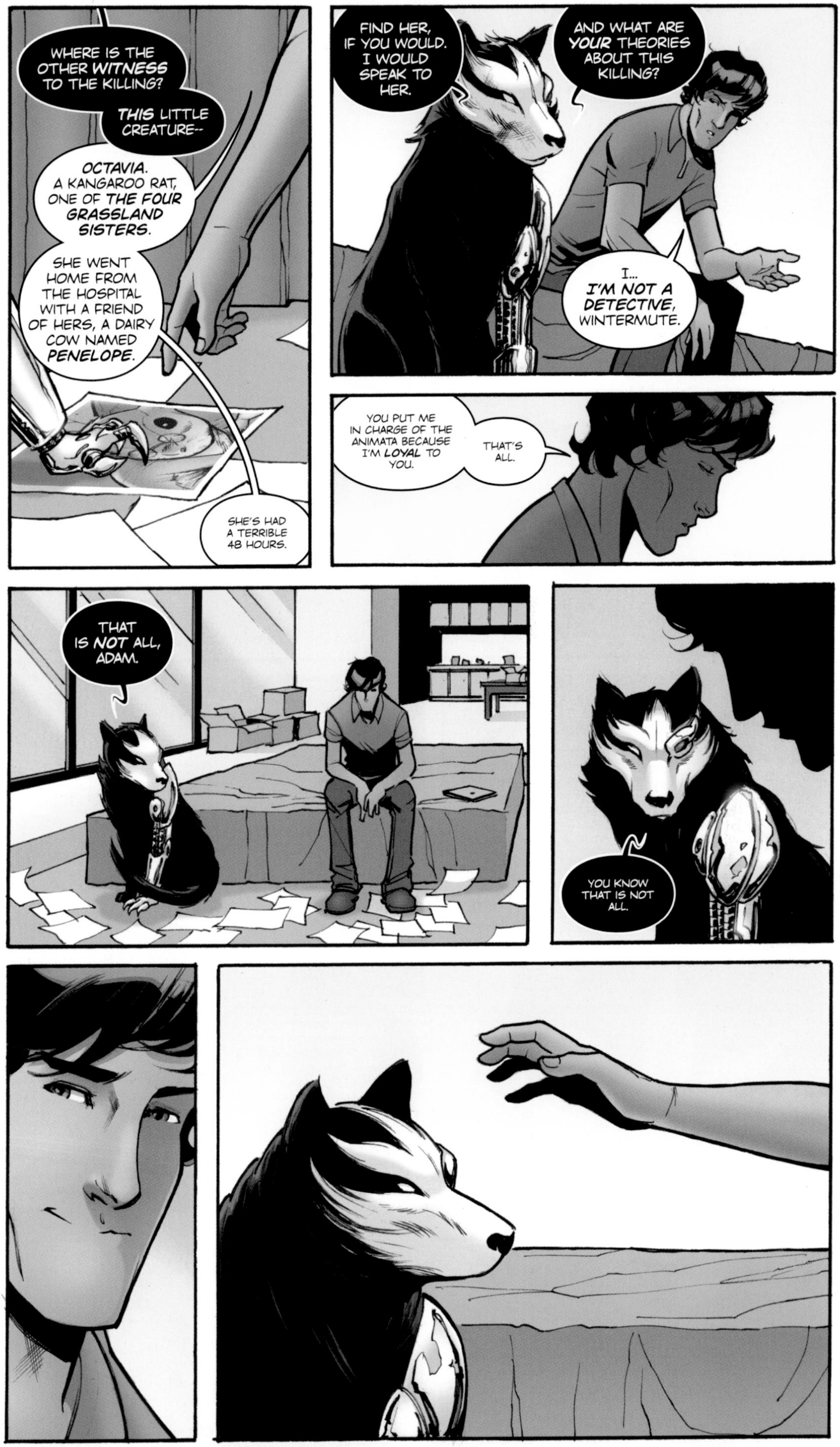
WHERE IS THE OTHER WITNESS TO THE KILLING?
THIS LITTLE CREATURE--
OCTAVIA. A KANGAROO RAT, ONE OF THE FOUR GRASSLAND SISTERS.
SHE WENT HOME FROM THE HOSPITAL WITH A FRIEND OF HERS, A DAIRY COW NAMED PENELOPE.
SHE'S HAD A TERRIBLE 48 HOURS.
FIND HER, IF YOU WOULD. I WOULD SPEAK TO HER.
AND WHAT ARE YOUR THEORIES ABOUT THIS KILLING?
I... I'M NOT A DETECTIVE, WINTERMUTE.
YOU PUT ME IN CHARGE OF THE ANIMATA BECAUSE I'M LOYAL TO YOU.
THAT'S ALL.
THAT IS NOT ALL, ADAM.
YOU KNOW THAT IS NOT ALL.

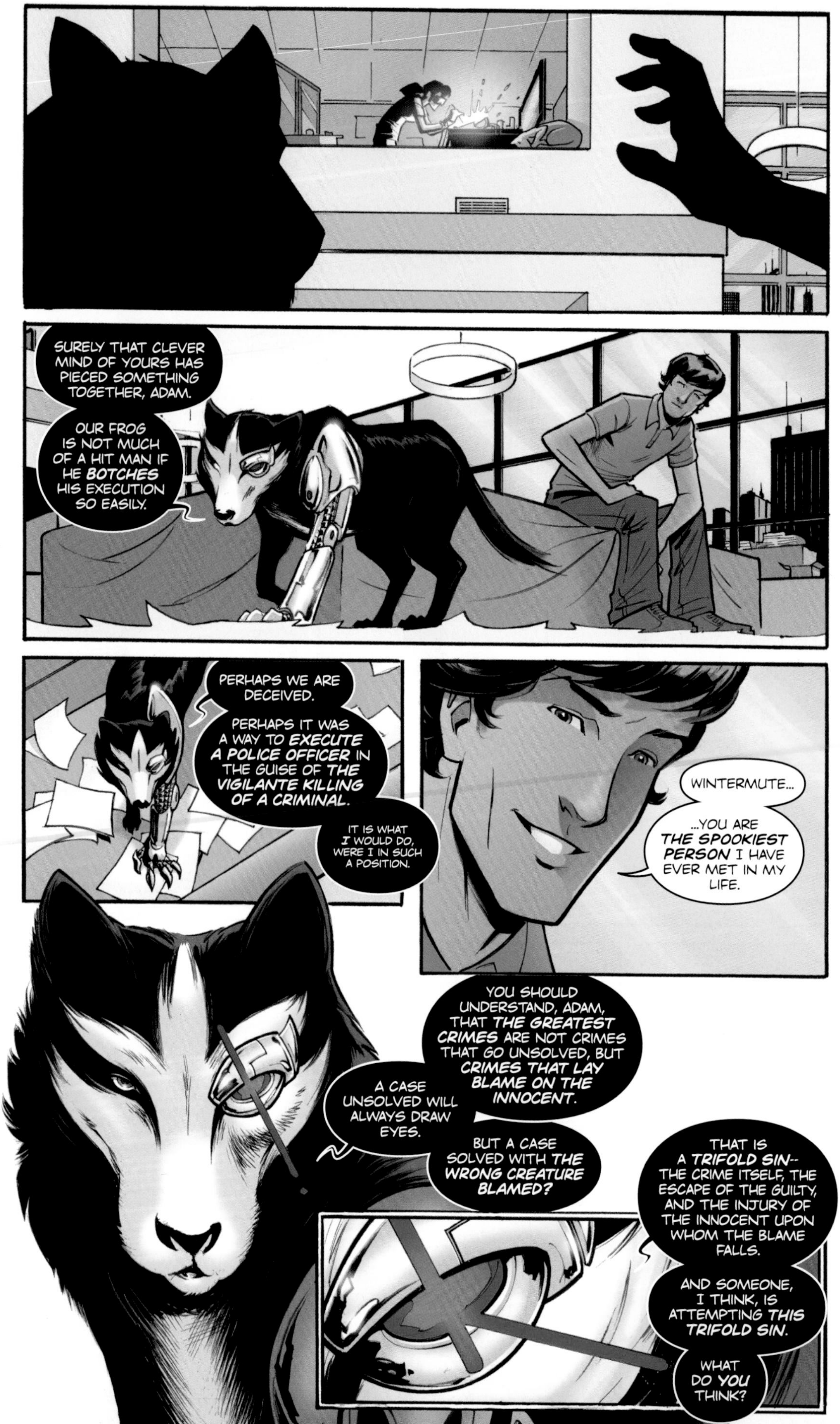
SURELY THAT CLEVER MIND OF YOURS HAS PIECED SOMETHING TOGETHER, ADAM.
OUR FROG IS NOT MUCH OF A HIT MAN IF HE BOTCHES HIS EXECUTION SO EASILY.
PERHAPS WE ARE DECEIVED.
PERHAPS IT WAS A WAY TO EXECUTE A POLICE OFFICER IN THE GUISE OF THE VIGILANTE KILLING OF A CRIMINAL.
IT IS WHAT I WOULD DO, WERE I IN SUCH A POSITION.
WINTERMUTE...
...YOU ARE THE SPOOKIEST PERSON I HAVE EVER MET IN MY LIFE.
YOU SHOULD UNDERSTAND, ADAM, THAT THE GREATEST CRIMES ARE NOT CRIMES THAT GO UNSOLVED, BUT CRIMES THAT LAY BLAME ON THE INNOCENT.
A CASE UNSOLVED WILL ALWAYS DRAW EYES.
BUT A CASE SOLVED WITH THE WRONG CREATURE BLAMED?
THAT IS A TRIFOLD SIN-- THE CRIME ITSELF, THE ESCAPE OF THE GUILTY, AND THE INJURY OF THE INNOCENT UPON WHOM THE BLAME FALLS.
AND SOMEONE, I THINK, IS ATTEMPTING THIS TRIFOLD SIN.
WHAT DO YOU THINK?

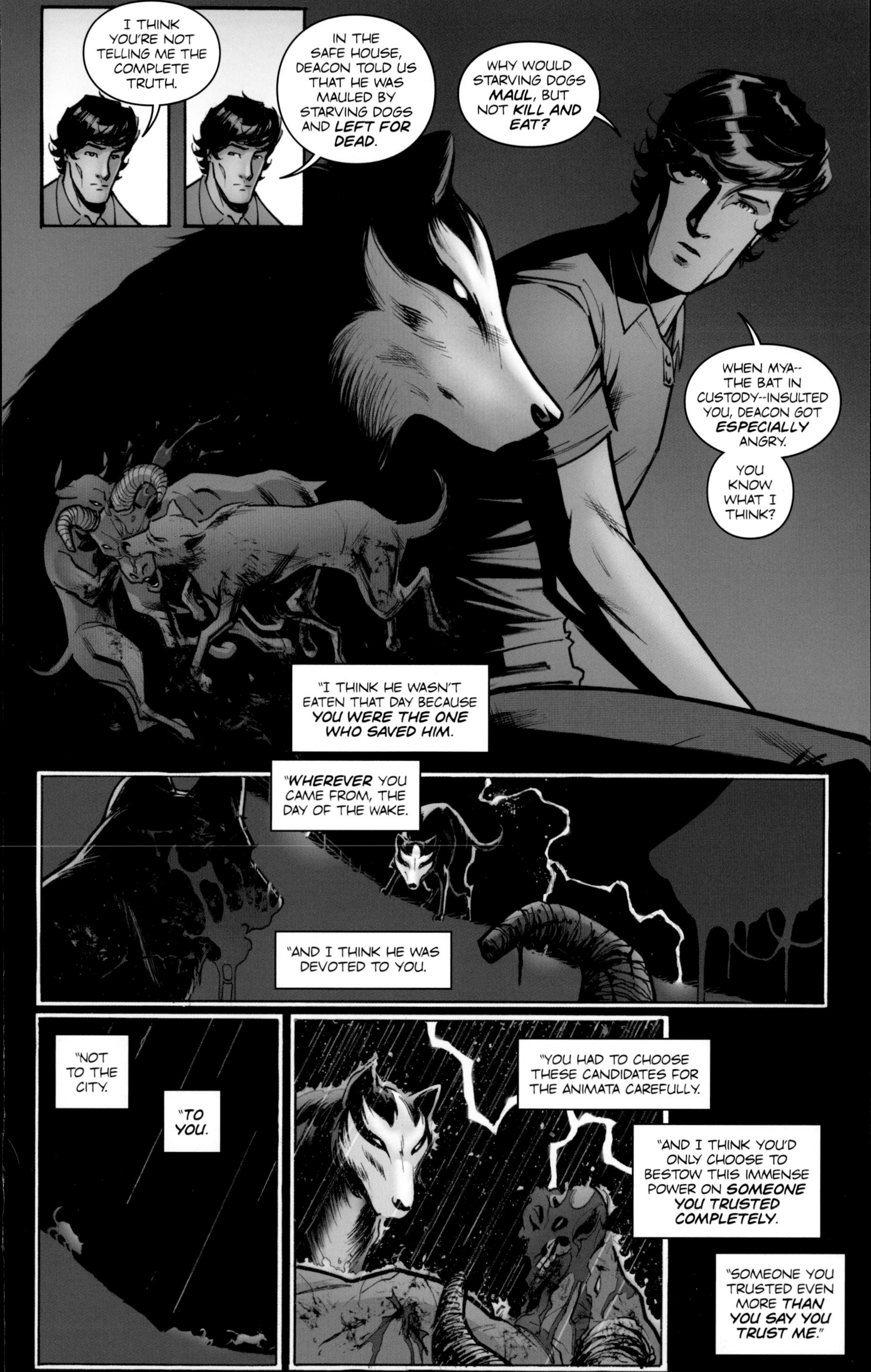
I THINK YOU'RE NOT TELLING ME THE COMPLETE TRUTH.
IN THE SAFE HOUSE, DEACON TOLD US THAT HE WAS MAULED BY STARVING DOGS AND **LEFT FOR DEAD**.
WHY WOULD STARVING DOGS **MAUL**, BUT NOT **KILL AND EAT?**
WHEN MYA--THE BAT IN CUSTODY--INSULTED YOU, DEACON GOT **ESPECIALLY** ANGRY.
YOU KNOW WHAT I THINK?
"I THINK HE WASN'T EATEN THAT DAY BECAUSE **YOU WERE THE ONE WHO SAVED HIM**.
"**WHEREVER** YOU CAME FROM, THE DAY OF THE WAKE.
"AND I THINK HE WAS DEVOTED TO YOU.
"NOT TO THE CITY.
"*TO YOU*.
"YOU HAD TO CHOOSE THESE CANDIDATES FOR THE ANIMATA CAREFULLY.
"AND I THINK YOU'D ONLY CHOOSE TO BESTOW THIS IMMENSE POWER ON **SOMEONE YOU TRUSTED COMPLETELY**.
"SOMEONE YOU TRUSTED EVEN MORE **THAN YOU SAY YOU TRUST ME**."

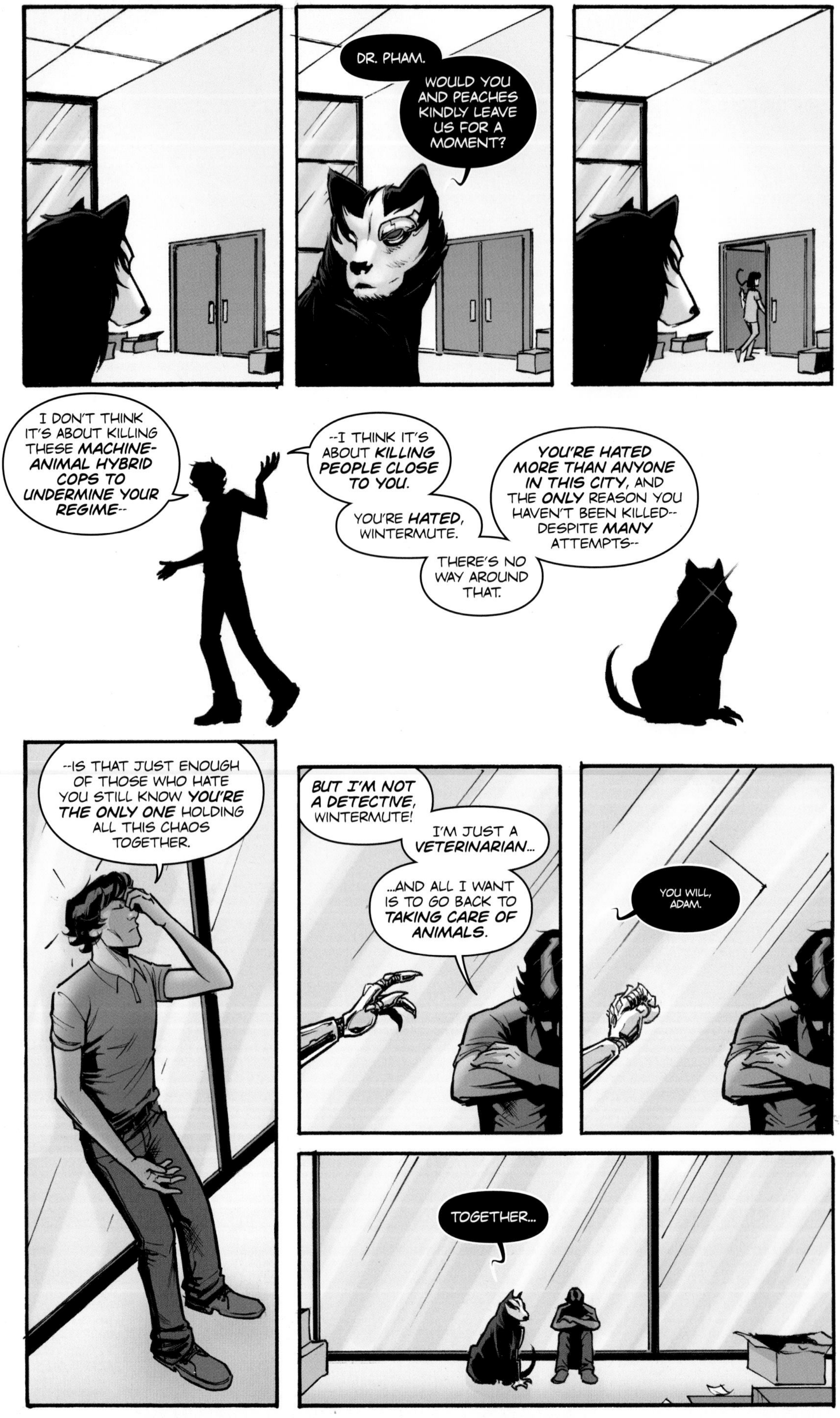
DR. PHAM.
WOULD YOU AND PEACHES KINDLY LEAVE US FOR A MOMENT?
I DON'T THINK IT'S ABOUT KILLING THESE MACHINE-ANIMAL HYBRID COPS TO UNDERMINE YOUR REGIME--
--I THINK IT'S ABOUT KILLING PEOPLE CLOSE TO YOU.
YOU'RE HATED, WINTERMUTE.
THERE'S NO WAY AROUND THAT.
YOU'RE HATED MORE THAN ANYONE IN THIS CITY, AND THE ONLY REASON YOU HAVEN'T BEEN KILLED-- DESPITE MANY ATTEMPTS--
--IS THAT JUST ENOUGH OF THOSE WHO HATE YOU STILL KNOW YOU'RE THE ONLY ONE HOLDING ALL THIS CHAOS TOGETHER.
BUT I'M NOT A DETECTIVE, WINTERMUTE!
I'M JUST A VETERINARIAN...
...AND ALL I WANT IS TO GO BACK TO TAKING CARE OF ANIMALS.
YOU WILL, ADAM.
TOGETHER...

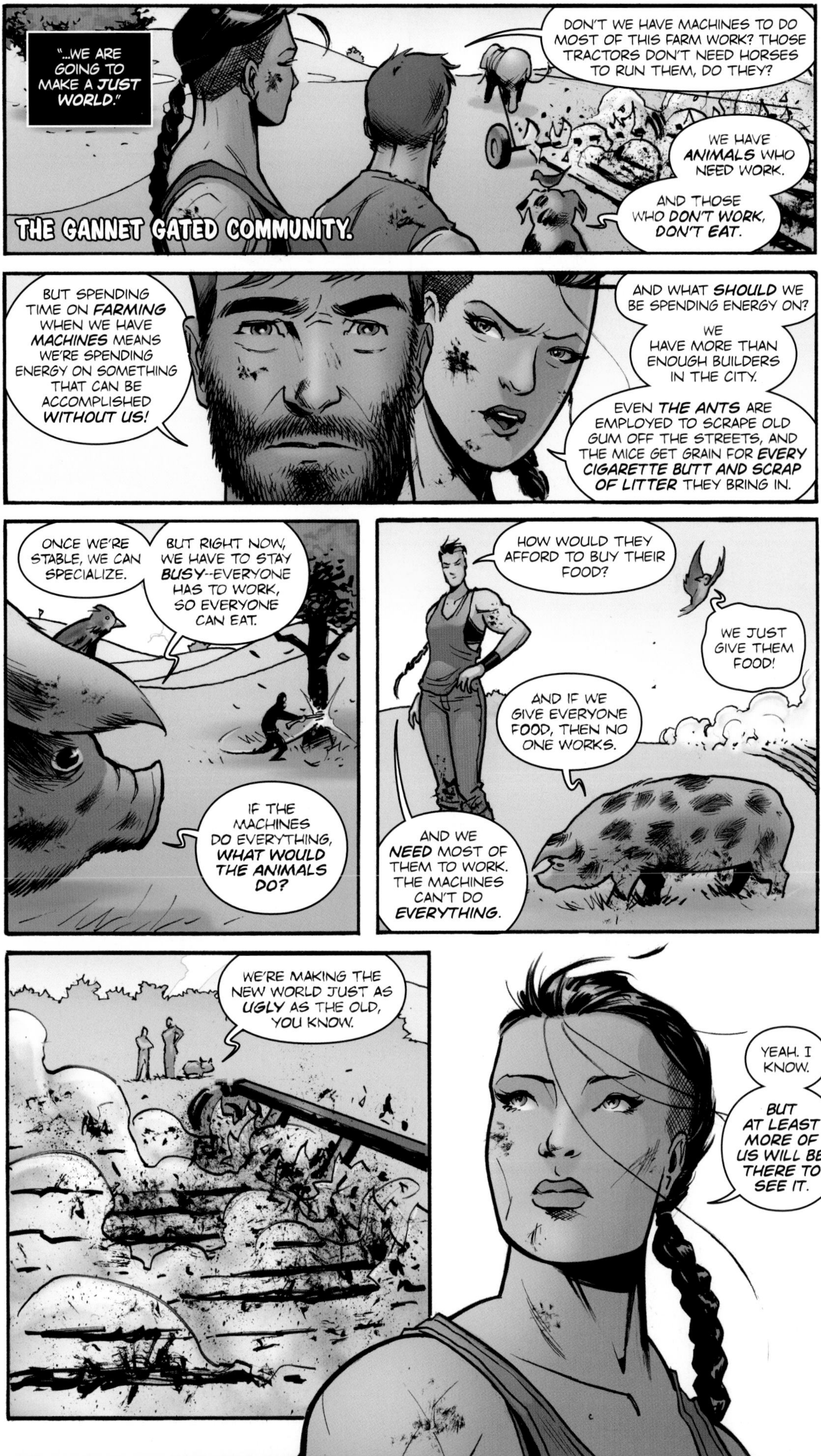
"...WE ARE GOING TO MAKE A JUST WORLD."
THE GANNET GATED COMMUNITY.
DON'T WE HAVE MACHINES TO DO MOST OF THIS FARM WORK? THOSE TRACTORS DON'T NEED HORSES TO RUN THEM, DO THEY?
WE HAVE ANIMALS WHO NEED WORK.
AND THOSE WHO DON'T WORK, DON'T EAT.
BUT SPENDING TIME ON FARMING WHEN WE HAVE MACHINES MEANS WE'RE SPENDING ENERGY ON SOMETHING THAT CAN BE ACCOMPLISHED WITHOUT US!
AND WHAT SHOULD WE BE SPENDING ENERGY ON?
WE HAVE MORE THAN ENOUGH BUILDERS IN THE CITY.
EVEN THE ANTS ARE EMPLOYED TO SCRAPE OLD GUM OFF THE STREETS, AND THE MICE GET GRAIN FOR EVERY CIGARETTE BUTT AND SCRAP OF LITTER THEY BRING IN.
ONCE WE'RE STABLE, WE CAN SPECIALIZE.
BUT RIGHT NOW, WE HAVE TO STAY BUSY--EVERYONE HAS TO WORK, SO EVERYONE CAN EAT.
IF THE MACHINES DO EVERYTHING, WHAT WOULD THE ANIMALS DO?
HOW WOULD THEY AFFORD TO BUY THEIR FOOD?
WE JUST GIVE THEM FOOD!
AND IF WE GIVE EVERYONE FOOD, THEN NO ONE WORKS.
AND WE NEED MOST OF THEM TO WORK. THE MACHINES CAN'T DO EVERYTHING.
WE'RE MAKING THE NEW WORLD JUST AS UGLY AS THE OLD, YOU KNOW.
YEAH. I KNOW.
BUT AT LEAST MORE OF US WILL BE THERE TO SEE IT.

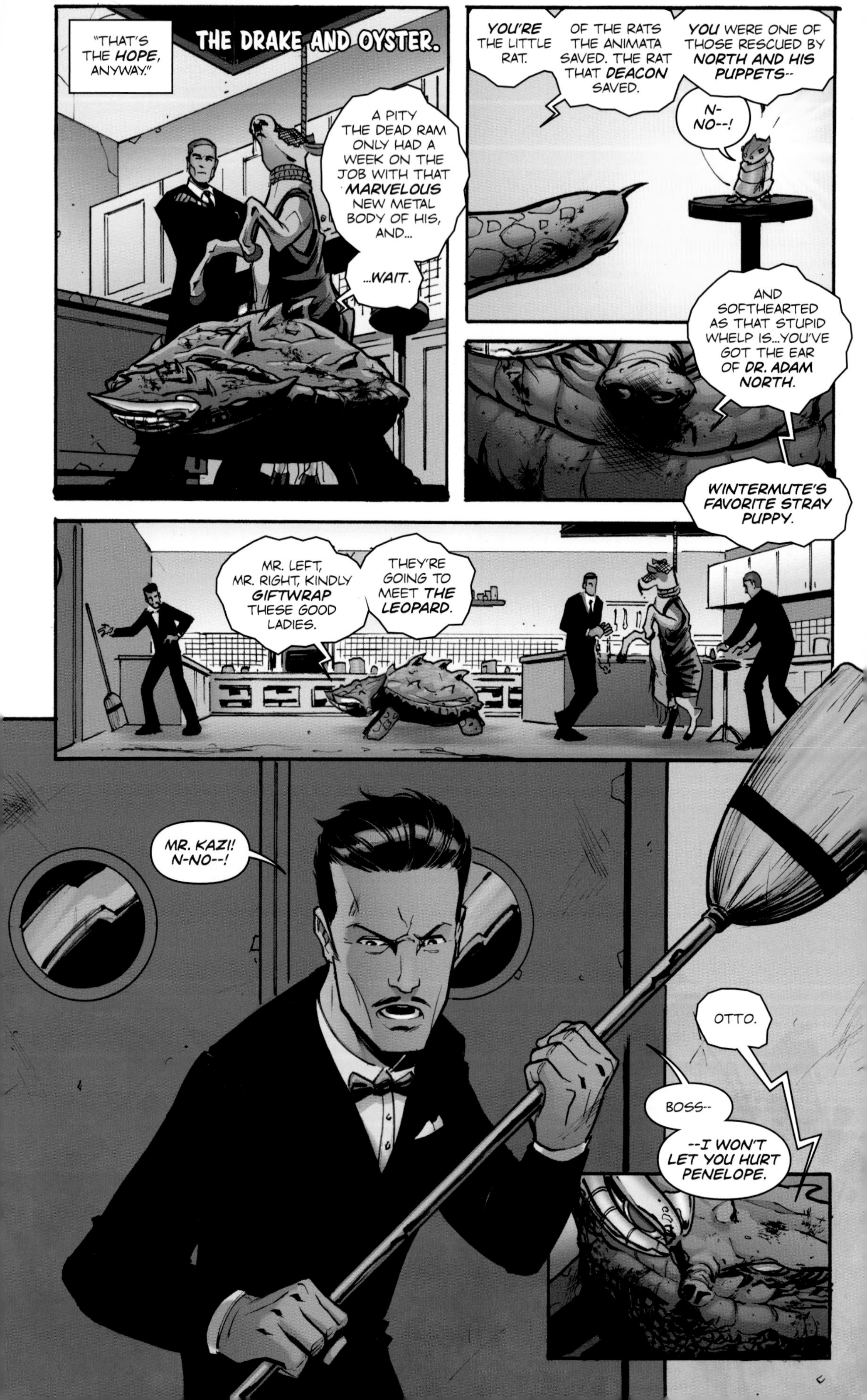
"THAT'S THE HOPE, ANYWAY."
THE DRAKE AND OYSTER.
A PITY THE DEAD RAM ONLY HAD A WEEK ON THE JOB WITH THAT MARVELOUS NEW METAL BODY OF HIS, AND...
...WAIT.
YOU'RE THE LITTLE RAT.
OF THE RATS THE ANIMATA SAVED. THE RAT THAT DEACON SAVED.
YOU WERE ONE OF THOSE RESCUED BY NORTH AND HIS PUPPETS--
N-NO--!
AND SOFTHEARTED AS THAT STUPID WHELP IS...YOU'VE GOT THE EAR OF DR. ADAM NORTH.
WINTERMUTE'S FAVORITE STRAY PUPPY.
MR. LEFT, MR. RIGHT, KINDLY GIFTWRAP THESE GOOD LADIES.
THEY'RE GOING TO MEET THE LEOPARD.
MR. KAZI! N-NO--!
OTTO.
BOSS--
--I WON'T LET YOU HURT PENELOPE.

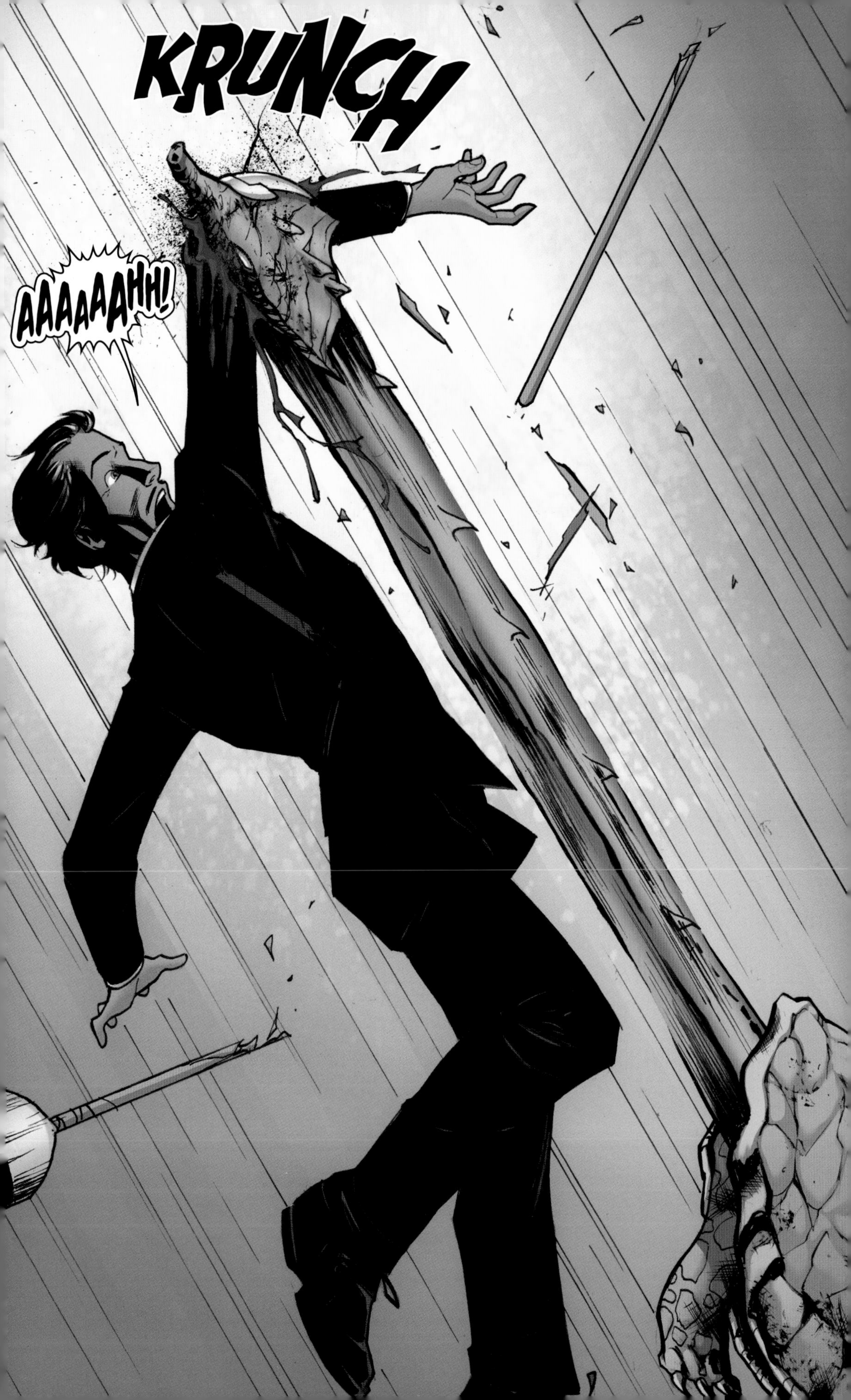
KRUNCH
AAAAAAHH!

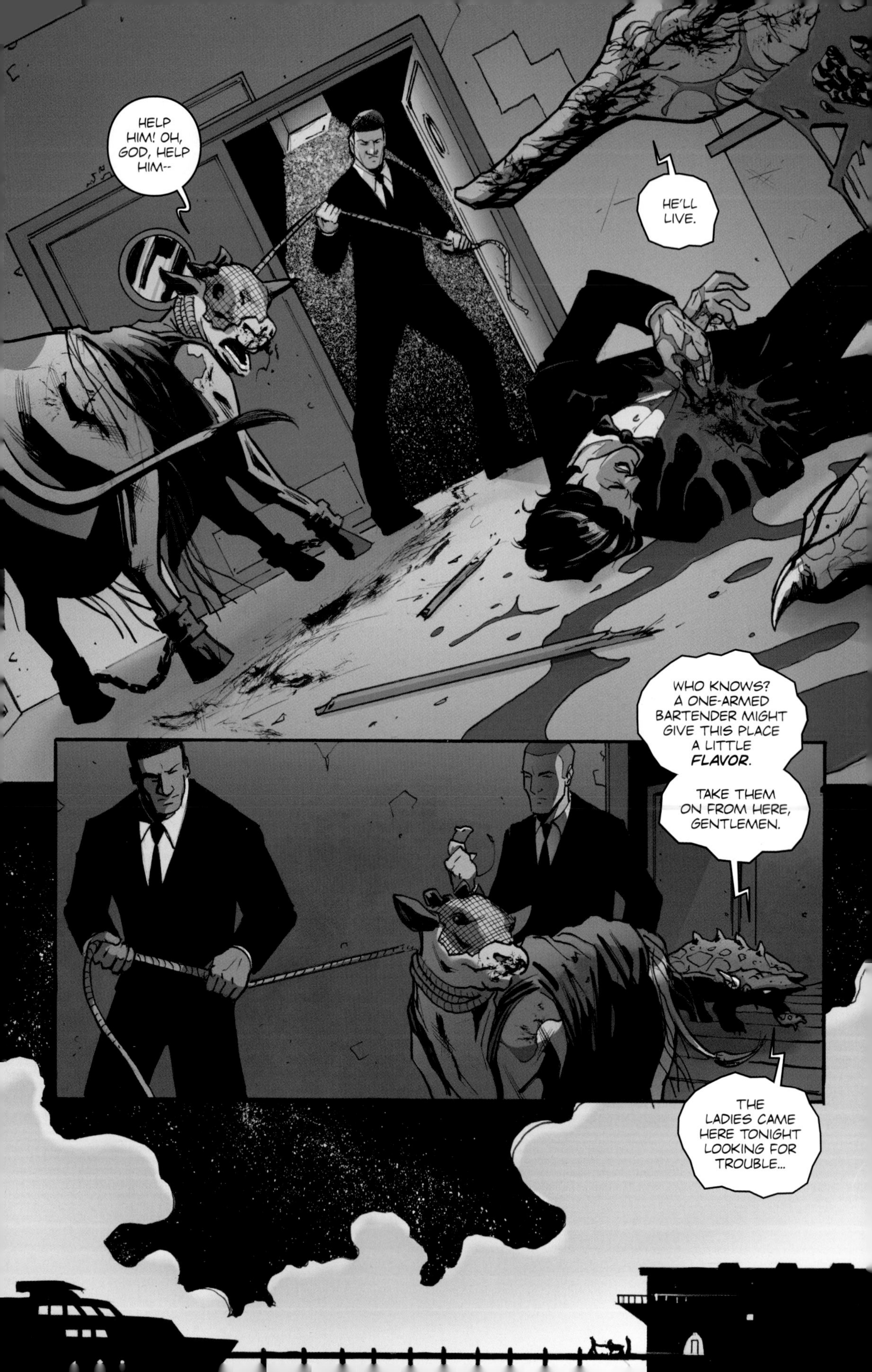
HELP HIM! OH, GOD, HELP HIM--
HE'LL LIVE.
WHO KNOWS? A ONE-ARMED BARTENDER MIGHT GIVE THIS PLACE A LITTLE **FLAVOR**.
TAKE THEM ON FROM HERE, GENTLEMEN.
THE LADIES CAME HERE TONIGHT LOOKING FOR TROUBLE...

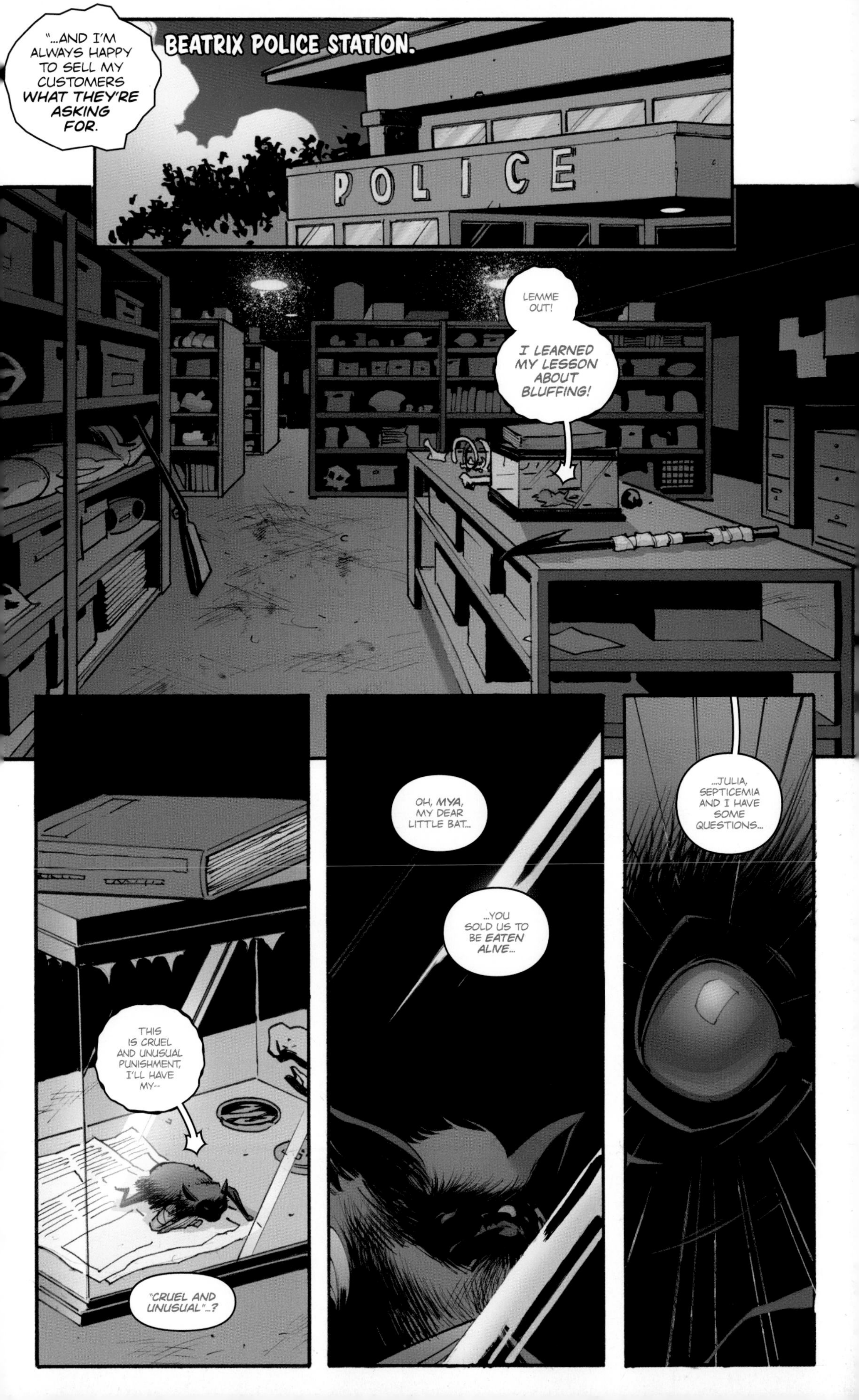
"...AND I'M ALWAYS HAPPY TO SELL MY CUSTOMERS *WHAT THEY'RE ASKING* FOR.
BEATRIX POLICE STATION.
POLICE
LEMME OUT!
I LEARNED MY LESSON ABOUT BLUFFING!
THIS IS CRUEL AND UNUSUAL PUNISHMENT, I'LL HAVE MY--
"CRUEL AND UNUSUAL"...?
OH, *MYA*, MY DEAR LITTLE BAT...
...YOU SOLD US TO BE *EATEN ALIVE*...
...JULIA, SEPTICEMIA AND I HAVE SOME QUESTIONS...

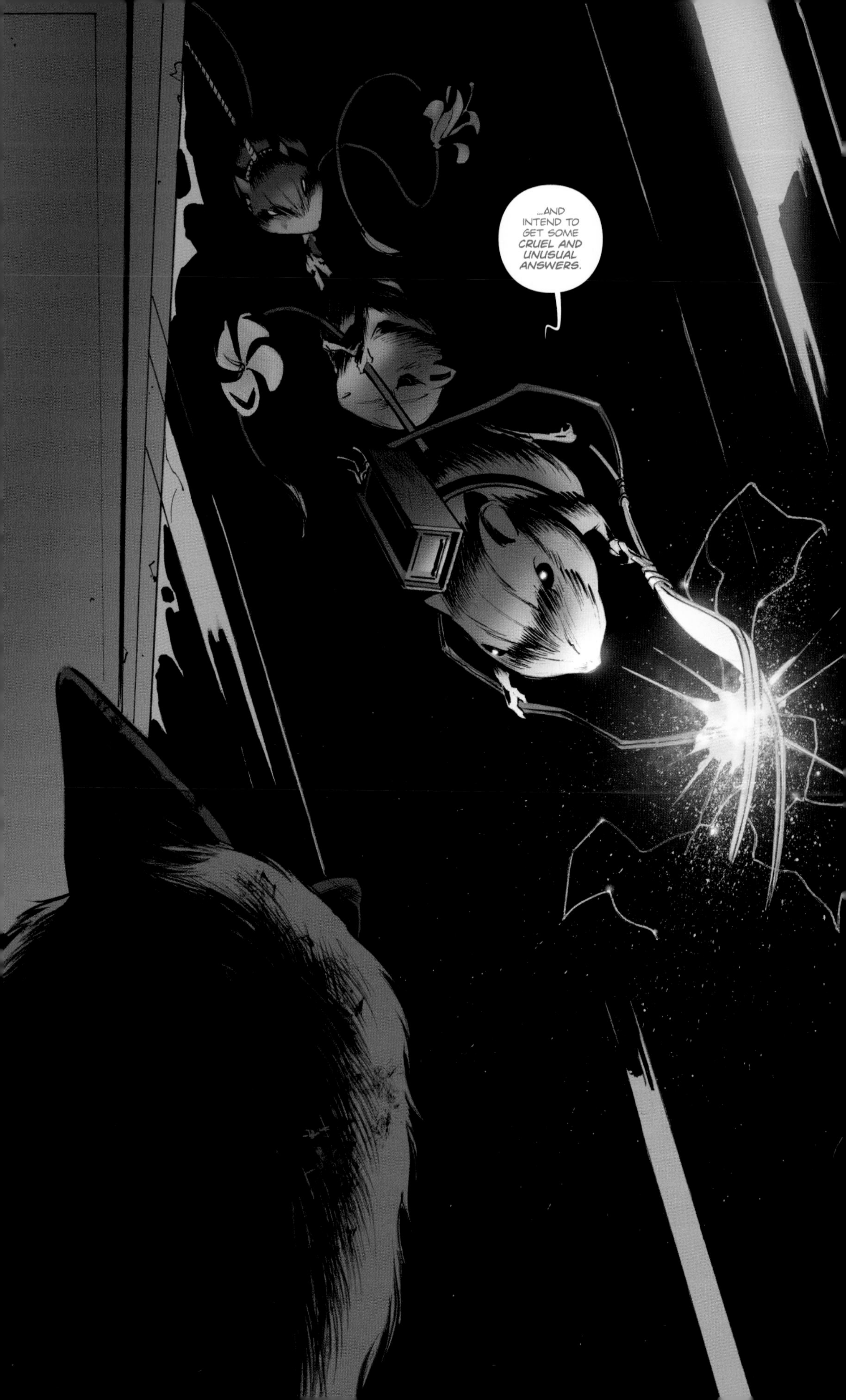
...AND INTEND TO GET SOME CRUEL AND UNUSUAL ANSWERS.

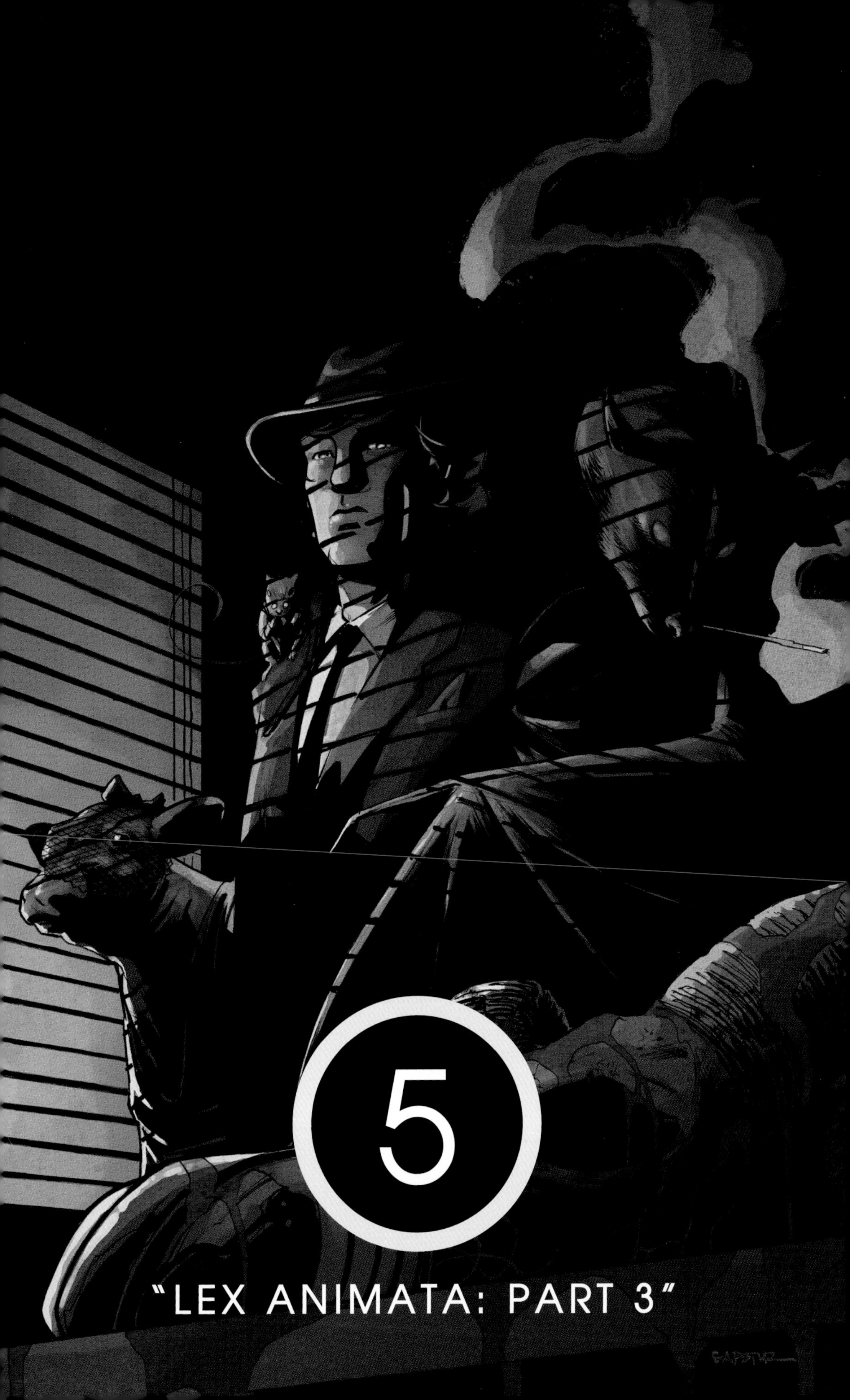

5

"LEX ANIMATA: PART 3"

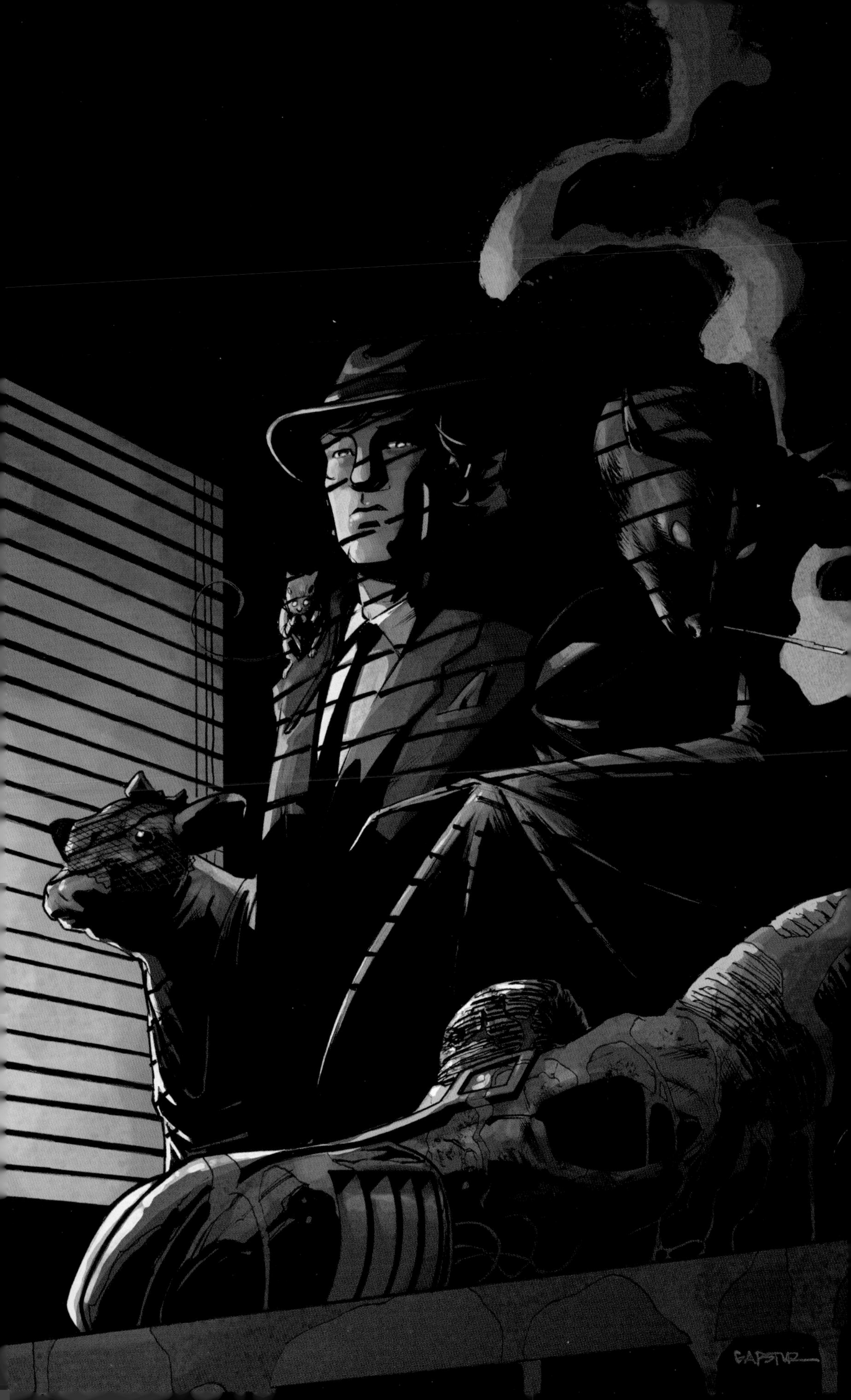
GAPSTUR

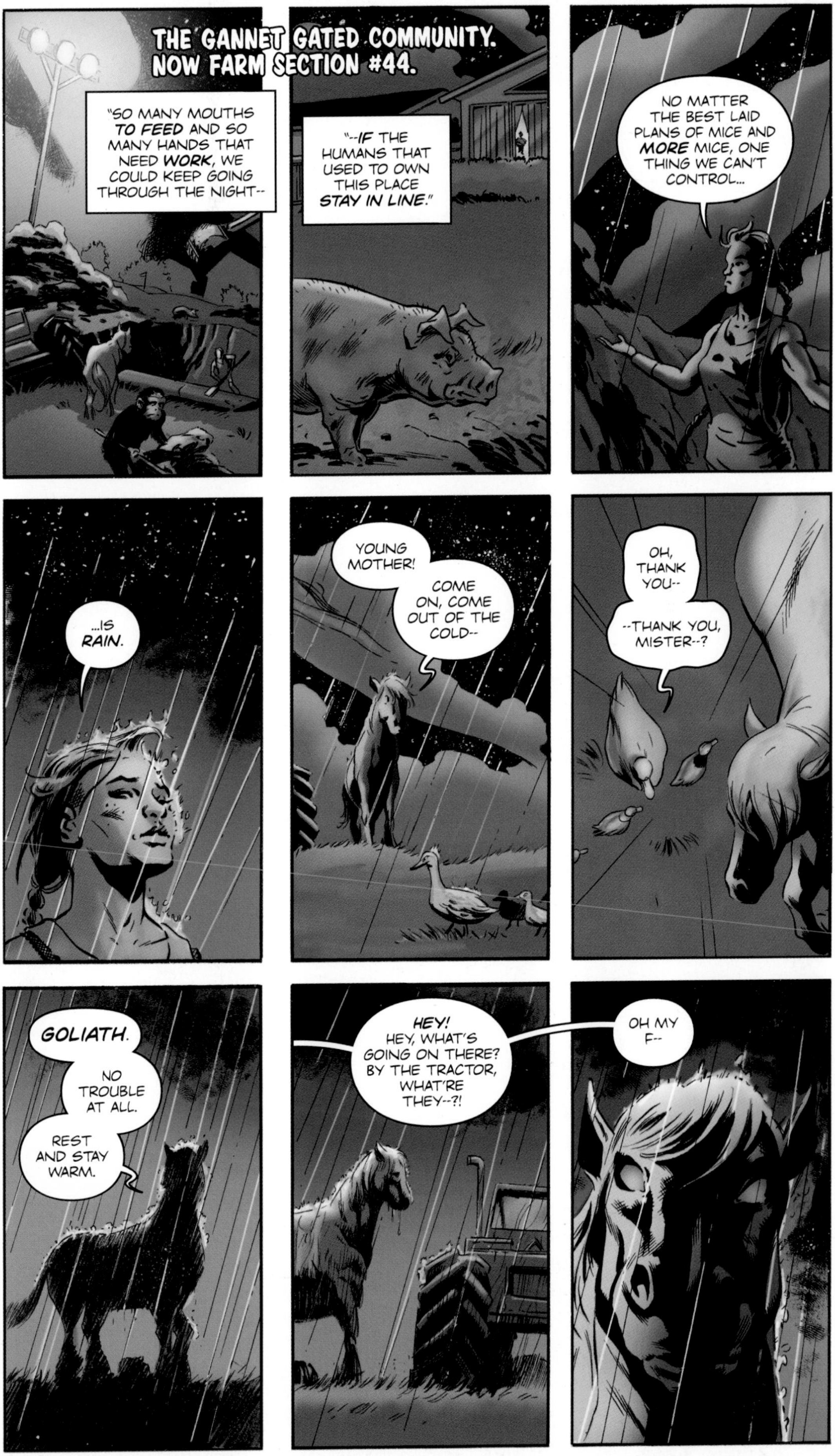
THE GANNET GATED COMMUNITY. NOW FARM SECTION #44.
"SO MANY MOUTHS TO FEED AND SO MANY HANDS THAT NEED WORK, WE COULD KEEP GOING THROUGH THE NIGHT--
"--IF THE HUMANS THAT USED TO OWN THIS PLACE STAY IN LINE."
NO MATTER THE BEST LAID PLANS OF MICE AND MORE MICE, ONE THING WE CAN'T CONTROL...
...IS RAIN.
YOUNG MOTHER!
COME ON, COME OUT OF THE COLD--
OH, THANK YOU--
--THANK YOU, MISTER--?
GOLIATH.
NO TROUBLE AT ALL.
REST AND STAY WARM.
HEY! HEY, WHAT'S GOING ON THERE? BY THE TRACTOR, WHAT'RE THEY--?!
OH MY F--

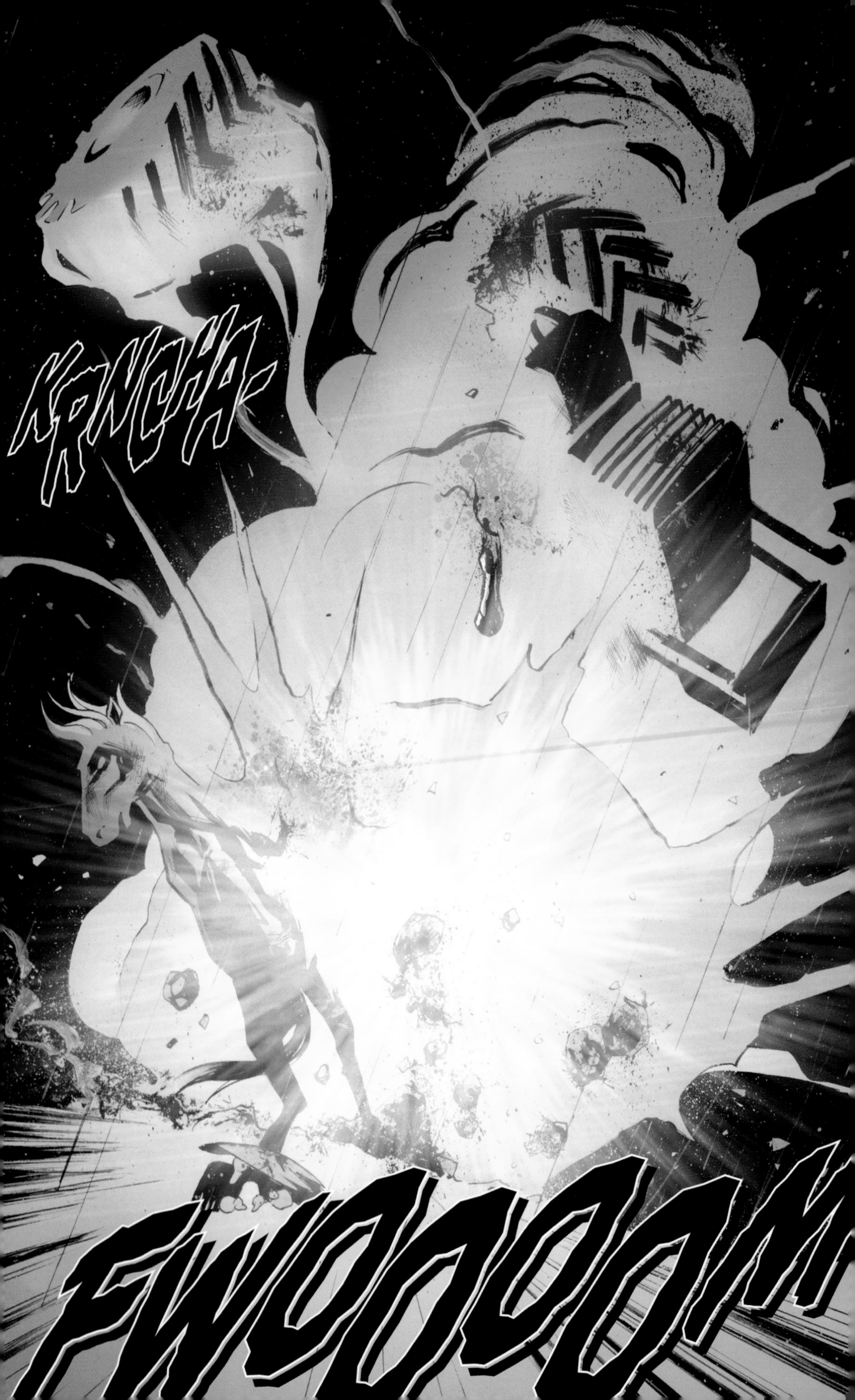

KRNCHA-
FWOOOOM

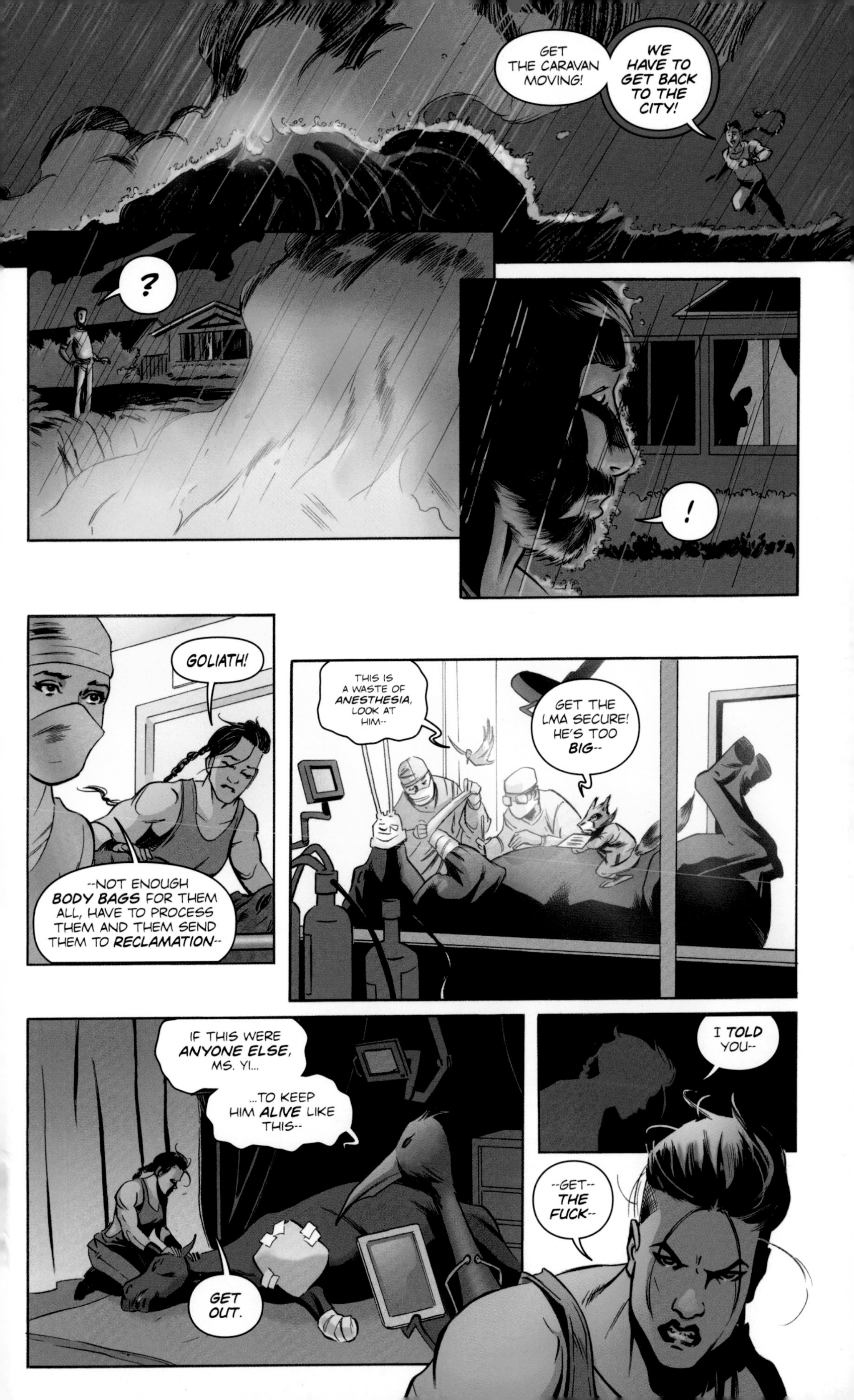
GET THE CARAVAN MOVING!
WE HAVE TO GET BACK TO THE CITY!
?
!
GOLIATH!
--NOT ENOUGH BODY BAGS FOR THEM ALL, HAVE TO PROCESS THEM AND THEM SEND THEM TO RECLAMATION--
THIS IS A WASTE OF ANESTHESIA, LOOK AT HIM--
GET THE LMA SECURE! HE'S TOO BIG--
IF THIS WERE ANYONE ELSE, MS. YI...
...TO KEEP HIM ALIVE LIKE THIS--
GET OUT.
I TOLD YOU--
--GET-- THE FUCK--

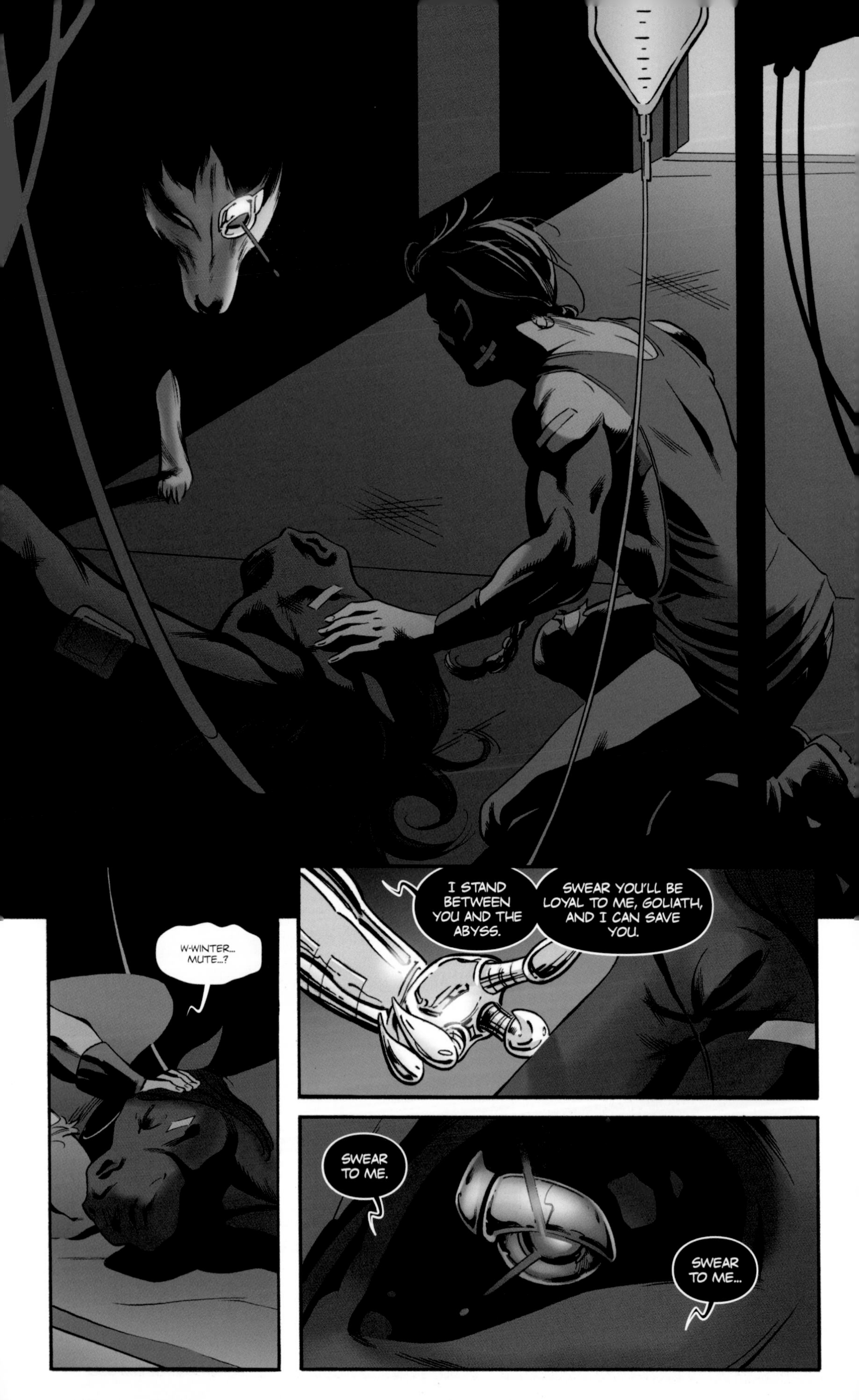
W-WINTER... MUTE...?
I STAND BETWEEN YOU AND THE ABYSS.
SWEAR YOU'LL BE LOYAL TO ME, GOLIATH, AND I CAN SAVE YOU.
SWEAR TO ME.
SWEAR TO ME...

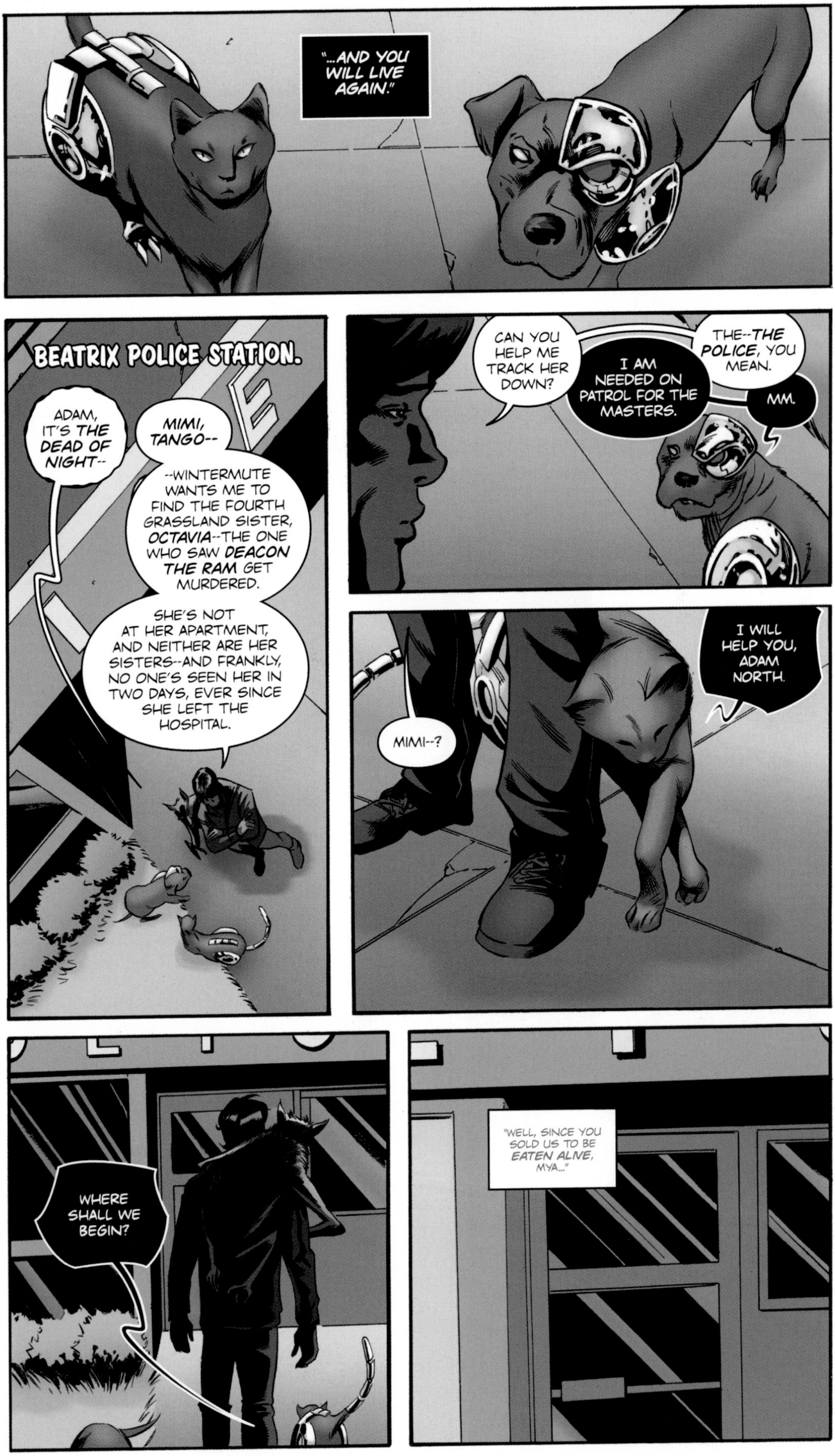
"...AND YOU WILL LIVE AGAIN."
BEATRIX POLICE STATION.
ADAM, IT'S THE DEAD OF NIGHT--
MIMI, TANGO--
--WINTERMUTE WANTS ME TO FIND THE FOURTH GRASSLAND SISTER, OCTAVIA--THE ONE WHO SAW DEACON THE RAM GET MURDERED.
SHE'S NOT AT HER APARTMENT, AND NEITHER ARE HER SISTERS--AND FRANKLY, NO ONE'S SEEN HER IN TWO DAYS, EVER SINCE SHE LEFT THE HOSPITAL.
CAN YOU HELP ME TRACK HER DOWN?
I AM NEEDED ON PATROL FOR THE MASTERS.
THE--THE POLICE, YOU MEAN.
MM.
I WILL HELP YOU, ADAM NORTH.
MIMI--?
WHERE SHALL WE BEGIN?
"WELL, SINCE YOU SOLD US TO BE EATEN ALIVE, MYA..."

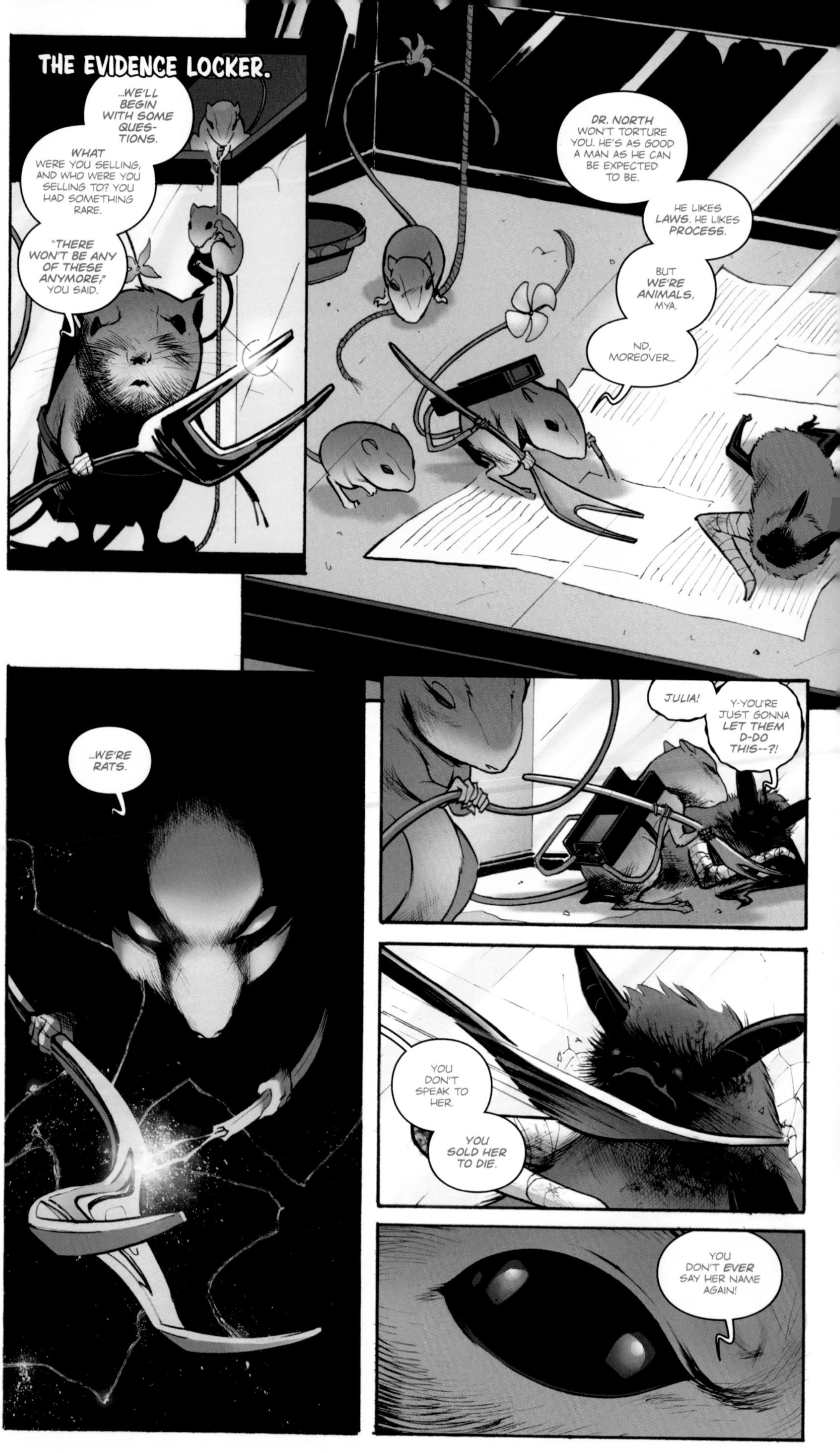
THE EVIDENCE LOCKER.
...WE'LL BEGIN WITH SOME QUES-TIONS.
WHAT WERE YOU SELLING, AND WHO WERE YOU SELLING TO? YOU HAD SOMETHING RARE.
"THERE WON'T BE ANY OF THESE ANYMORE," YOU SAID.
DR. NORTH WON'T TORTURE YOU. HE'S AS GOOD A MAN AS HE CAN BE EXPECTED TO BE.
HE LIKES LAWS. HE LIKES PROCESS.
BUT WE'RE ANIMALS, MYA.
ND, MOREOVER...
...WE'RE RATS.
JULIA!
Y-YOU'RE JUST GONNA LET THEM D-DO THIS--?!
YOU DON'T SPEAK TO HER.
YOU SOLD HER TO DIE.
YOU DON'T EVER SAY HER NAME AGAIN!

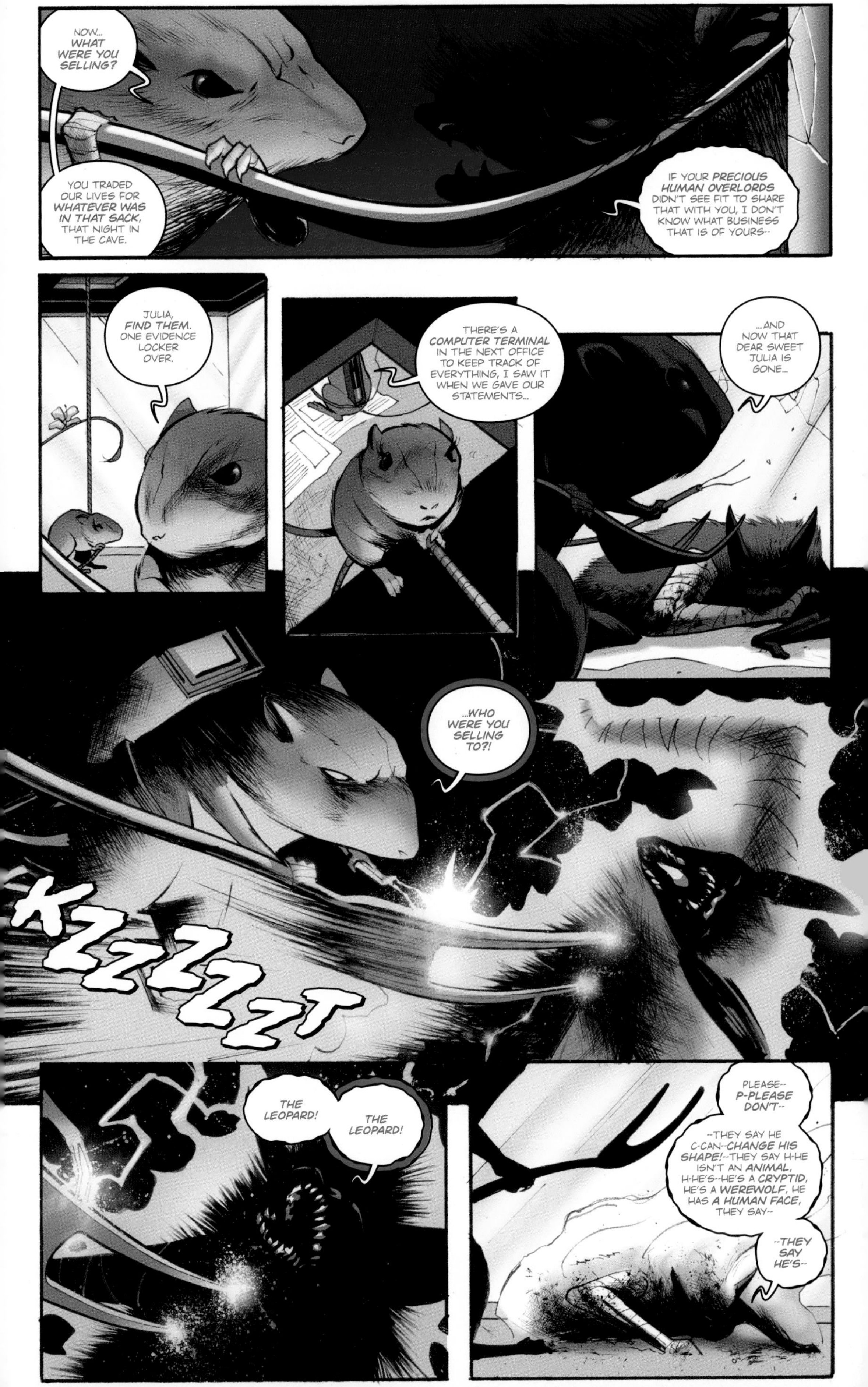
NOW... WHAT WERE YOU SELLING?
YOU TRADED OUR LIVES FOR WHATEVER WAS IN THAT SACK, THAT NIGHT IN THE CAVE.
IF YOUR PRECIOUS HUMAN OVERLORDS DIDN'T SEE FIT TO SHARE THAT WITH YOU, I DON'T KNOW WHAT BUSINESS THAT IS OF YOURS--
JULIA, FIND THEM. ONE EVIDENCE LOCKER OVER.
THERE'S A COMPUTER TERMINAL IN THE NEXT OFFICE TO KEEP TRACK OF EVERYTHING, I SAW IT WHEN WE GAVE OUR STATEMENTS...
...AND NOW THAT DEAR SWEET JULIA IS GONE...
...WHO WERE YOU SELLING TO?!
KZZZZZZT
THE LEOPARD!
THE LEOPARD!
PLEASE-- P-PLEASE DON'T--
--THEY SAY HE C-CAN--CHANGE HIS SHAPE!--THEY SAY H-HE ISN'T AN ANIMAL, H-HE'S--HE'S A CRYPTID, HE'S A WEREWOLF, HE HAS A HUMAN FACE, THEY SAY--
--THEY SAY HE'S--

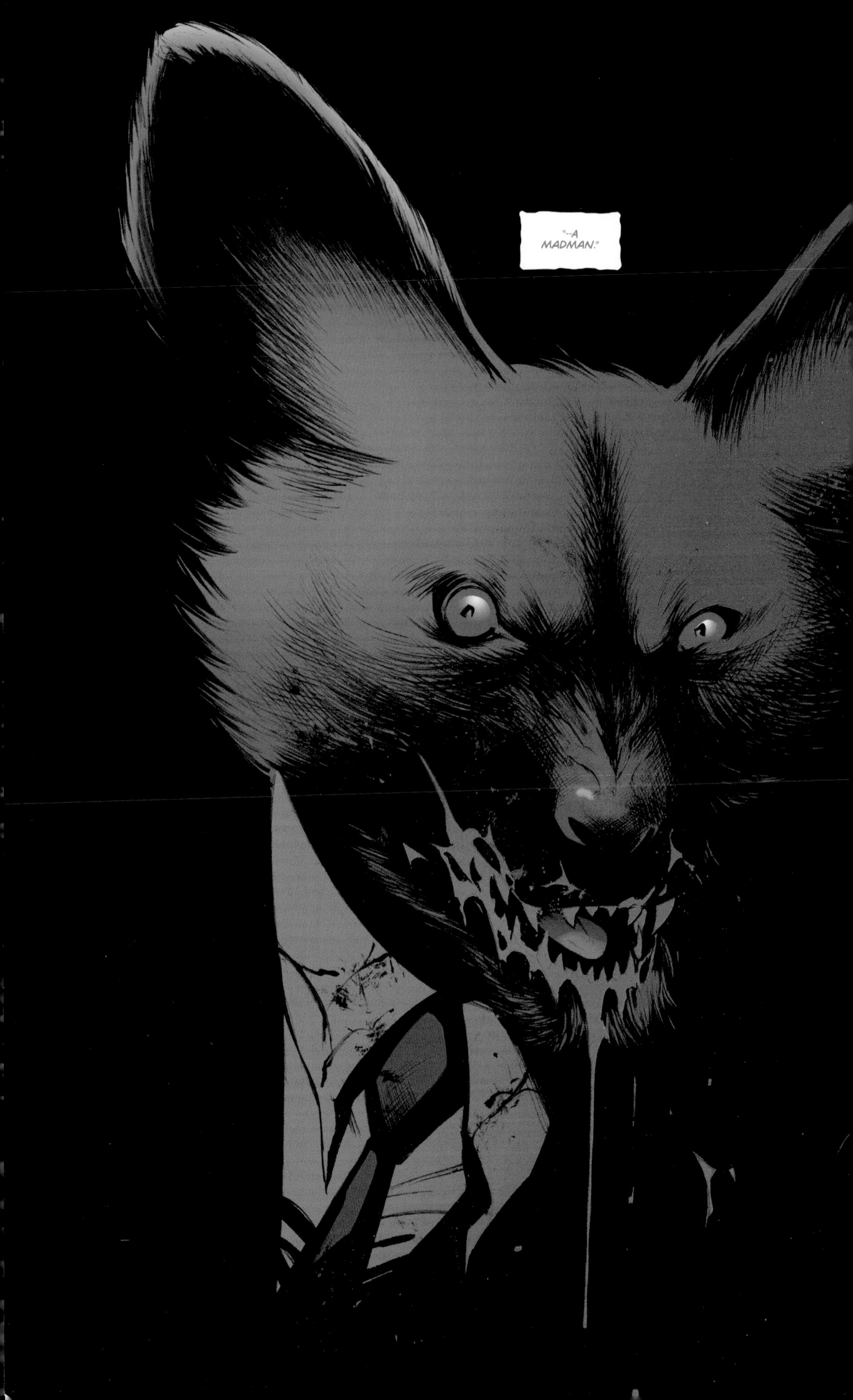
"--A MADMAN."

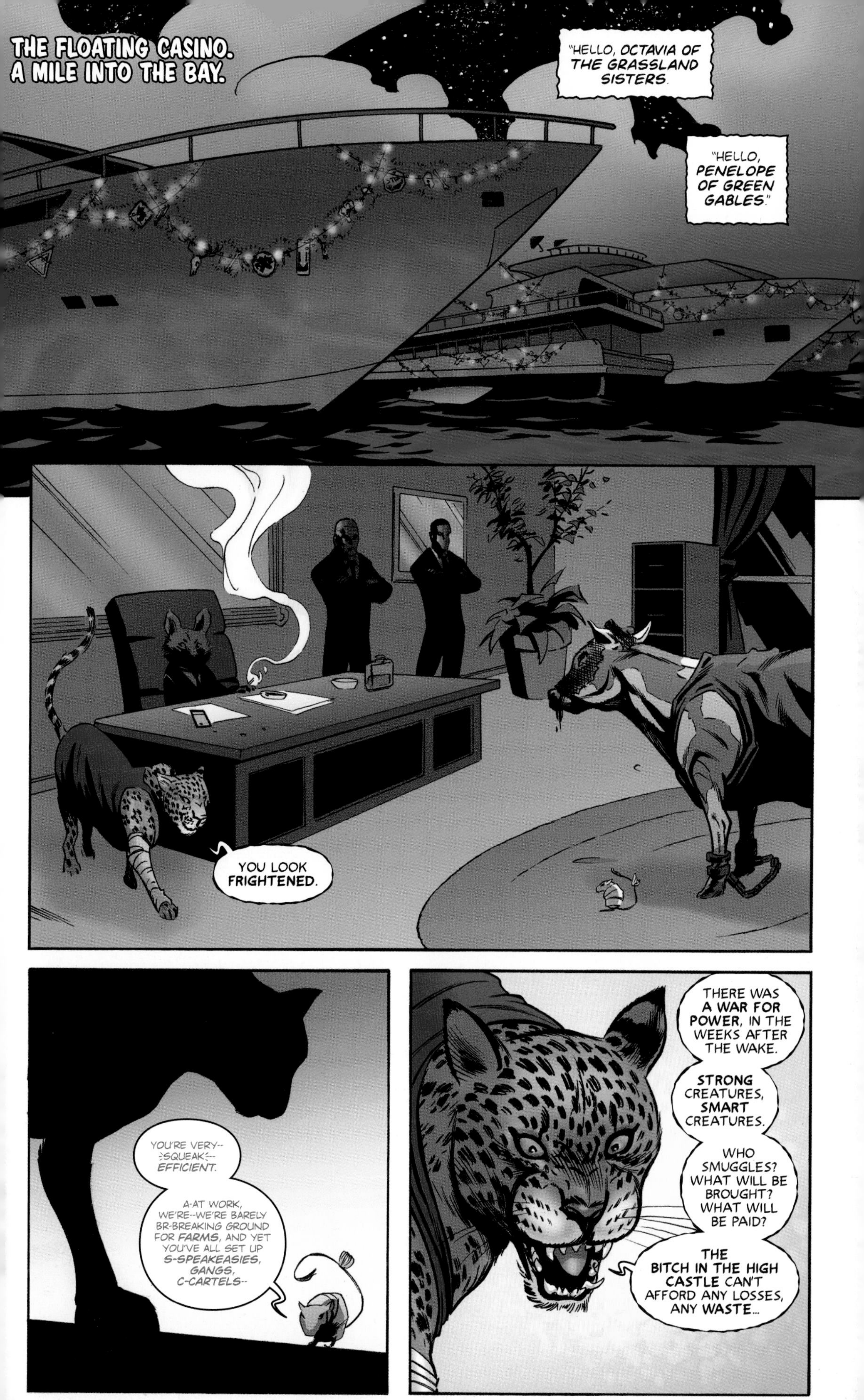
THE FLOATING CASINO. A MILE INTO THE BAY.
"HELLO, OCTAVIA OF THE GRASSLAND SISTERS.
"HELLO, PENELOPE OF GREEN GABLES."
YOU LOOK FRIGHTENED.
YOU'RE VERY-- ~SQUEAK~-- EFFICIENT.
A-AT WORK, WE'RE--WE'RE BARELY BR-BREAKING GROUND FOR FARMS, AND YET YOU'VE ALL SET UP S-SPEAKEASIES, GANGS, C-CARTELS--
THERE WAS A WAR FOR POWER, IN THE WEEKS AFTER THE WAKE.
STRONG CREATURES, SMART CREATURES.
WHO SMUGGLES? WHAT WILL BE BROUGHT? WHAT WILL BE PAID?
THE BITCH IN THE HIGH CASTLE CAN'T AFFORD ANY LOSSES, ANY WASTE...

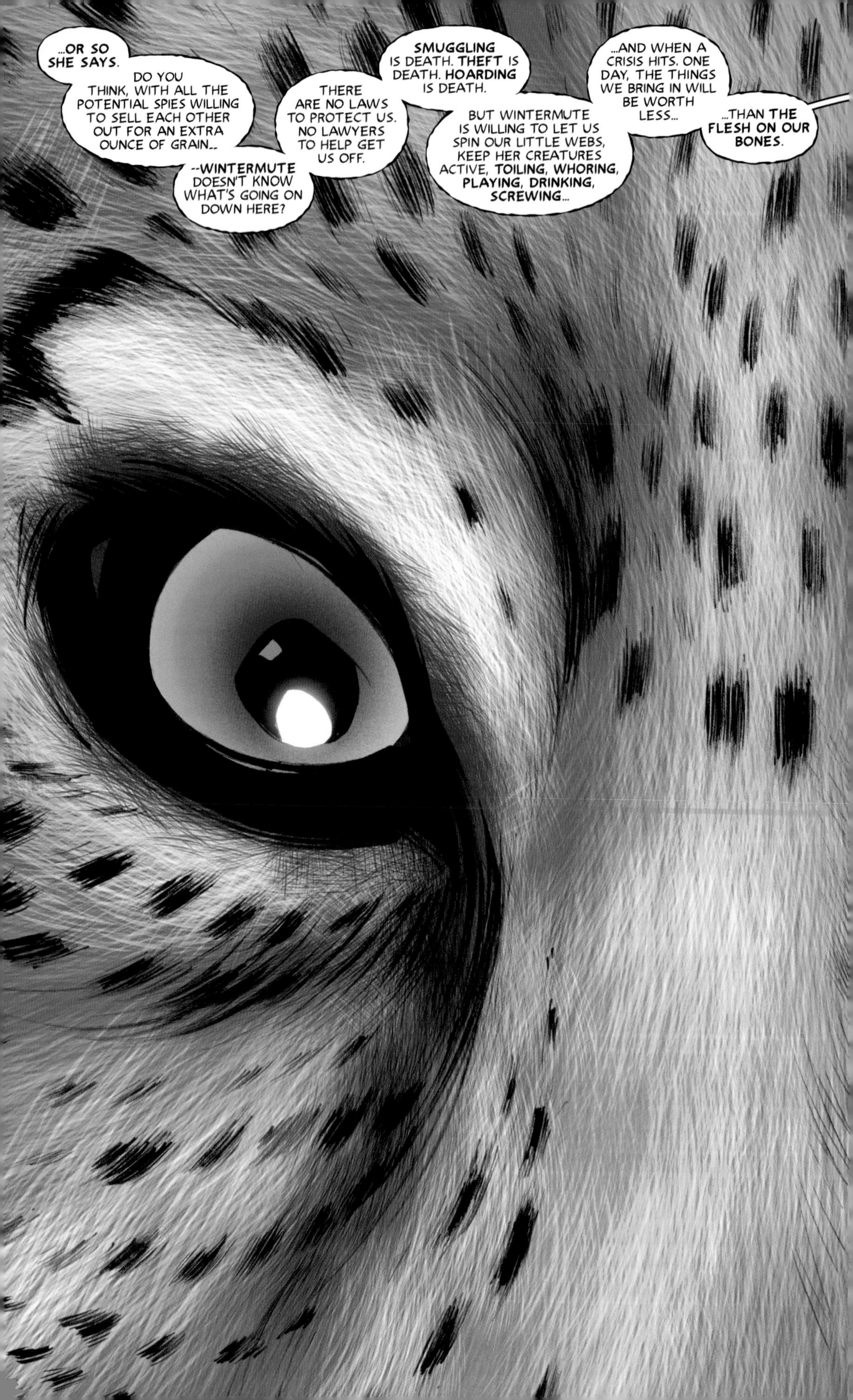
...OR SO SHE SAYS.
DO YOU THINK, WITH ALL THE POTENTIAL SPIES WILLING TO SELL EACH OTHER OUT FOR AN EXTRA OUNCE OF GRAIN--
--WINTERMUTE DOESN'T KNOW WHAT'S GOING ON DOWN HERE?
THERE ARE NO LAWS TO PROTECT US. NO LAWYERS TO HELP GET US OFF.
SMUGGLING IS DEATH. THEFT IS DEATH. HOARDING IS DEATH.
BUT WINTERMUTE IS WILLING TO LET US SPIN OUR LITTLE WEBS, KEEP HER CREATURES ACTIVE, TOILING, WHORING, PLAYING, DRINKING, SCREWING...
...AND WHEN A CRISIS HITS. ONE DAY, THE THINGS WE BRING IN WILL BE WORTH LESS...
...THAN THE FLESH ON OUR BONES.

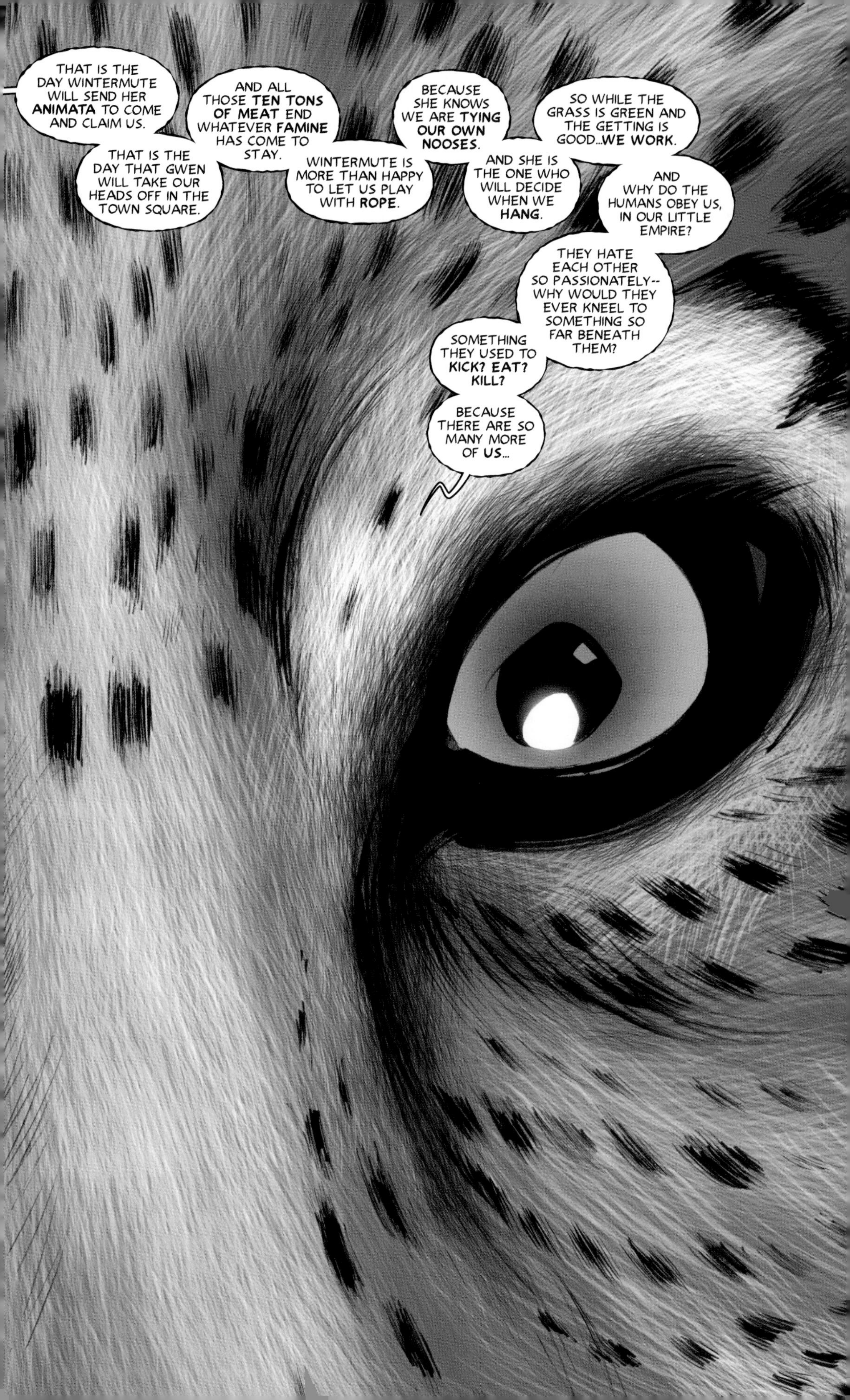

THAT IS THE DAY WINTERMUTE WILL SEND HER ANIMATA TO COME AND CLAIM US.
THAT IS THE DAY THAT GWEN WILL TAKE OUR HEADS OFF IN THE TOWN SQUARE.
AND ALL THOSE TEN TONS OF MEAT END WHATEVER FAMINE HAS COME TO STAY.
WINTERMUTE IS MORE THAN HAPPY TO LET US PLAY WITH ROPE.
BECAUSE SHE KNOWS WE ARE TYING OUR OWN NOOSES.
AND SHE IS THE ONE WHO WILL DECIDE WHEN WE HANG.
SO WHILE THE GRASS IS GREEN AND THE GETTING IS GOOD...WE WORK.
AND WHY DO THE HUMANS OBEY US, IN OUR LITTLE EMPIRE?
THEY HATE EACH OTHER SO PASSIONATELY-- WHY WOULD THEY EVER KNEEL TO SOMETHING SO FAR BENEATH THEM?
SOMETHING THEY USED TO KICK? EAT? KILL?
BECAUSE THERE ARE SO MANY MORE OF US...

"...THAN THERE ARE OF **THEM**."

THE EVIDENCE LOCKERS.

AUGUSTA! I FOUND WHAT MYA WAS SMUGGLING--

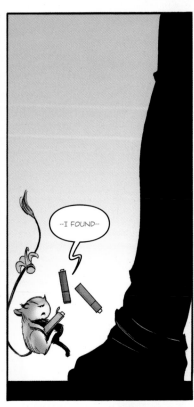

--I FOUND--

J-JULIA?

OF THE GRASSLAND SISTERS?

WHAT ARE YOU DOING HERE IN THE DEAD OF--

--HOW DID YOU KNOW **OCTAVIA WAS MISSING?**

WHAT DO YOU **HAVE** THERE, JULIA?

M-MYA.

SH-SHE-- SMUGGLED THESE--

--THESE ARE WHAT SHE RECEIVED AS **P-PAYMENT**, THE NIGHT SHE TRIED TO **SELL** AUGUSTA, OCTAVIA, SEPTICEMIA, AND ME TO **THE S-SERPENT**...

KIRI... **WHAT'S ON THESE?**

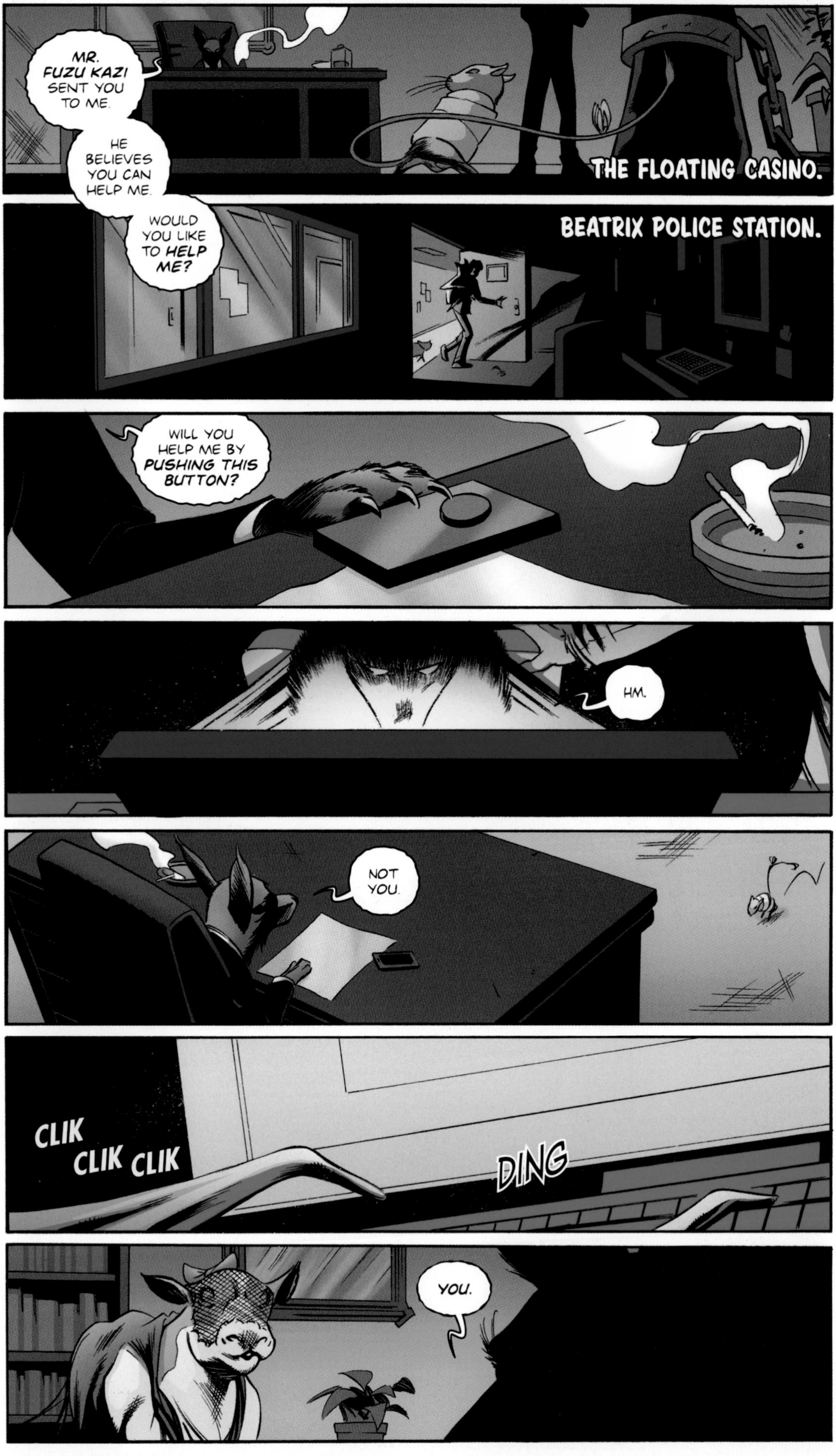
MR. FUZU KAZI SENT YOU TO ME.
HE BELIEVES YOU CAN HELP ME.
THE FLOATING CASINO.
WOULD YOU LIKE TO HELP ME?
BEATRIX POLICE STATION.
WILL YOU HELP ME BY PUSHING THIS BUTTON?
HM.
NOT YOU.
CLIK
CLIK CLIK
DING
YOU.

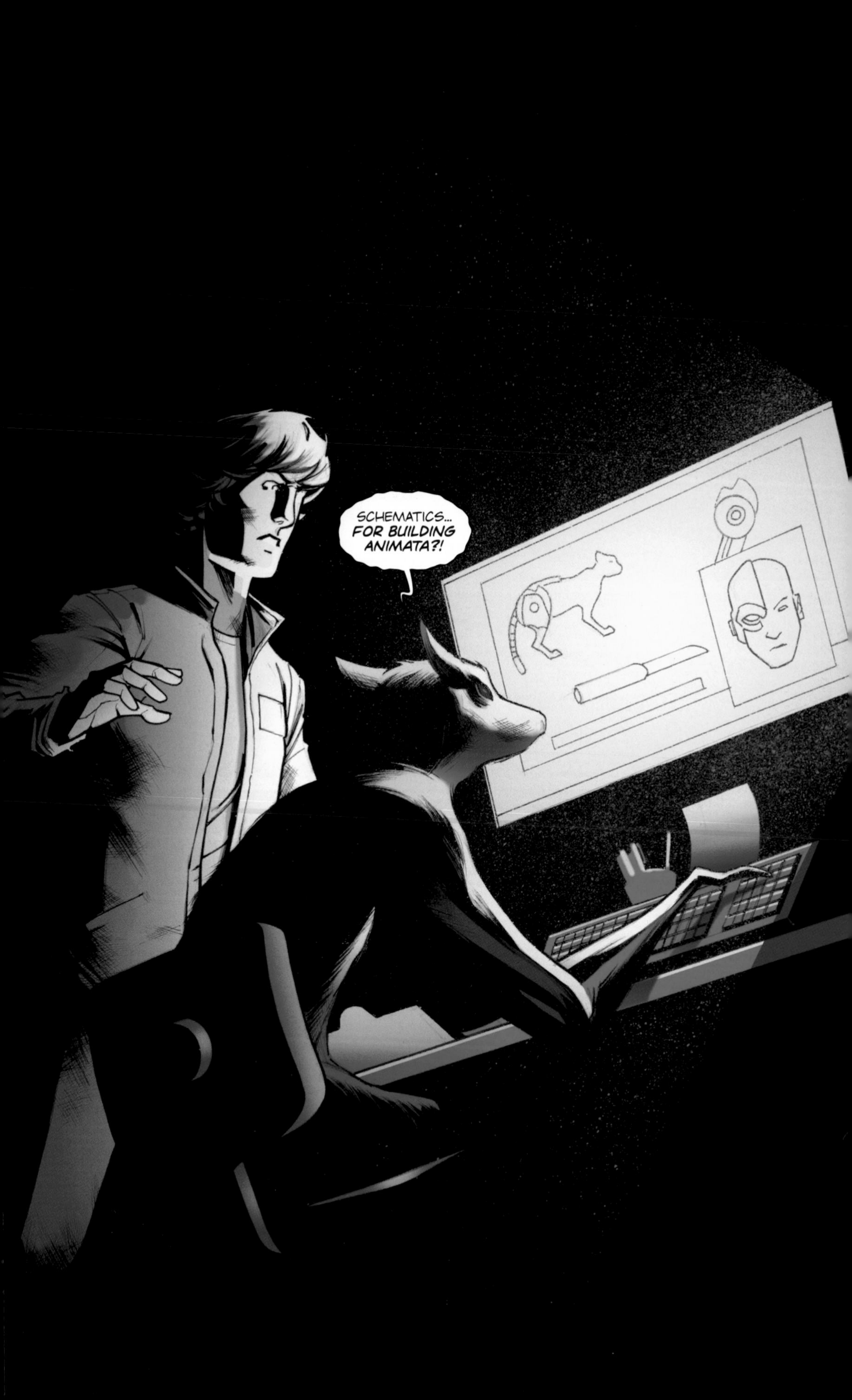
SCHEMATICS... FOR BUILDING ANIMATA?!

PLEASE.

MY **SON** IS AT HOME, I SHOULDN'T **BE** HERE--

YOUR SON WILL BE **VEAL** IF THE HUMANS HAVE THEIR WAY.

HE WILL DO THESE THINGS, BECAUSE **SOON**, THERE WON'T BE ANY **DR. NORTH**.

THERE WON'T BE ANY MORE **WINTER-MUTE**.

BUT IF YOU HELP ME, HE WILL GROW UP **SAFE** AND **FREE** AND **HAPPY**.

AND THERE WON'T BE ANY MORE **ANIMATA**.

PLEASE-- PLEASE, *I DON'T UNDERSTAND!*

OH, MADAME...

...YOU DON'T NEED TO.

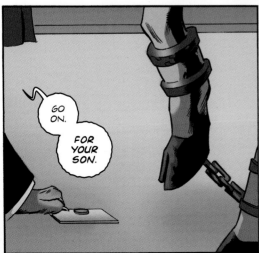

GO ON.

FOR YOUR SON.

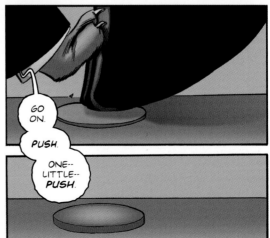

GO ON.

PUSH.

ONE-- LITTLE-- **PUSH.**

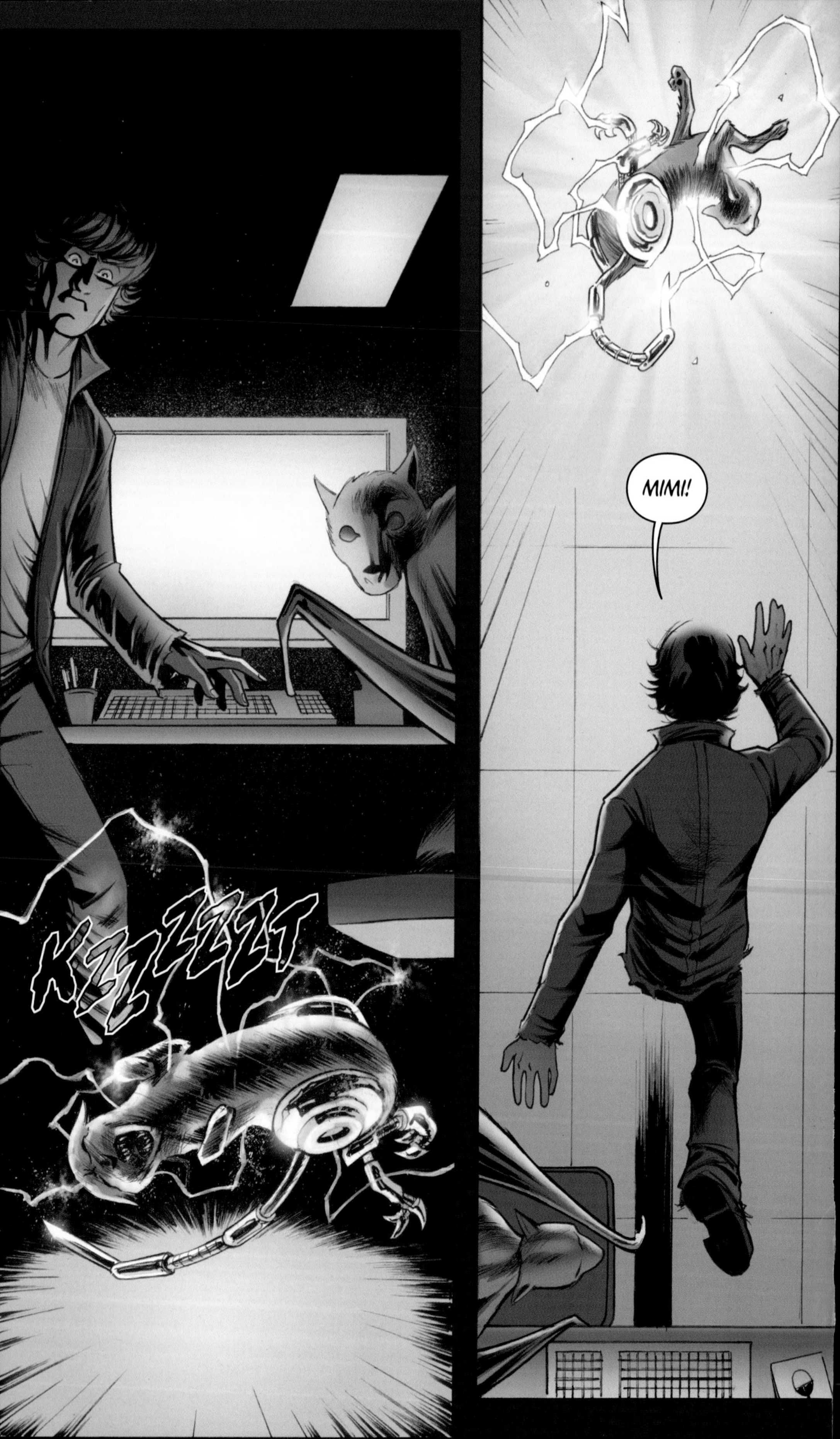
KZZZZZT
MIMI!

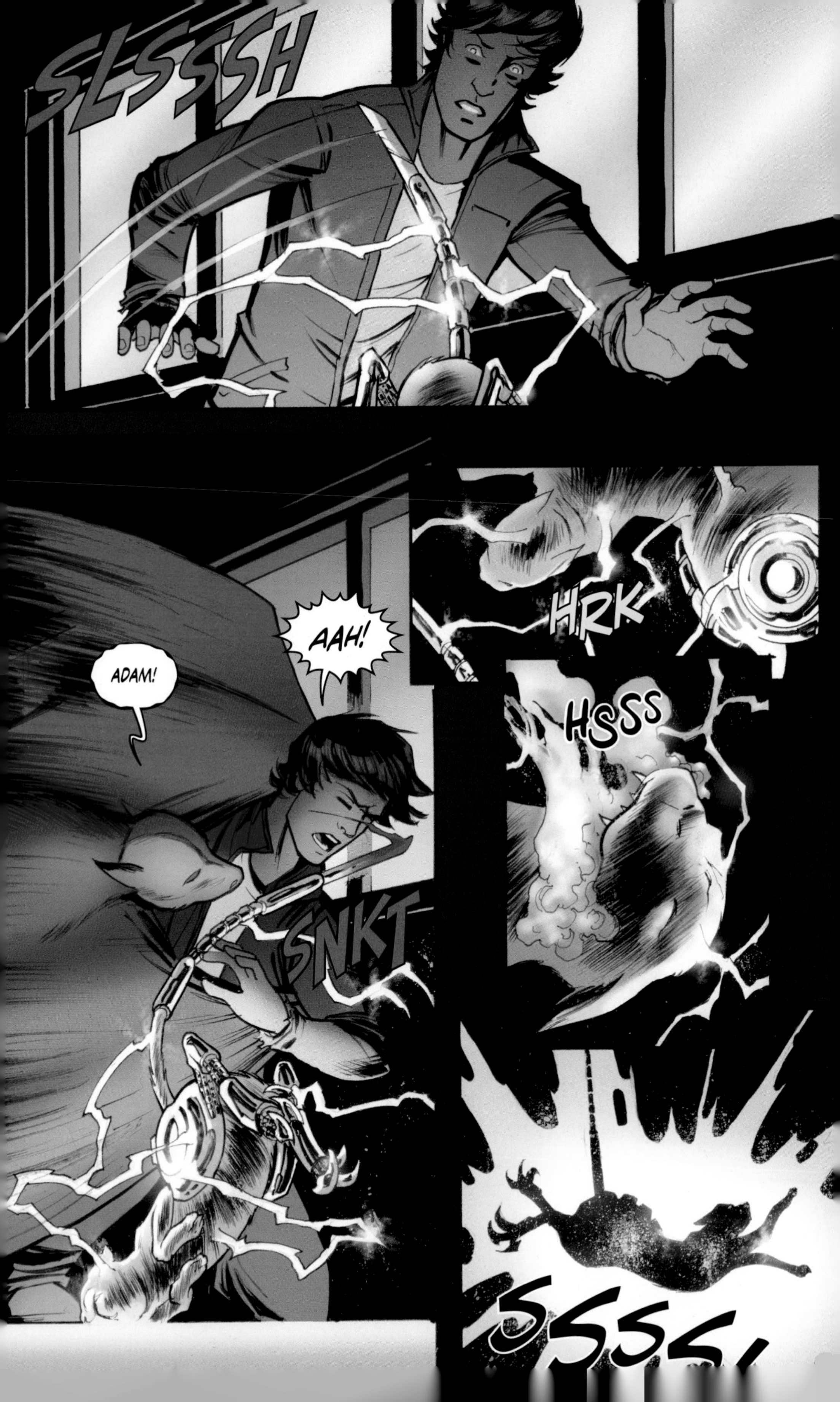
SLSSSH
ADAM!
AAH!
SNKT
HRK
HSSS
SSSS

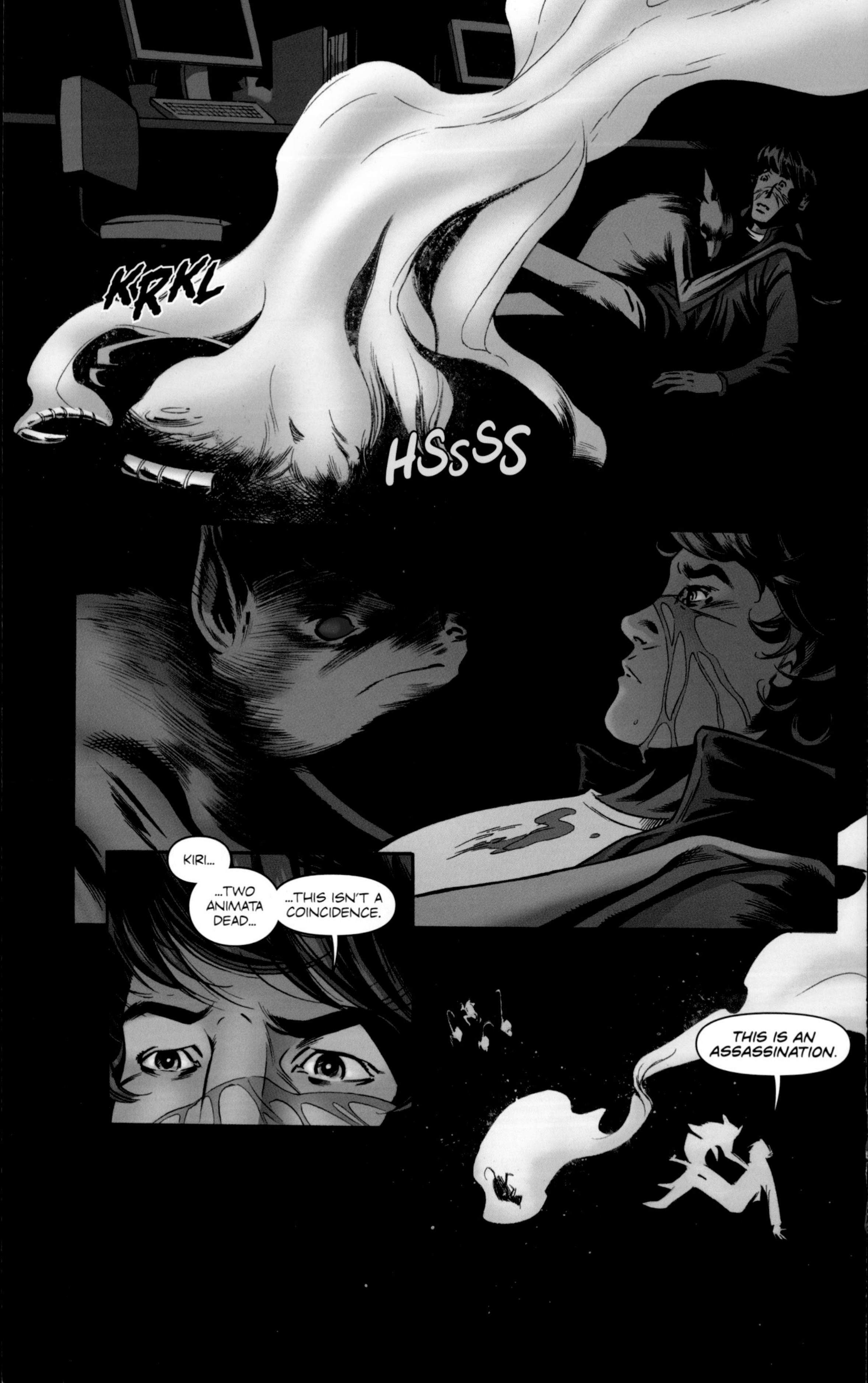
KRKL
HSSSS
KIRI...
...TWO ANIMATA DEAD...
...THIS ISN'T A COINCIDENCE.
THIS IS AN ASSASSINATION.

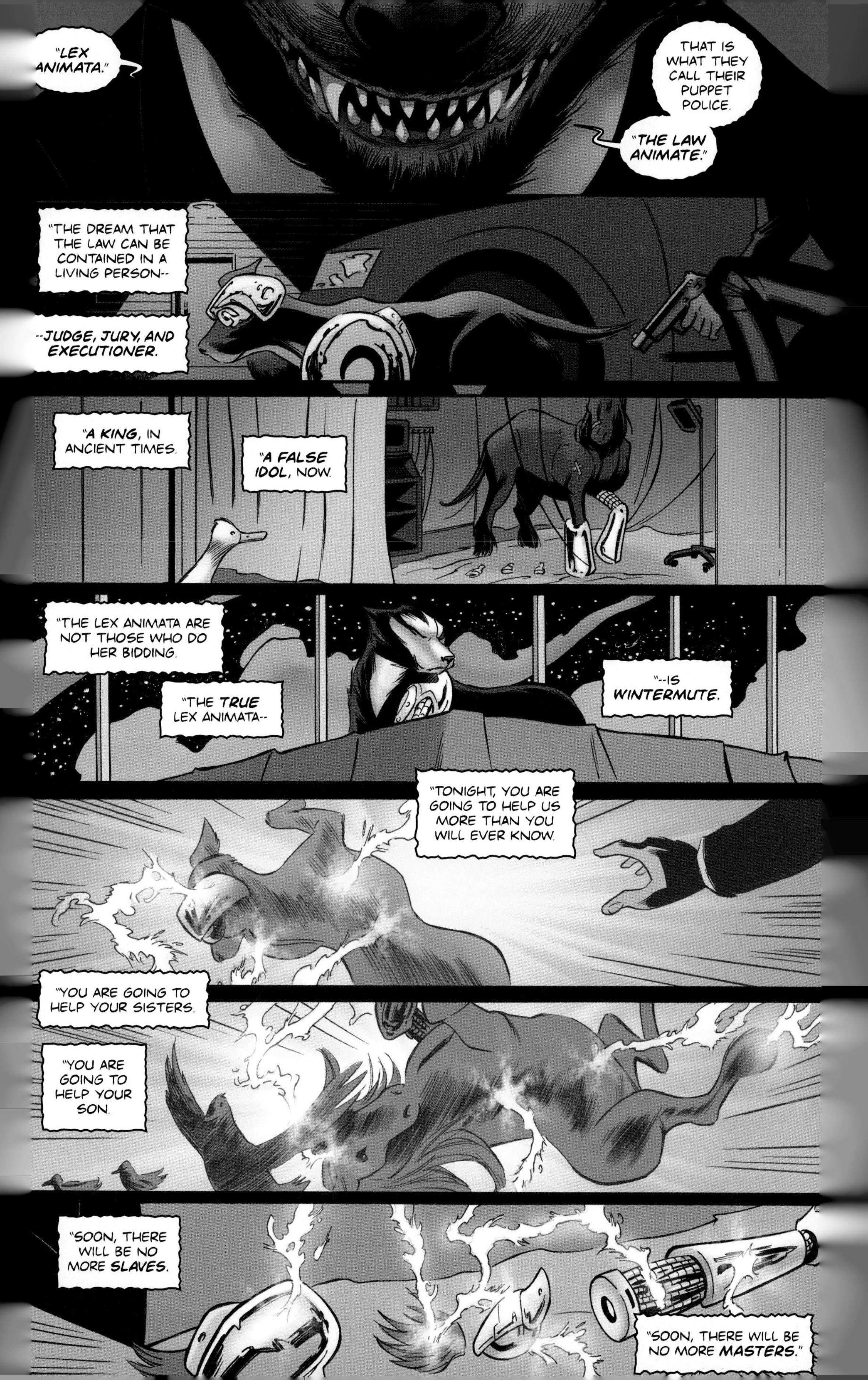
"LEX ANIMATA."
THAT IS WHAT THEY CALL THEIR PUPPET POLICE.
"THE LAW ANIMATE."
"THE DREAM THAT THE LAW CAN BE CONTAINED IN A LIVING PERSON--
--JUDGE, JURY, AND EXECUTIONER.
"A KING, IN ANCIENT TIMES.
"A FALSE IDOL, NOW.
"THE LEX ANIMATA ARE NOT THOSE WHO DO HER BIDDING.
"THE TRUE LEX ANIMATA--
"--IS WINTERMUTE.
"TONIGHT, YOU ARE GOING TO HELP US MORE THAN YOU WILL EVER KNOW.
"YOU ARE GOING TO HELP YOUR SISTERS.
"YOU ARE GOING TO HELP YOUR SON.
"SOON, THERE WILL BE NO MORE SLAVES.
"SOON, THERE WILL BE NO MORE MASTERS."

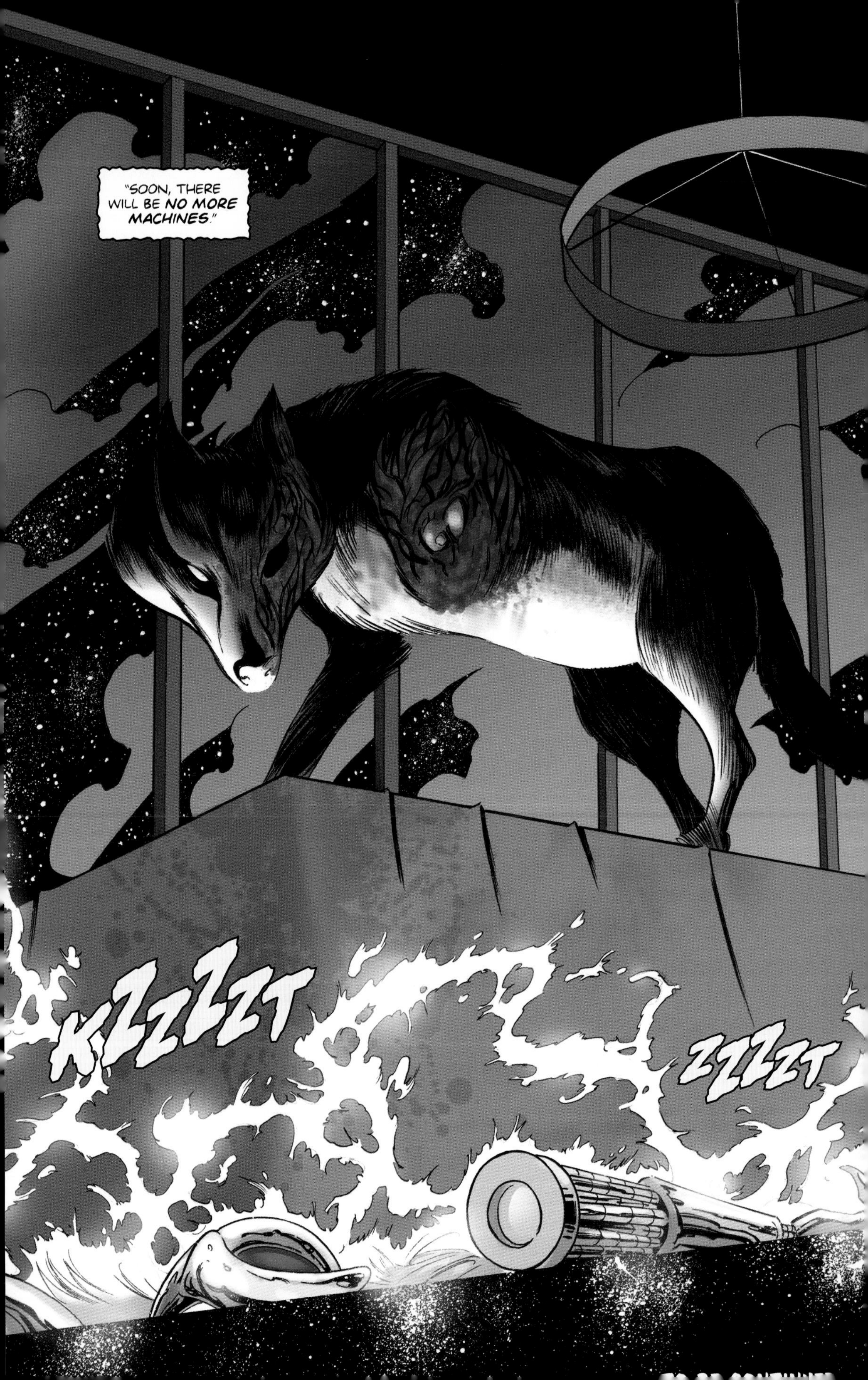
"SOON, THERE WILL BE NO MORE MACHINES."
KZZZZT
ZZZZT

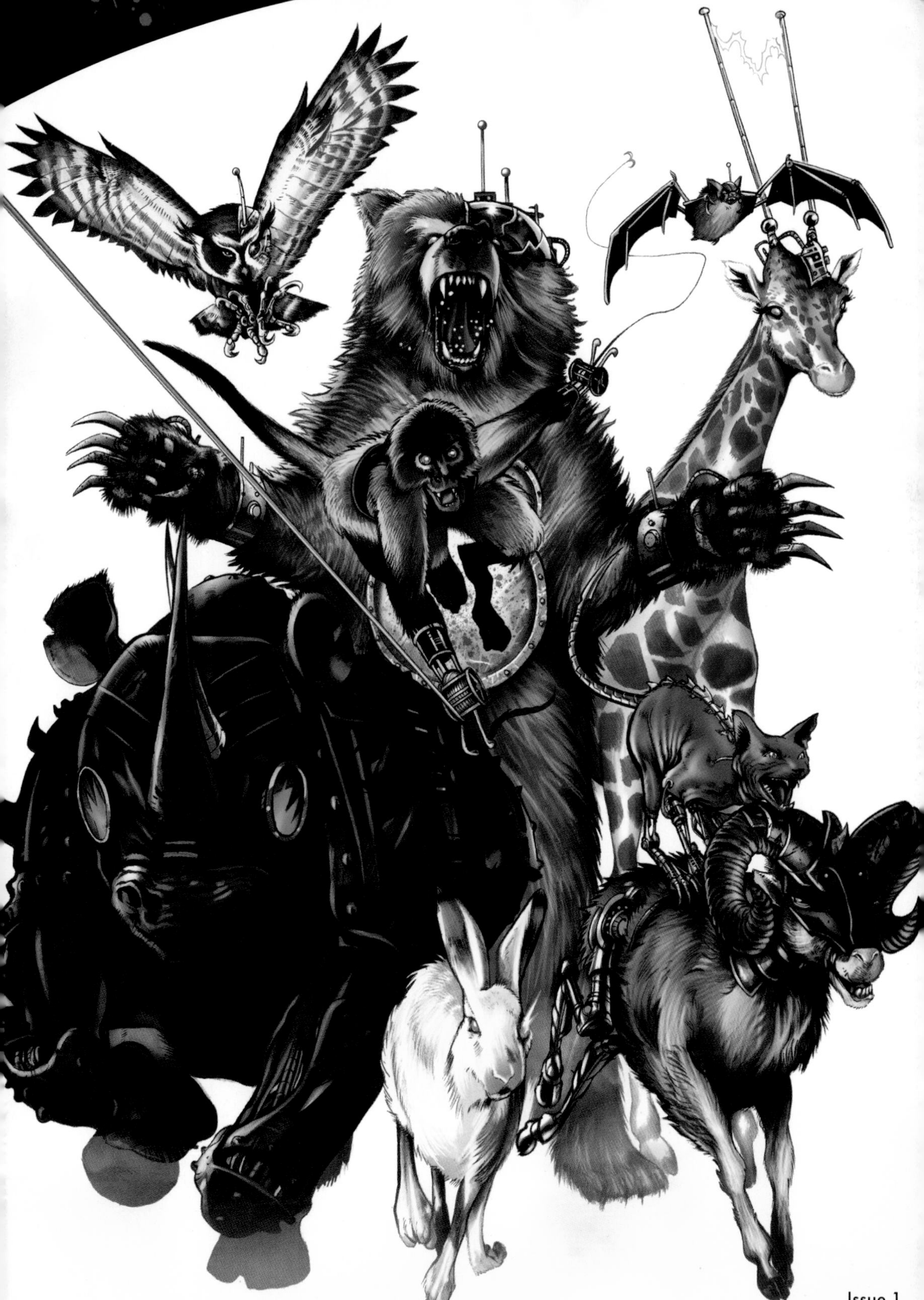

Issue 1
MIKE ROOTH
cover B

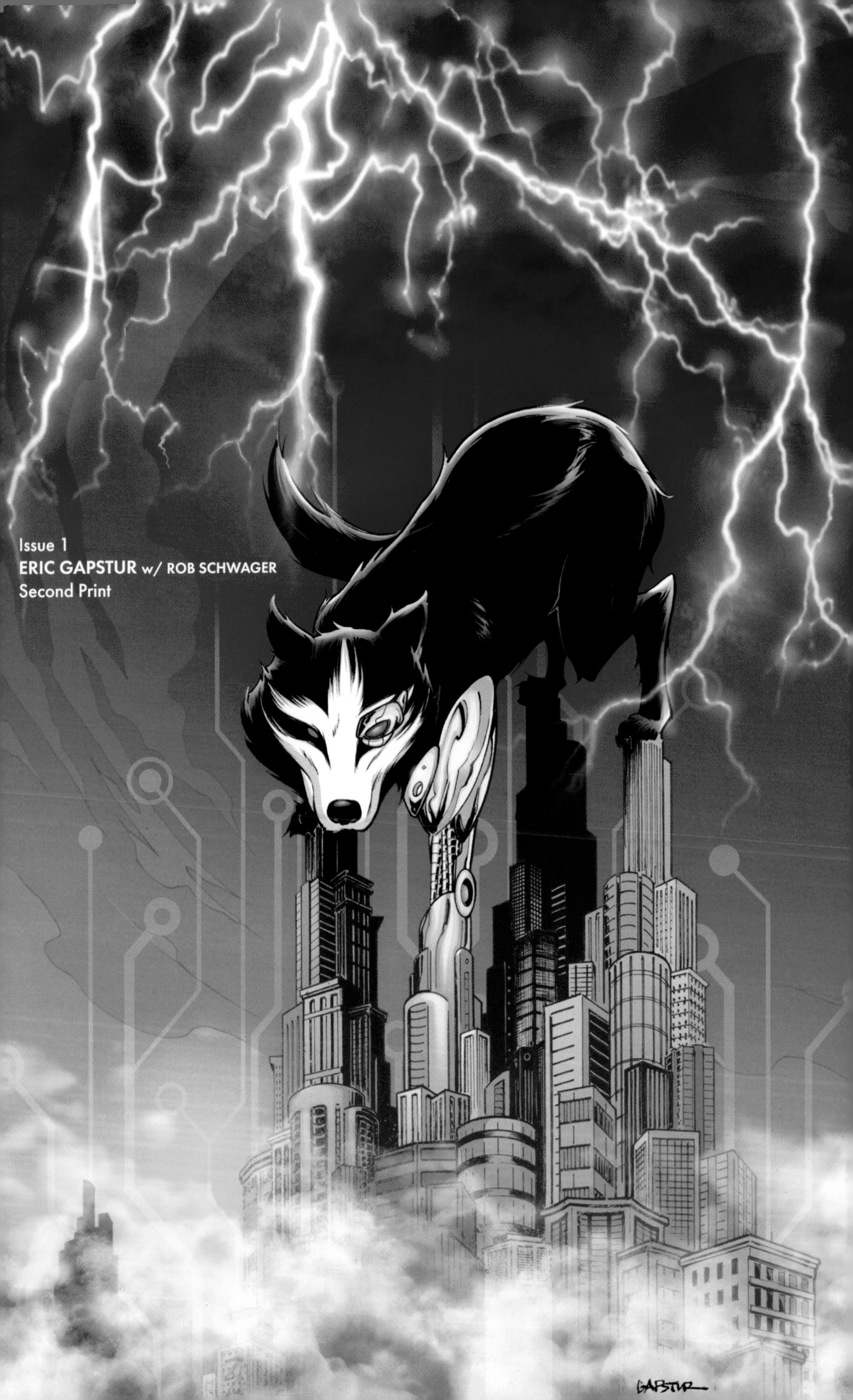
Issue 1
ERIC GAPSTUR w/ ROB SCHWAGER
Second Print
GAPSTUR

Issue 1
RAFAEL DE LATORRE w/ MARCELO MAIOLO
Fried Pie Variant Cover

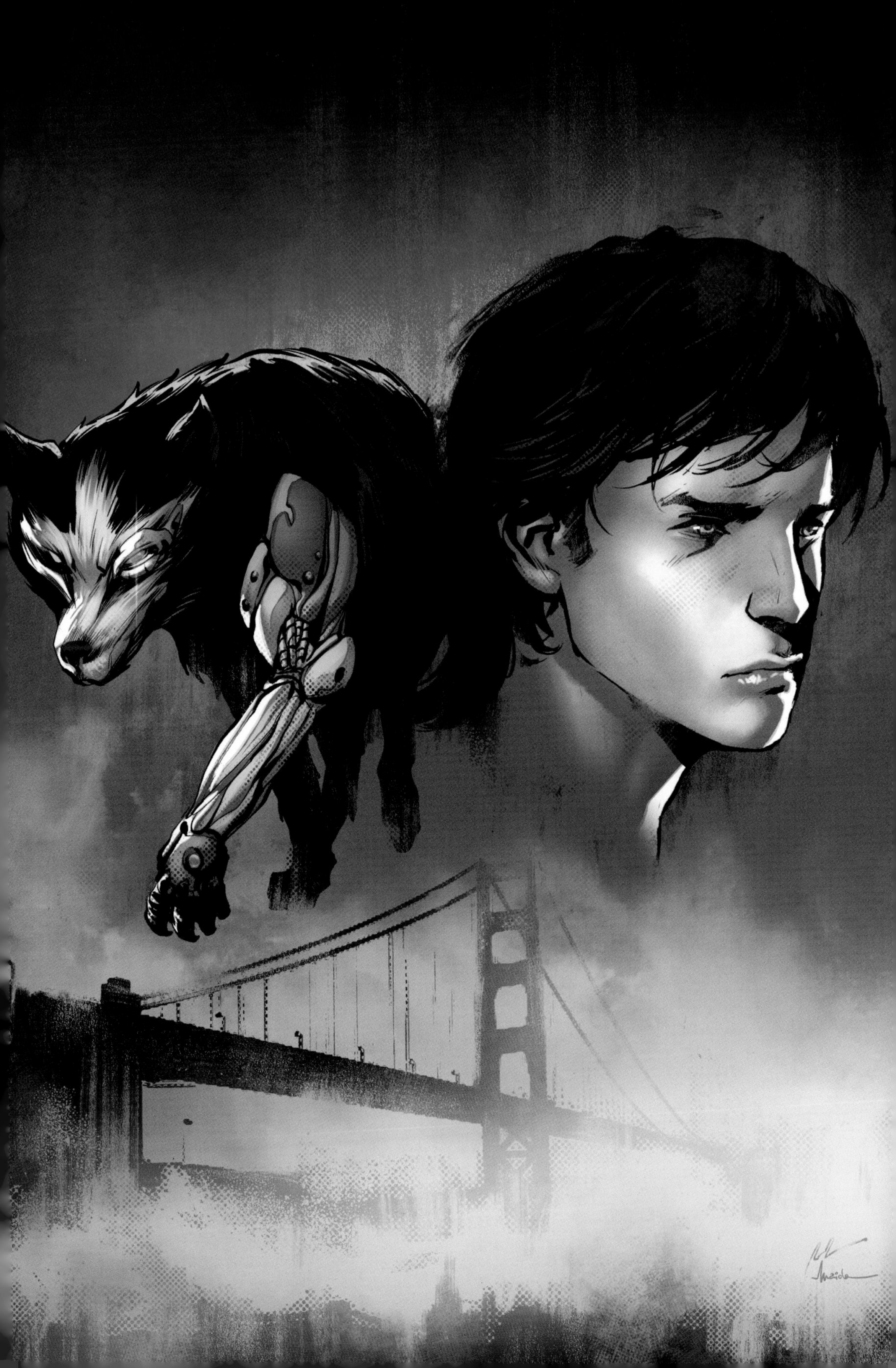

Issue 1
BLAKE OVARD
Geek Out Variant Cover

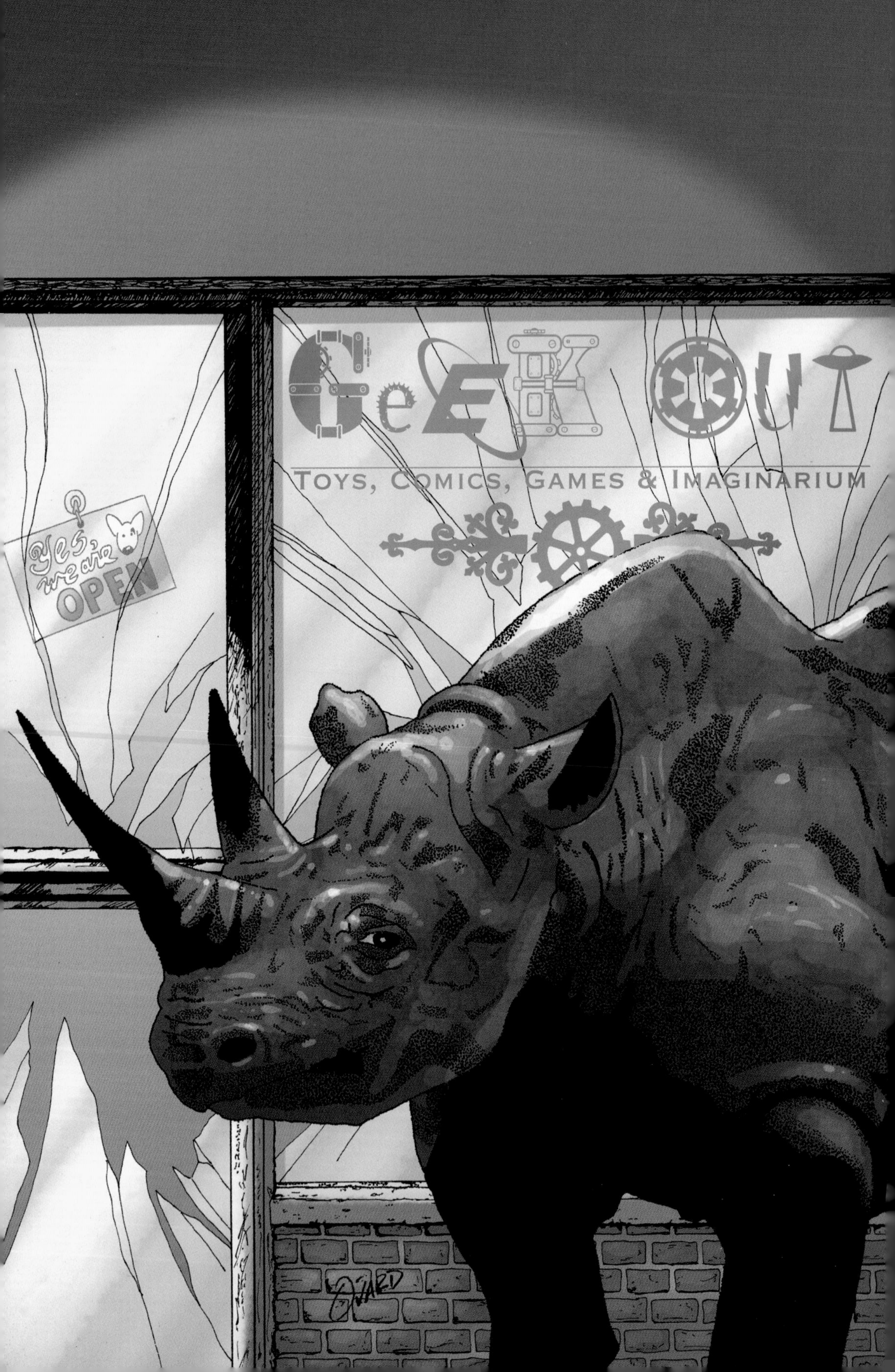
GEEK OUT
TOYS, COMICS, GAMES & IMAGINARIUM
Yes, we are OPEN
OVARD

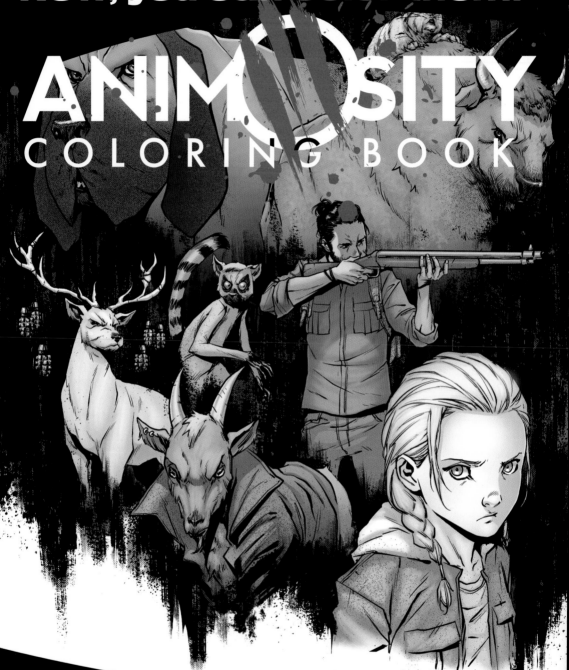

ANIMOSITY: EVOLUTION™ #1

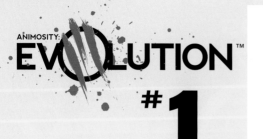

PAGE FOURTEEN

14.1
The PLANE smashes into the water.

1 SFX: KR-SMASSSSH

14.2
Around the sinking BODY of the twisted remains of the PLANE, DOLPHINS are swarmin furious and aggressive.

2 DOLPHINS: GET IT! GET IT!

14.3
The DOLPHINS are ripping at the plane, carrying off PIECES of the tech.

3 DOLPHINS: GET ALL OF IT, TAKE IT ALL!

14.4
A DOLPHIN kills the DROWNING PILOT.

4 DOLPHIN: ***TAKE IT ALL TO THE UR-KING!***

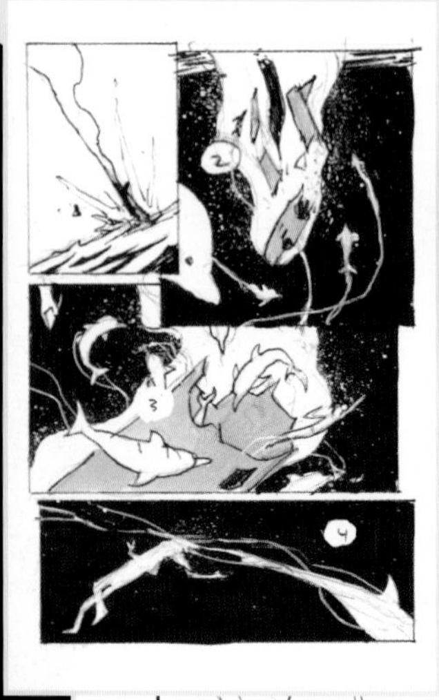

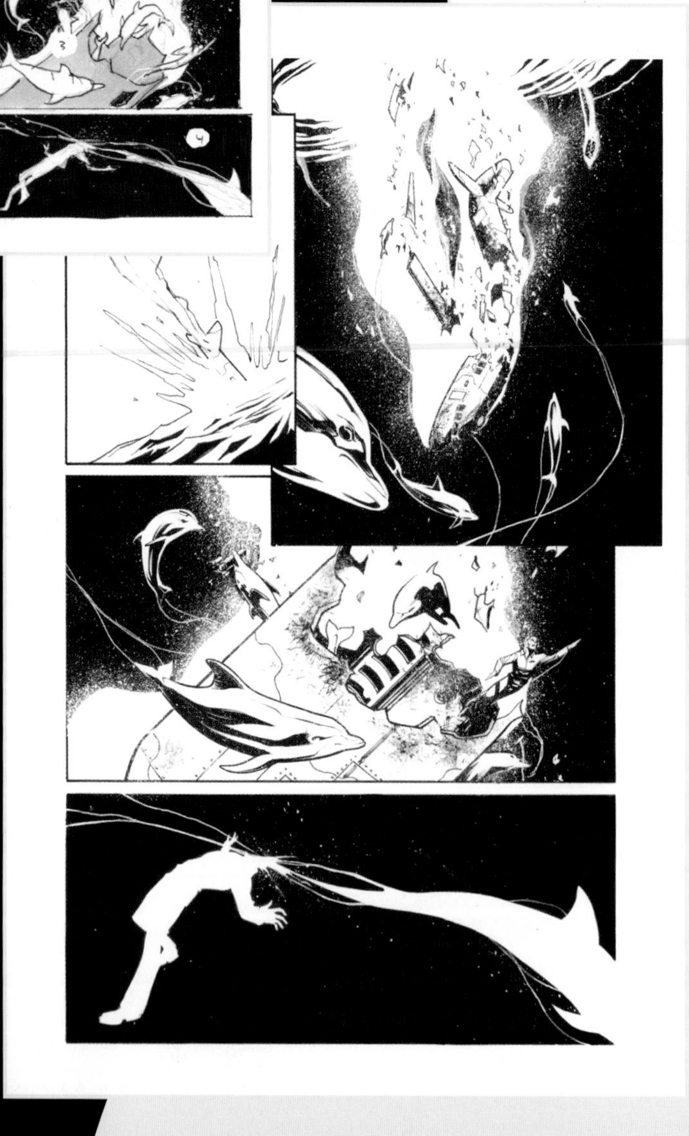

script by
MARGUERITE BENNETT

PAGE 14 PROCESS

art by
ERIC GAPSTUR

colors by
ROB SCHWAGER

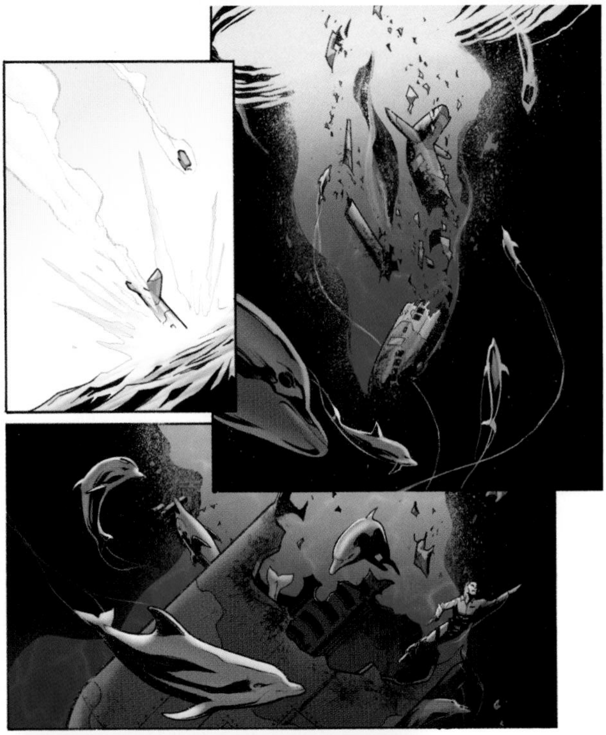

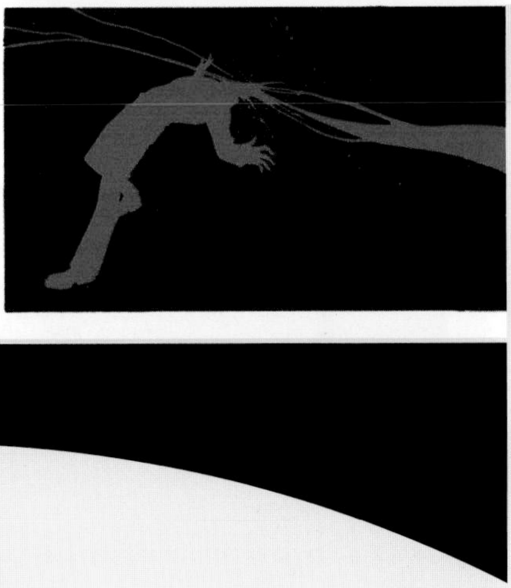

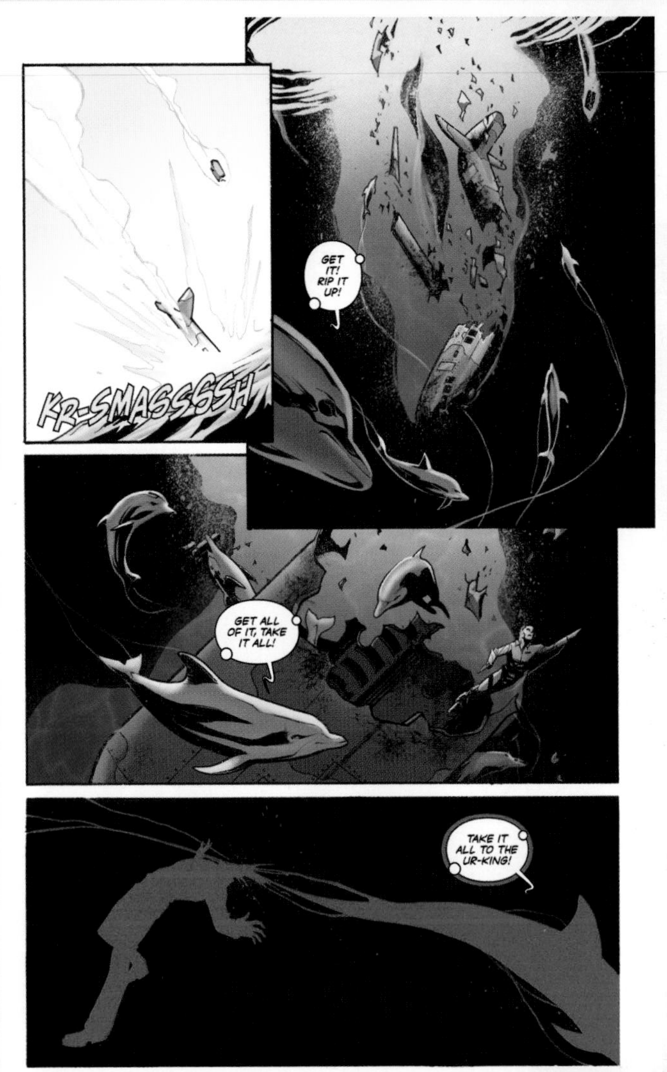
KR-SMASSSSH
GET IT! RIP IT UP!
GET ALL OF IT, TAKE IT ALL!
TAKE IT ALL TO THE UR-KING!

lettering by
MARSHALL DILLON

ANIMOSITY: EVOLUTION™
#1

PAGE TWENTY-ONE

21.1

Splash page.

WINTERMUTE stands on three feet. She has a PROSETHETIC leg and EYE, both much h tech than common prostheses. She has her fourth (and PROSTHETIC) LIMB raised (one of front legs – whatever is on the cover for #1). The PROSTHETIC has THREE OPPOSABLI FINGERS and ONE THUMB (a bit FURIOSA - https://s-media-cache-ak0.pinimg.com/ originals/b9/07/90/b90790f384c37cdaec7b009a9844a158.jpg). WINTERMUTE is now sem mechanical. She is examining it.

    1 WINTERMUTE: What to you know, Adam…

21.2

WINTERMUTE admires her new "hand." She is SPOOKY AS FUCK.

    2 WINTERMUTE: "*Thumbs*," indeed.

scri
MARGUERITE BENN

PAGE
21
PROCESS

art by
ERIC GAPSTUR

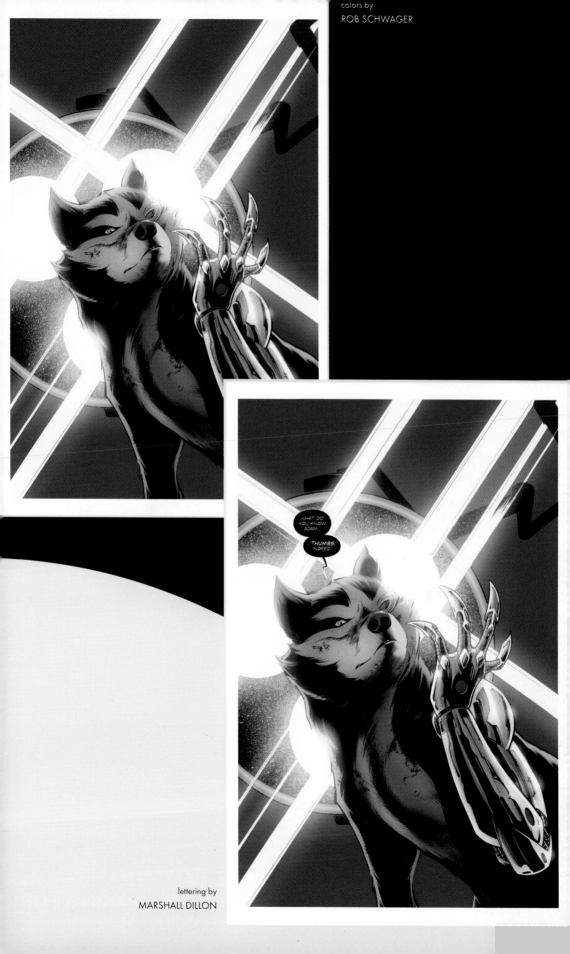

colors by
ROB SCHWAGER

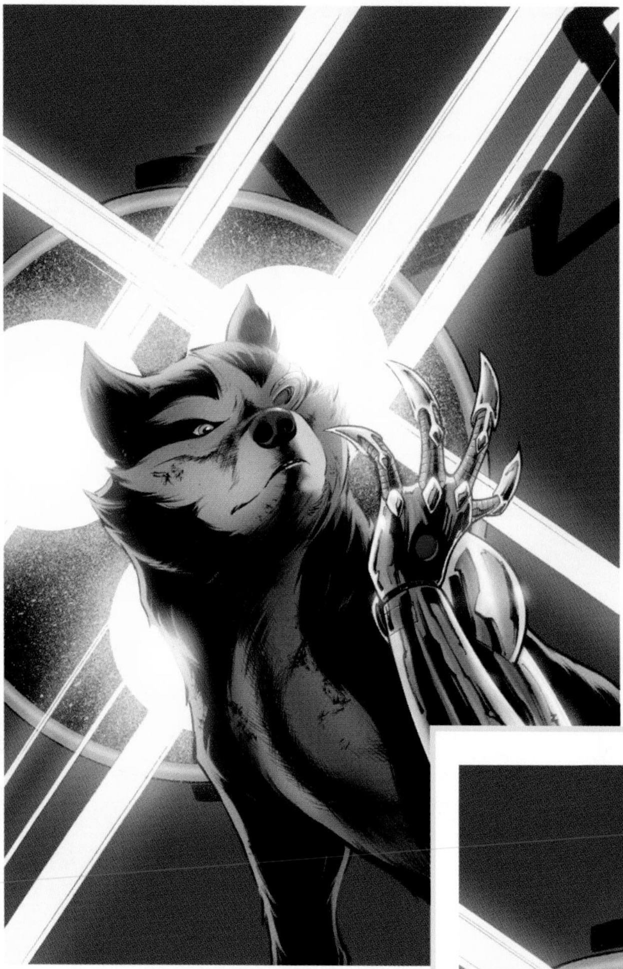

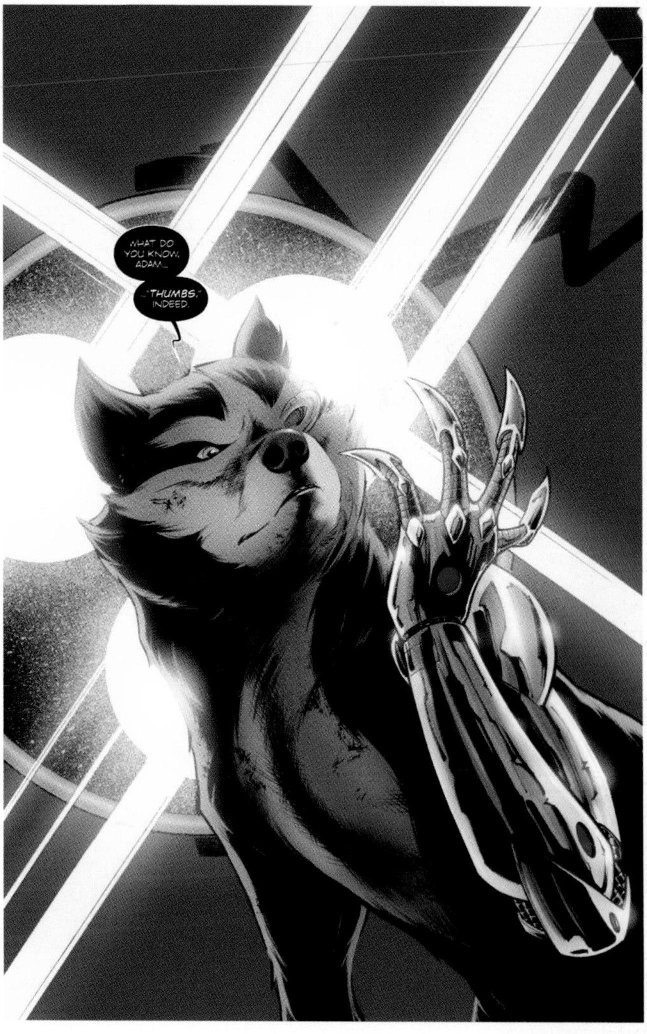
WHAT DO YOU KNOW, ADAM...
..."THUMBS," INDEED.

lettering by
MARSHALL DILLON

TOP TALENT
SOPHISTICATED STORIES
ONE COLLECTION

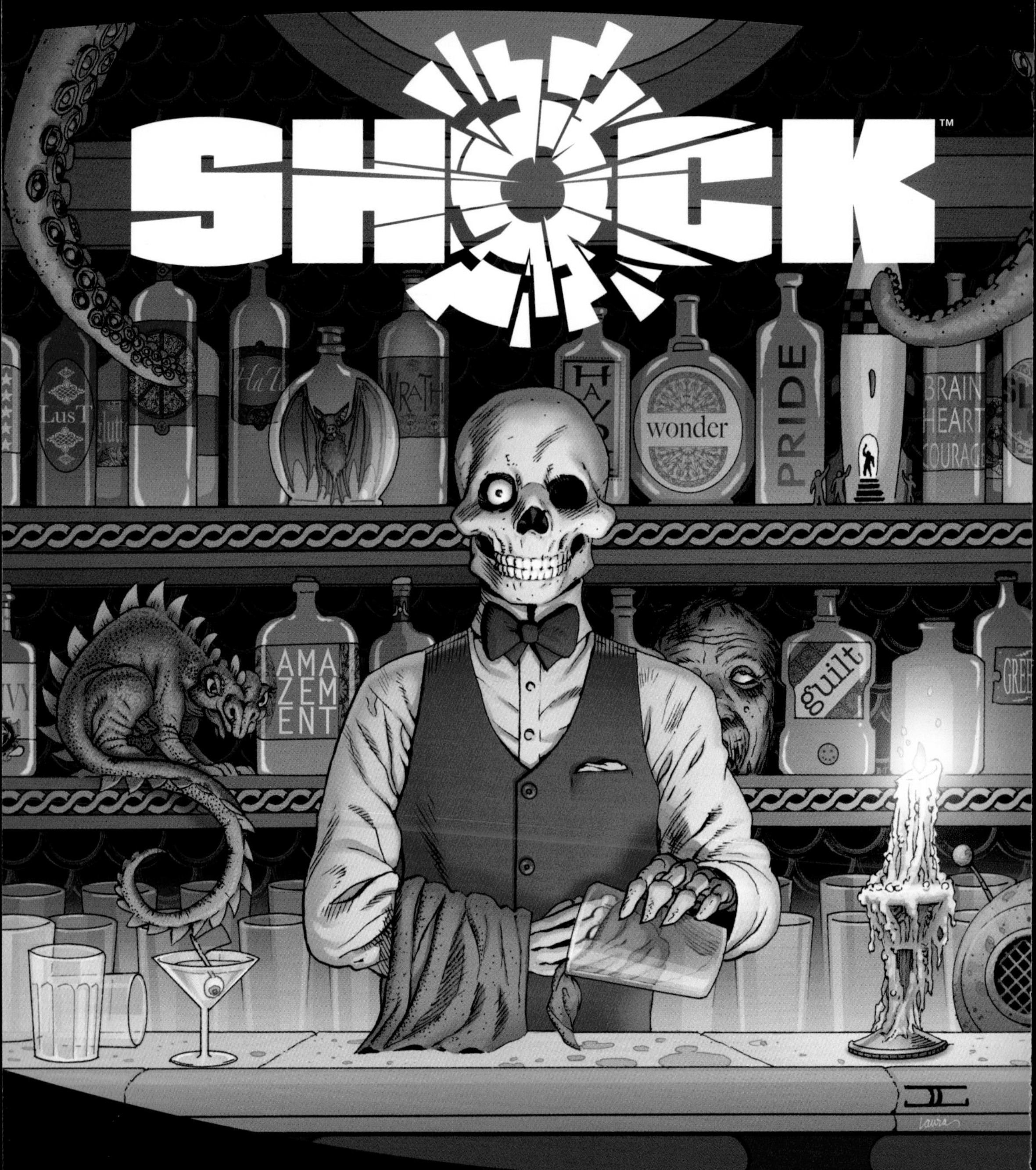
SHOCK™
LusT
WRATH
wonder
PRIDE
BRAIN
HEART
COURAGE
AMA
ZEM
ENT
guilt

Featuring original stories by Brian Azzarello, Marguerite Bennett, Cullen Bunn, Neil Gaiman, Michael Gaydos, Marc Guggenheim, Andrew Robinson, Jim Starlin, Frank Tieri, Charles Vess, Bill Willingham, Francesco Francavilla and many more!

AFTERSHOCK™

AVAILABLE NOW!

THESE ARE THE COMICS YOU'RE LOOKING FOR

CHECK OUT THESE GREAT AFTERSHOCK
COLLECTIONS!

ALTERS VOL 1
PAUL JENKINS / LEILA LEIZ

AMERICAN MONSTER VOL 1
BRIAN AZZARELLO / JUAN DOE

ANIMOSITY YEAR ONE, VOL 1 & VOL 2
MARGUERITE BENNETT / RAFAEL DE LATORRE

ANIMOSITY: THE RISE HARDCOVER
MARGUERITE BENNETT / JUAN DOE

BABYTEETH VOL 1
DONNY CATES / GARRY BROWN

BLACK-EYED KIDS VOL 1, VOL 2 & VOL 3
JOE PRUETT / SZYMON KUDRANSKI

CAPTAIN KID VOL 1
MARK WAID / TOM PEYER / WILFREDO TORRES

DARK ARK VOL 1
CULLEN BUNN / JUAN DOE

DREAMING EAGLES HARDCOVER
GARTH ENNIS / SIMON COLEBY

ELEANOR & THE EGRET VOL 1
JOHN LAYMAN / SAM KIETH

INSEXTS VOL 1
MARGUERITE BENNETT / ARIELA KRISTANTINA

JIMMY'S BASTARDS VOL 1
GARTH ENNIS / RUSS BRAUN

PESTILENCE VOL 1
FRANK TIERI / OLEG OKUNEV

REPLICA VOL 1
PAUL JENKINS / ANDY CLARKE

ROUGH RIDERS VOL 1 & VOL 2
ADAM GLASS / PATRICK OLLIFFE

SECOND SIGHT VOL 1
DAVID HINE / ALBERTO PONTICELLI

SUPERZERO VOL 1
AMANDA CONNER / JIMMY PALMIOTTI / RAFAEL DE LATORRE

SHOCK HARDCOVER
VARIOUS

UNHOLY GRAIL VOL 1
CULLEN BUNN / MIRKO COLAK

WORLD READER VOL 1
JEFF LOVENESS / JUAN DOE

ABOUT THE CREATORS OF

ANIMOSITY: EVOLUTION

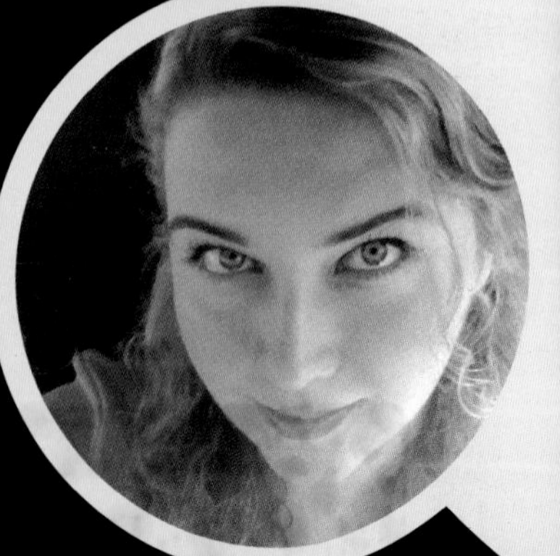

MARGUERITE BENNETT writer

@EvilMarguerite

Marguerite Bennett is a comic book writer from Richmond, Virginia, who currently splits her time between Los Angeles and New York City. She received her MFA in Creative Writing from Sarah Lawrence College in 2013 and quickly went on to work for DC Comics, Marvel, BOOM! Studios, Dynamite and IDW on projects ranging from *Batman, Bombshells,* and *A-Force* to *Angela: Asgard's Assassin, Red Sonja,* and FOX TV's *Sleepy Hollow.*

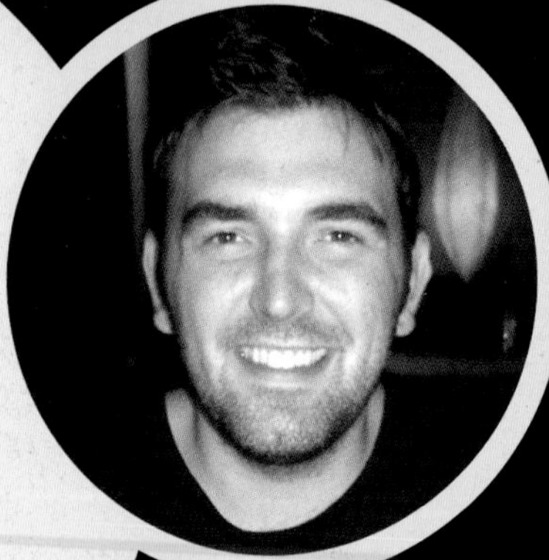

ERIC GAPSTUR artist

@EricGapstur

Eric has been creating comics professionally since 2011, most notably inking Phil Hester on such titles as *Legends of the Dark Knight, Adventures of Superman* and *Batman Beyond 2.0.* Additionally, Eric is pencilling *Flash: Season Zero.* He lives in Eastern Iowa with his wife, Michelle, and son, Liam.

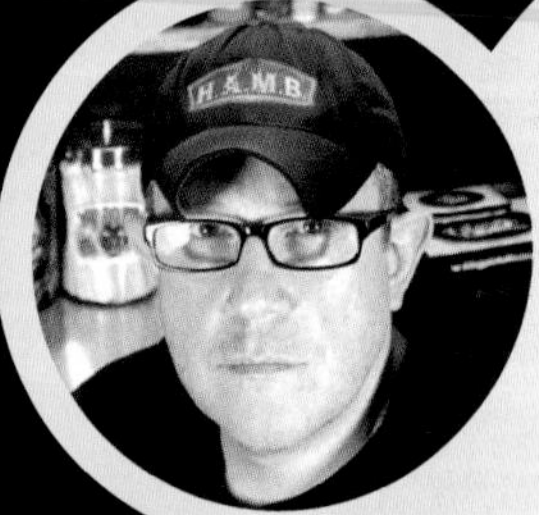

ROB SCHWAGER colorist

@RobSchwager

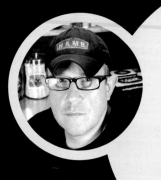

Rob Schwager is a self taught artist with over twenty-five years experience as a colorist in the comic book industry. He's worked on such iconic titles as *Batman, Superman, Green Lantern, Jonah Hex, Ghost Rider, Deadpool, Spider-Man, X-Men* and many others. He currently resides in the Tampa Bay area with his wife and three children and is extremely excited to be part of the AfterShock family of creators.

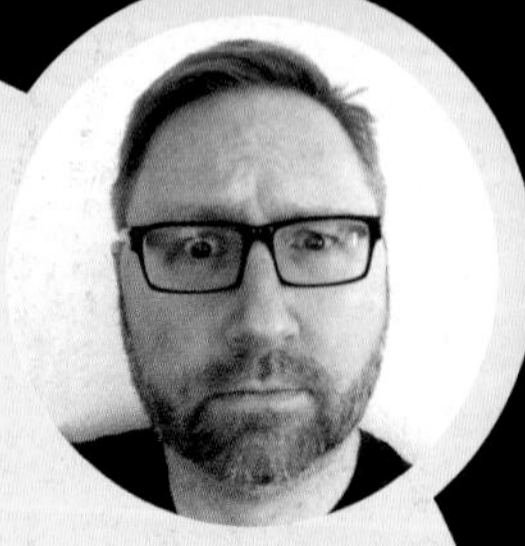

MARSHALL DILLON letterer

@MarshallDillon

A comic book industry veteran, Marshall got his start in 1994, in the midst of the indie comic boom. Over the years, he's been everything from an independent self-published writer to an associate publisher working on properties like *G.I.Joe, Voltron* and *Street Fighter.* He's done … everything except draw a comic book, and worked for just … publisher except the "big two." Primarily a father and lettere… he also dabbles in old-school paper and dice RPG gam… can catch up with Marshall at firstdraftpress.net.